MW00784297

Clouds of Witnesses

Christian Voices from Africa and Asia

Mark A. Noll
Carolyn Nystrom

16
EasyRead Large

RHYW

Copyright Page from the Original Book

InterVarsity Press
P.O. Box 1400, Downers Grove, IL 60515-1426
World Wide Web: www.ivpress.com
E-mail: email@ivpress.com

InterVarsity Press® is the book-publishing division of InterVarsity Christian Fellowship/USA®, a movement of students and faculty active on campus at hundreds of universities, colleges and schools of nursing in the United States of America, and a member movement of the International Fellowship of Evangelical Students. For information about local and regional activities, write Public Relations Dept., InterVarsity Christian Fellowship/USA, 6400 Schroeder Rd., P.O. Box 7895, Madison, WI 53707-7895, or visit the IVCF website at <www.intervarsity.org>.

See p. 285 for interior image credits.

Design: Cindy Kiple

Images: African sunset: Graeme Purdy/iStockphoto
Sari borders: Heidi Kalyani/iStockphoto
Kil photo: First ordained Korean clergymen/Samuel and Eileen Moffett
Chilembwe photo: George Shepperson, Independent African; John Chilembwe and the Origins, Setting and Significance of the Nyasaland Native Rising of 1915 (Edinburgh: Edinburgh University Press, 1958), p. 87.

ISBN 978-0-8308-3834-9

Printed in the United States of America ∞

green press INITIATIVE *InterVarsity Press is committed to protecting the environment and to the responsible use of natural resources. As a member of Green Press Initiative we use recycled paper whenever possible. To learn more about the Green Press Initiative, visit <www.greenpressinitiative.org>.*

Library of Congress Cataloging-in-Publication Data

Noll, Mark A., 1946-
Clouds of witnesses: christian voices from africa and asia / Mark A. Noll, Carolyn Nystrom.
Includes bibliographical references and indexs.
ISBN 978-0-8308-3834-9 (hardcover: alk. paper)
1. Christian biography—Asia. 2. Asia—Church history—20th Century. 3. Christian biography—Africa. 4. Africa—Church History—20th century. I. Nystrom, Carolyn. II. Title.
BR17520.3..N65 2010
276—dc22
[B]

2010040603

P 20 19 18 17 16 15 14 13 12 11 10 9 8 7 6 5 4 3 2 1
Y 28 27 26 25 24 23 22 21 20 19 18 17 16 15 14 13 12 11

This optimized ReadHowYouWant edition contains the complete, unabridged text of the original publisher's edition. Other aspects of the book may vary from the original edition.

Set in 16 pt. Verdana

TABLE OF CONTENTS

"Most of us have heard of Christianity's monumental shift from global north to global south. But shifts are impersonal things. They don't breathe, evangelize, repent, worship or die for their faith. Only people do that. These seventeen snapshots of global Christian luminaries put a much-needed face on the rise of world Christianity.... Highly recommended."

Mark Shaw, Nairobi Evangelical Graduate School of Theology

"A remarkable book helping us, through the lives of seventeen Christians from outside Europe and North America, to understand how the "center of gravity" in world Christianity has shifted from North to South and from West to East. A novel way to help us change perspective."

Gerald J. Pillay, Liverpool Hope University

"The authors have shown again and again through the stories of these heroes that, with a few exceptions like Y.T. Wu (and they are indeed the exceptions), the old, old Story is still very much alive in ways that have long been forgotten by a beleaguered Christianity in the West. My hope is that their effort will help to rekindle confidence in the gospel as the power of God unto salvation."

Simon Chan, Trinity Theological College, Singapore

To

Carol and Jim Plueddemann

Paul and Priscilla Heidebrecht

LIST OF MAPS

INTRODUCTION

The purpose of this book is to introduce readers in the Western world to noteworthy Christian believers from the recent history of the non-Western world. The momentous changes that have reconstructed the shape of Christianity in the world make introductions like this imperative. Today, in the early twenty-first century, there are far more active church participants in Africa than in Europe; a strong majority of the adherents to major denominational families like Pentecostals, Anglicans and Catholics live outside of North America and Europe; more missionaries are being sent out from places like South Korea, Brazil or Nigeria than from any European country; and it is not beyond the realm of possibility that within a few more years churchgoers in China may outnumber churchgoers in the United States of America. Respected historians and missiologists have provided a growing number of solid books charting the major features of the current situation and how it came about. (A few of these volumes are listed at the end of this book.) *Clouds of Witnesses* supplements these general studies by providing biographical accounts of seventeen significant individuals who made important contributions as Christian leaders during the century reaching from the 1880s to the 1980s.

The figures treated in this book come from Africa, India, Korea and China. These are by no means the only regions of rapid Christian advance (the newer Christian heartlands) that need to be introduced to believers in North America and Europe (the older Christian heartlands). Studies of other significant Christian lives would be equally instructive from South and Central America, the Philippines, the South Sea islands, southeast Asia, some parts of the Middle East and other places where flourishing believing communities have come to exist. But limiting subjects to just these four regions makes it possible to achieve some cohesion among the biographical sketches and also to produce a volume of manageable size.

Even with these geographical limits, the chapters of this book make only the barest beginning. Still, they do open up histories from which names may arise that one day count for the world Christian community the way that Evangeline Booth, William Carey, Billy Graham, Madam Guyon, Charles Haddon Spurgeon, Hudson Taylor, John Wesley, George Whitefield and Francis Xavier now count among Western Christians.

As a book intending to make introductions, the chapters that follow provide basic information and some historical context, but only a little assessment. This strategy is intentional. At the present stage in history, as Western believers begin to learn about Christian developments elsewhere, the result is bound to be considerable wonder and some bewilderment. The marvel comes from facing up to the fact that in 1900 more than four-fifths of the world's Christian population lived in Europe and North America, while a century later about two-thirds live outside those regions. The challenge for American and European believers who become aware of this epochal transformation is to grasp what it has meant for Christianity to take root in societies with often very different cultural norms from those in the West. Focused biographical attention is not all that is needed, but it can be a valuable strategy for entering the pathway of understanding that promotes sympathetic engagement and charitable discussion with brothers and sisters in Christ from around the world.

THE BIOGRAPHIES

Clouds of Witnesses is organized partly by region and partly by chronology, with three biographies of significant leaders from the southern part of Africa coming first. It is particularly fitting that we begin with **Bernard Mizeki,** a crosscultural missionary, a lay catechist and a martyr, because the gospel has advanced most dramatically in the recent past where local believers have spread the faith and endured through great trial to the end. Next is **John Chilembwe,** whose activities as pastor, development worker and political rebel led to his early death and the apparent collapse of his far-sighted enterprises but that have made him a hero in contemporary Africa. **Albert Luthuli** was a tribal chief and faithful Christian before he assumed leadership in the African National Congress; his life story sheds light on the vitality of indigenous Christian faith in the complex and conflicted modern history of South Africa.

Our two chapters from West Africa feature lives from the first and last parts of the twentieth century. **William Wadé Harris** was one of the most visible "prophets" early in the twentieth century; his brief but spectacular preaching career helped much of his region move from missionary Christianity to African Christianity. **Byang Kato** offers a record of serious theological achievement that left a continuing legacy not only in his native Nigeria but also in many other African regions.

The two chapters from the other side of the continent tell a nearly continuous story. **Simeon Nsibambi** played a key role in the beginnings of the East African Revival that, with recent revivals in China, was certainly one of the twentieth century's most important Christian renewal movements of any kind. The Anglican bishop **Janani Luwum** was a later product of the East African Revival whose faithfulness unto death left a sterling record to imitate in his native Uganda but also in a much wider circle.

These seven African "lives" represent only a few of the continent's major Christian movements, but they nonetheless suggest the wealth of wisdom to be won by paying attention to Africa as a center of rapid Christian maturation as well as simple expansion.

From Africa our biographies move to India, where three studies explore how Indian believers deliberately adjusted their own cultural inheritances in accepting Christian faith but also how they adapted Western Christian traditions to Indian conditions. **Pandita Ramabai** was a pioneer traveler, institution builder and distinctly Indian teacher whose independent path made her a key figure in the rooting of Protestant-like Christianity in modern India. **Vedanayagam Samuel Azariah** enjoyed the distinction of serving as the first Anglican bishop in India to come from Indian stock; his long record of sacrificial service to the poor in his diocese and well beyond is, however, even more impressive than the ecclesiastical prominence he achieved. **Sundar Singh,** who earned the honorific title *Sadhu* (the teacher), was an independent thinker and evangelist about whose life considerable controversy accumulated. These controversies perhaps reveal more about Singh's Western connections than about his noteworthy Indian ministry.

The book's next portrait is of **Sun Chu Kil,** a Korean at the center of one of the most significant revivals of the early twentieth century and also of a landmark Korean attempt to obtain national independence. Because affairs of religion and politics mixed differently in Kil's life than has become customary in the West, it only adds reasons for attending carefully to this important early leader in Korea's momentous twentieth-century Christian history.

The book concludes with six studies from China, presented in roughly chronological order. Close attention to these biographies provides some historical clues for understanding the dramatic surge recently of Christianity in the world's largest and also strongest Communist nation. **Dora Yu** was one of the most effective evangelists in the early history of modern Chinese Christianity; her significance is suggested by the fact that the celebrated Watchman Nee came to Christ under her ministry. The life of physician **Mary Stone** offers intriguing insights about a medical professional who carried out her work despite significant obstacles in China, as well as about the occasionally fraught relationship between Chinese and American forms of education, organization and ministry. **John Sung** was one of Mary Stone's younger colleagues, who like her pursued advanced scientific study in the United States. How this talented chemist with a Ph.D. changed the direction of his career and in the 1930s became one of the world's most effective evangelists offers much to ponder about sacrifice, discretion, zeal and more.

The sketches of the near contemporaries **Y.T. Wu, Wang Mingdao** and **Ignatius Cardinal Kung** are connected by their efforts to serve Christ and his people in China during desperate tumults in the 1930s and 40s and then under the Communist regime. In the face of extraordinary political, psychological and social pressures, Wu chose the path of negotiation as a way to preserve what he considered the essential elements of his Protestant training. By contrast, Wang took the road of resistance. Kung resembled Wang in his stance toward the regime, but as a Roman Catholic he differed considerably from his Protestant peers. Together, these lives communicate some of the drive, insight and tension that have made the recent history of Christianity in China such a powerful but also complicated story.

It is important to repeat that our primary purpose in presenting the biographies is to inform. But because these lives were so obviously shaped by powerful spiritual commitments, we pause at the end for a short afterword in order to reflect briefly on some of the general challenges presented to Western Christians by learning about such saints from around the world. A short list of books on the new conditions of world Christianity brings the book to a close.

PARAMETERS

As authors, we are aware of the limitations under which we have written this book. Neither of us is a scholar in the world regions from which we have drawn our subjects, though we have benefited tremendously from the writings of those who are truly expert. As evangelical Protestants, it has been easier to find and write about individuals with connections to evangelical movements, though we have also made a point to include nonevangelicals, one Catholic and several others who are difficult to categorize by the standard definitions of Western Christian traditions. Obviously, more representative biographical coverage would have displayed a much broader ecumenical balance. Our justification for *Clouds of Witnesses,* despite such limitations, is the unusual degree to which we ourselves have been intellectually simulated, historically instructed and spiritually challenged by studying even a small and skewed sampling of biographical possibilities. We are aware that the book is fragmentary and preliminary, but we are also confident that even efforts of this kind can help Western believers learn about and learn from the new regions of world Christianity.

Our choice of subjects obviously reflect considerable bias. We selected individuals who we thought were significant, who struck us as personally interesting and about whom we could find accessible materials in English. Originally we had hoped to include several figures from Central and South America, but in the end we concluded that most Latin American biographies involved too much Catholic-Protestant conflict for a book focused on the world's newer Christian regions. A few obviously important figures, like Watchman Nee and Samuel Ajayi Crowther, the first African Anglican Bishop, we did not include because they are already well known in Western Christian circles.

Other limitations are also inevitable for such a book. For some of the chapters, like our sketch of Bernard Mizeki, who died at the dawn of Christian expansion in southern Africa, documentary sources are fragmentary. For others, sources in English can be confusing, as with the seven or eight spellings and arrangement of names we found for the Korean we call Sun Chu Kil in chapter eleven. Furthermore, controversy attended some of our figures when they were living and in some instances long after their deaths. Was John Chilembwe a responsible patriot or a dangerous political agitator? Did the Sadhu Sundar Singh fabricate the stories he told about mystical encounters in Tibet? How secure is the documentation for the miracles recorded about the work of William Wadé Harris? Was Y.T. Wu wise or traitorous in accommodating Mao Zedong and the new regime of the People's Republic of China, and was his contemporary Wang Mingdao courageous or foolhardy in resisting the Communists? These and similar interpretive questions, which can be raised for almost all of our figures, are good ones that deserve close attention. But they are not questions we try to answer in this book. Our intention, rather, has been to offer as much information in short compass as possible, to present controversial matters as fairly as we can, to try to communicate something about the humanity of each figure and then deliberately to step back. One of the benefits in this approach is to grasp how much sympathetic engagement is required even to begin serious assessment of peoples, cultures and activities very different from our own.

CLOUDS OF WITNESSES

We have taken our title from the memorable words of Hebrews 12:1-2: "Therefore, since we are surrounded by so great a cloud of witnesses, let us also lay aside every weight, and sin which clings so closely, and let us run with perseverance the race that is set before us, looking to Jesus the pioneer and perfecter of our faith" (RSV). In the section of Hebrews right before these verses, the author sketches the lives of Old Testament "witnesses"—from Abel through Noah, Abraham and Moses, to an unnamed throng of men and women—who had remained faithful to God in the face of great opposition and repeated traumas. Now he calls on readers to remember these ones as an encouragement for running "the race" with perseverance. The sketches were to help believers from latter-day times and faraway places follow Jesus who endured "the cross" and "the shame" in order to accomplish his saving work. Our "witnesses," while not on the same plane as these biblical exemplars, may also serve as examples from other times and places of those who prevailed in their Christian profession. We call them "clouds" of witnesses to emphasize the many world regions in which the faith now flourishes.

The reference in our subtitle to "voices" is connected to another theme in the book of Hebrews, where we read about believers who "confessed" their faith. The "voices" heard in this book were, in the term from Hebrews, "confessors." In several places the epistle speaks of Christian confession as that which believers profess about the Son of God, thus Jesus is "the high priest of our confession" (3:1). The author then urges believers, as they remember Christ's high-priestly work, to "hold fast our confession" (4:14 RSV). Most expansively, the author urges his readers to draw on Christ's faithfulness to them as they persevere in the hope that they have professed and as they stimulate one another to love and compassionate action. "Let us hold fast the confession of our hope without wavering, for he who promised is faithful; and let us consider how to stir up one another to love and good works" (10:23-24 RSV).

The lives sketched in this book belonged to individuals who held fast their confession of Christ but did so in circumstances different from what most Western believers have experienced. Our hope is that these stories encourage all who read the book to persevere in following Christ. It is an appeal to realize that the work of encouragement in Christ, which is so central to the book of Hebrews, has now taken on striking international dimensions. The clouds of witnesses who have been faithful, often through stresses that parallel what was described in Hebrews, are numerous; and they come from everywhere. How these witnesses confessed Christ in many tongues deepens, expands and enriches the story of salvation that the book of Hebrews proclaims.

Of course, our sketches are not inspired Scripture and so will contain mistakes, misapprehensions and misapplications. But since the biblical foundation holds—the truth that believers alive today can receive great encouragement from saints who have gone before—we are pleased to offer these sketches as an indication of how numerous and diverse the clouds of witnesses to God's mercy have become and how wide that mercy continues to stretch in our present age.

ACKNOWLEDGMENTS

Clouds of Witnesses is a companion volume to an earlier book published by InterVarsity Press, Mark Noll's *The New Shape of World Christianity: How American Experience Reflects Global Faith* (2009). Where, however, that book explains new Christian realities in relationship to American history, this book focuses directly on events, persons and circumstances in the world's newer Christian regions. Both books owe much to past and present editors at InterVarsity Press, including Joel Scandrett for initiating the projects, David Zimmerman and Dan Reid for shepherding the books into print, Krista Carnet for working hard at publicity, and especially Andy LePeau for a long and much-valued friendship with both authors. We offer heartfelt thanks to Maggie Noll for contributing indispensable research, organizing, fact-checking, editing and much else to both books. Mark Noll would like to thank classes in the recent world history of Christianity at Wheaton College, Regent College and the University of Notre Dame who have contributed a great deal to his understanding of recent Christian history. Carolyn Nystrom thanks several librarians at Wheaton College—including Nancy Falciani-White, Gregory Morrison and David Malone—for study space, friendly assistance and research diligence. We owe a special debt to Dan Bays for his assistance on our Chinese chapters. The notes on "Sources" that end each chapter include grateful acknowledgment of welcome help we received in preparing several of the individual chapters.

The book is dedicated with respect and affection to four individuals who for the authors and their families have been exemplary pastors, friends, teachers and role models as world Christians.

SOUTHERN AFRICA

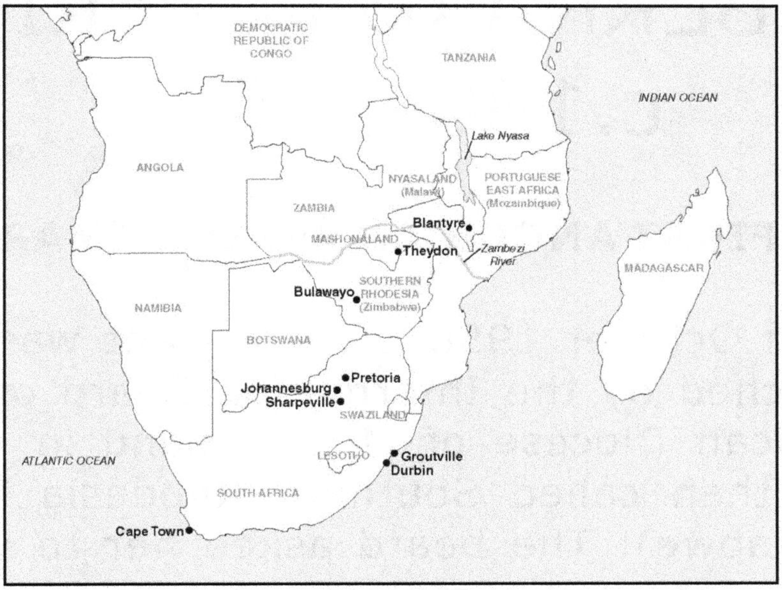

1

BERNARD MIZEKI c.1861-1896

THE FIRST ANGLICAN AFRICAN MARTYR

In October 1958, Jean Farrant was approached by the Information Board of the Anglican Diocese of Mashonaland in what was then called Southern Rhodesia (now Zimbabwe). The board asked her to write a modest sized pamphlet that could be distributed with a map to aid pilgrims who came annually to the Bernard Mizeki Shrine at Theydon, a site near Marandellas, which is itself located about an hour east of the Zimbabwe capital, Harare. Ms. Farrant took on this task reluctantly because, apart from being an Anglican herself and living in this district, she knew little about Bernard Mizeki. The assignment came at a delicate moment in the Christian, as well as political, history of southern Africa. The authority of the British colonial rulers was beginning to crumble, and the signs of rising African nationalism were unmistakable.

Bernard Mizeki

Upon setting to work, Farrant soon found much more material about the last ten years of Mizeki's life than she could have imagined. But she was stymied in her quest for information about Mizeki's early years. Then in an unexpected response to one last random request for information, she was directed to a small book, published in German in 1898, by a P.D. von Blomberg, of which the only known copies were housed at the British Museum and the Africana collection of the South African Public Library. Once translated, it turned out that this volume's author was Paula Dorothea von Blomberg, a missionary in Cape Town, South Africa, who had conducted a school for Africans during the 1880s. It also turned out that Fräulein von Blomberg had identified Bernard Mizeki as her "most-loved pupil" and that she had recorded many heretofore unknown details about his early life. With this unexpected assistance, Farrant could record Mizeki's life in considerable detail, which she proceeded to do in a book called *Mashonaland Martyr,* published in 1966 by Oxford University Press in Cape Town.

But the Mizeki story also witnessed several other unexpected turns after the publication of Farrant's compelling biography. Those turns concerned the great transformation of political life in Southern Rhodesia that took place from the 1960s and even more the extraordinary transformation of Christianity in this same part of the world over the same time. For this later part of the Mizeki story, the distinguished historian of world Christianity Dana Robert provided a discerning update in 2006. She shows that Bernard Mizeki's life is not only instructive for what happened while he was alive but also for how his memory has continued to be a living presence. A final introductory word is to note that the fragile quality of sources about Mizeki's life illustrates some of the problems faced in reconstructing the early history of Christianity in areas that have recently become heartlands of the faith.

EARLY LIFE AND EDUCATION

Mamiyeri Mizeka Gwambe was born in Portuguese East Africa (now Mozambique), probably in the year 1861. His childhood seems to have been an ordinary one for the early days of European colonial expansion on the continent, since the boy was raised in traditional African fashion but also worked for a time in a trader's store where he learned a little Portuguese. Sometime between the ages of ten and fifteen, he left the place of his birth with a cousin who convinced the young Mamiyeri to go with him to Cape Town, South Africa. In that rapidly expanding city, which anchored the British empire in Africa's southern cone, the lad found a new name, "Barns," and a variety of jobs—on the docks, as a house servant, as a gardener. He also avoided common vices like the intemperance that beset many who came from the countryside into Africa's growing cities. In 1885 or shortly before, Barns made the connections that changed his life and that would influence the course of African Christianity more generally: he was introduced to the Cowley Fathers, and he entered a night school taught by Fräulein von Blomberg. The Cowley Fathers was the informal name of the Society of St. John the Evangelist, a religious order of high-church Anglicans founded in the Oxford district of Cowley in 1865. It carried out its mission—to promote spiritual growth and education—in several cities of the British Empire during that empire's rapid expansion in the second half of the nineteenth century. In Cape Town the

Cowley Fathers linked their work to the school run by the Fräulein.

Barns soon became a favorite of the Fathers and at school because of his conscientious demeanor, but even more because of his intense interest in the Scriptures. On March 7, 1886, he was baptized along with six other young Africans. At the baptism he received the name "Bernard Mizeki." It was the feast day of Saint Perpetua, who about the year 203 at Carthage had become one of Africa's first Christian martyrs. Almost immediately thereafter, Bernard and several others asked the Cowley Fathers to train them as mission helpers. The baptismal photo that has been preserved shows him as short, square of face and with a determined countenance. He was then about twenty-five years old.

For the next five years Bernard attended Zonnebloem College, an institution that taught white, black, and colored (mixed-race) men and boys together. He assisted the Fräulein at her evening school and remained in close touch with the Cowley Fathers. Europeans found him shy, diffident and not particularly quick on the uptake. Yet over time they gave him an increasing range of duties assisting with various Anglican enterprises, which he fulfilled with honesty and efficiency. When Fräulein von Blomberg took him along on outings to villages, she discovered that he could be a warm and effective speaker. Only toward the end of his training did Mizeki's intellectual paralysis in the presence of Europeans begin to give way; later the Cowley Fathers would look back and recall that Bernard's gentleness had made the gospel message particularly attractive to other Africans.

INTO MASHONALAND

In January 1891, Mizeki met George Wyndham Hamilton Knight-Bruce, the newly appointed bishop of the recently created Anglican diocese of Mashonaland. Knight-Bruce, an earnest and enthusiastic young graduate of Eton and Oxford, had been the Bishop of Bloemfontein in South Africa. Now he was recruiting native helpers for his new diocese, which he had already explored on a long and arduous journey by foot.

As the control of the British Empire spread inland from the African coasts, so too did the Anglican Church. Elsewhere in southern Africa, missionaries had preceded empire, which led to conflict between the churches and the empire when colonial administrations arrived. In Mashonaland, where empire and church moved into African territory together, the problems were created by how native peoples responded to the incursion of church and empire.

Mashonaland, the region of the Shona people, lay in the north of what is now Zimbabwe, a landlocked region between the Zambezi River to the north and the Munyati River to the south that includes Zimbabwe's capital city of Harare, which was known as Salisbury during Mizeki's years. Earlier in the nineteenth century the Shona had been brutally conquered by the Ndebele people, but now both Shona and Ndebele were coming under the sway of the British, in particular the British South African Company of Cecil Rhodes. As part of "the scramble for Africa," Rhodes and the company's directors hoped to organize trading, mining and settlement in order to enrich themselves and bring civilization to the Africans. Bishop Knight-Bruce spoke out strongly against the political decisions that put Mashonaland under Rhodes's control, but there was little he could do to hold back the tide of empire.

In April 1891, Bishop Knight-Bruce sailed with Mizeki and one other lay catechist from Cape Town to a port in Mozambique, from where they trekked westwards overland, carrying their own loads into the twenty thousand square miles of Mashonaland. The Africans went with the bishop as he met various subchiefs and sought suitable venues for their work. Mizeki eventually settled in a territory known as Theydon. It was controlled by Chief Mangwende, who lived in stone buildings abandoned by Portuguese traders. For the bishop's gift of three pieces of calico and a few strings of beads, the chief allowed Mizeki to build a large mission hut near the chief's imposing stone structure. That hut soon came to serve as church, school and dwelling. It was located on the banks of a river that supplied water for the garden Mizeki planted for growing his own food. He was on his own, sixty miles from the only other native catechist. For long stretches, his only outside visitor was Douglas Pelly, one of Bishop Knight-Bruce's very few European colleagues. Dana Robert summarizes his situation in 1891 with these words: "Thus Bernard Mizeki, born in Mozambique, minimally educated in South Africa, and with little knowledge of either the Shona people or their language, was settled in the territory of Chief Mangwende."

MISSIONARY MIZEKI

Almost immediately it became obvious that Mizeki had remarkable missionary gifts. Within a year he mastered the Shona language. Before he died, the student whose European teachers had worried about his intelligence became adept in eight different African languages, as well as English, Dutch and Portuguese. (He also acquired some French, Latin and Greek.)

Even more impressive than his linguistic ability were his practical talents, his amiability and his faithfulness. His garden was productive, he knew how to hunt and find firewood, and he showed his fondness for animal life by keeping three pet klipspringers (small antelopes). When smallpox threatened the region in 1895, Bernard administered vaccinations and so expanded the basic medical care he had been offering since coming to Mangwende's territory.

As Mizeki mastered the Shona language, so too he grew close to the Shona people. Early on he won the friendship of Zandiparira, Mangwende's head wife, who then served as his patroness in the community. Young children were drawn to him by his beautiful singing and by his willingness to teach them how to sing as well. Europeans who learned of his work sometimes complained that he wasted time on the Shona, who had a reputation for shiftlessness. But others were deeply impressed by how effectively Mizeki was reaching out through word, song and deed.

Day by day he said the Anglican daily offices of matins, prime, evensong and compline. He rose early to spend time reading the Scriptures and in prayer. And after catechumens had gathered to live around his mission hut, he began regular instruction in the basics of the Christian faith.

Mizeki taught the Shona that the deity they had known as Mwari—the creator God—was the Christian God and Father of Jesus. When locals warned him about the activity of other gods and spirits, who were thought to bring rain and control the unfolding of daily life, Mizeki insisted that it was Mwari, "our Father and Creator," who caused the rain to fall and compassionately provided individuals and families with the means for sustaining life.

Mizeki's first catechumen was John Kapuya, the son of a local *nganga,* a traditional diviner-healer. Bernard cared for this young man diligently, even to the point of finding a new place for him to live after members of his family and the *nganga* s began persecuting him. The first open convert was Chigwada Gawe, who took the name Joseph after he was baptized. Joseph's young son was a special object of Bernard's affection, although many observers remarked on his fondness for all children.

Bernard himself soon established a respected reputation as *Umfundisi,* the teacher. But he was also known as *Mukiti,* the celibate one, since in the face of local custom he remained single and chaste. After several years and much thought, however, he resolved to marry and took as his bride a young woman who had been an eager "hearer" at the missionary's hut. She was Mutwa, who had been raised by one of Mangwende's daughters after her own mother died. With this step, Mizeki entered into Mangwende's own kin network, a move that not only spoke of his identification with this people but also led to bitter resentment among other members of Mangwende's large family. The wedding took place in early 1896 and was performed by an African Anglican priest, Hezekiah Mtobi, who had only shortly before come to Mashonaland from Grahamstown, South Africa, as the first African cleric to join the Shona mission.

From his base in Mangwende's territory, Mizeki journeyed on foot throughout the locality to preach the Christian message. He also contributed substantially to translation efforts under the direction of Bishop Bruce-Knight, for which he traveled regularly to the bishop's home in Umtali. Bernard's linguistic abilities made him a leader in efforts that soon resulted in Seshona translations of the Lord's Prayer, the Ten Commandments, the creed and other passages from the Bible.

Mizeki's obvious talents drew the attention of colonial officials who from time to time asked him to serve as an official interpreter. It would have been easy for Mizeki to secure well-compensated employment as a translator in Umtali, but he chose to remain in Theydon. African catechists like Mizeki received only a sparse living allowance and occasional bits of cash for pocket money. His own catechumens reported that he remained entirely content.

After several years of labor Mizeki's work prospered to the point that it was necessary to think about a new setting for the mission. After some deliberation and with Mangwende's approval he decided to move his small community—several families and a number of small boys who had been entrusted to his care for education—across the river to a fertile site about two miles distant. The band of trees and the spring that marked this new location had a special significance, for it was considered a sacred grove inhabited by the spirits of the tribe's ancestral lions. Locals worried about desecrating this sacred place, but Mizeki forged ahead as part of a systematic plan to reform what he saw as the evil practices of the Shona, including the killing of twin babies, habitual drunkenness, the offering of sacrifices to spirits and the harsh treatment (or murder) of individuals named by the *nganga* s as sorcerers. When Bernard was urged to make a small offering to the ancestral spirits before taking up his new place of residence, he instead drew the sign of the cross in the air and carved crosses in the trees at the edge of the sacred grove. Soon after moving, Mizeki felled some trees in the grove to make room for a field of wheat. This action would later be reported as sparking particularly strong resentment.

THE END AND A BEGINNING

Local hostility against Mizeki along with aftershocks from British imperial expansion created the forces that brought Mizeki's promising mission to its fatal conclusion. In early 1896 the Shona were caught up in a rebellion, initiated by the Ndebele a few years earlier, against Cecil Rhodes's British South African Company. Although the Ndebele were harsh oppressors of the Shona, the Ndebele resistance against British rule inspired the Shona. British leaders, including the Anglican missionaries, were surprised when the Shona joined in rebellion. But the Shona had also reacted to the new colonial order, with its hut tax, its mandated inoculations and its burning of infected cattle. In addition, the mid-1890s witnessed a tumultuous period of drought, locust plagues, new diseases for cattle and widespread famine that further poisoned relations between Africans and their new imperial rulers.

Locally, one of Mangwende's many sons had taken particular offense at Mizeki's entrance into the community, especially his marriage to one of Mangwende's own grandchildren. This anger was fueled by several *nganga* s who, quite correctly, saw Mizeki's new religion as an assault on their traditional worldview and the authority they had exercised in the local community. In mid-June 1896, messengers brought news to Mizeki's local enemies that the Shona were attacking Europeans in nearby regions. This communication prompted a decision to go after Mizeki.

Shortly before, instructions had been sent to all Anglican catechists and teachers to gather for safety at a fortified mission farm. The message came from a member of Bishop Knight-Bruce's staff, since the bishop himself was absent in England, where he would die later that same year from malaria contracted in Mashonaland. Mizeki hesitated when this message arrived, since he felt bound by Bishop Knight-Bruce's earlier instructions to stay at Theydon. In addition, Mizeki had only recently given hospitality to an ill and incapacitated older man at the mission compound. Among the Shona it was a well-established cultural norm that the sick could be cared for only by family members; if Mizeki left this new patient, he knew that no one else would look after him.

The upshot was that Mizeki sent this reply: "Mangwende's people are suffering. The Bishop has put me here and told me to remain. Until the Bishop returns, here I must stay. I cannot leave my people now in a time of such darkness."

On Sunday, June 14, 1896, Bernard rang the mission bell for matins. No one came, not even Zandiparira, who had not missed a service in four years, nor those who were residing with Mizeki at the mission compound. Mutwa, his wife, had been told what was up: the local *nganga* was enraged; he had been informed by the spirits that Christianity was sorcery and Bernard was a sorcerer; for cutting down the sacred trees there was a sentence of death. Mutwa, who was pregnant, urged Mizeki to leave. He demurred.

On Wednesday evening, June 17, after taking in a stranger who arrived late and asked for lodging, Mizeki and Mutwa saw bonfires in the hills surrounding their residence. About midnight, Bernard answered a loud knocking at his door where someone announced that European troops had killed Mangwende. (They had not.) When Mizeki stepped outside, he was assaulted by three men, one of whom drove a spear deep into his side. Mutwa followed and threw herself on top of Bernard, but the men dragged her off and pitched her back into the hut. When she emerged, the men had gone and Mizeki seemed to be dead. Quickly she ran to find the wife of Chigwada Gawe ("Joseph"), who returned with her to the hut. Mizeki was not there. They called for him, and he answered from a short distance away beside a nearby spring. He told them that he had been attacked by three of her relatives, that he was dying, and that he wanted Mutwa and their child to be baptized. He said that other teachers would come and that all of Mutwa's people would become Christians. Then she and her companion returned to their hut to find blankets and prepare sustenance for her wounded husband.

At this point it is worth quoting Jean Farrant's book, since she exerted great pains collecting all possible sources of information and, in the late 1950s, actually interviewed Mutwa and several other Africans who as young people were at or close to the scene in June 1896.

> As [the women] left the hut to climb the slope again, they halted in terrified amazement. They were almost blinded by a great and brilliant white light. The whole of the hillside was lit up, and there was a noise "like many wings of great birds." The noise was coming lower and lower, and as they crouched on the ground, covering their eyes, the women saw through their fingers that in the centre of the light, where

> Bernard lay, there was a strange red glow. They were very frightened and hid themselves, shaking from head to foot. After a long time, the noise ceased and they dared to look again. The light had gone, and they crept up the hill to the rock above the spring. It was empty. Bernard had gone. They never saw him again.

Farrant also discovered alternative accounts that came second- and third-hand from both Africans and Europeans. After her own careful sifting of all the evidence she could find, she concluded: "It is left to the individual Christian mind to accept or reject the supernatural light, but it seems certain that something happened that night which to the Africans was beyond explanation, which frightened them very much, and made a deep impression."

COMMEMORATING A MARTYR

The Shona rebellion was finally put down in the fall of 1897. Mutwa and the daughter born after Mizeki's death were baptized, but for several decades the Christian work among the Shona advanced slowly. In 1899 a white Anglican priest returned to where Mizeki had established his mission and founded a school for boys. Later missionaries identified the site of the martyrdom, planted a cross and memorialized his death with an annual service on June

18. After more investigation of the site in the early 1930s, another white Anglican built a circular shrine. It was consecrated in June 1938 at a service attended by a hundred Europeans and a thousand Africans, including "Joseph" (Chigwada Gawe). In 1946, on the fiftieth anniversary of Mizeki's death, a larger crowd, which included Mutwa and her daughter, gathered for a celebratory service of Communion and to hear a message read from the governor of Rhodesia.

Into the mid-twentieth century, white Anglicans sponsored commemorations of Mizeki's death. The Cowley Fathers eagerly promoted Mizeki's story wherever their missionary work spread. The picture they offered was of the faithful convert, loyal friend and inspiring Anglican. Commemorations slowly picked up speed. By the time of Jean Farrant's book in 1966, memorials of many kinds—stained glass, reliquaries, murals, inclusion on provincial Anglican calendars in South and Central Africa—existed in Swaziland, Botswana, South Africa and Rhodesia.

With the rise of African independence the image of Mizeki changed. The meaning of his life was hotly contested especially during the anticolonial war that led to the transformation of Rhodesia into Zimbabwe. Some ardent nationalists called him a colonial collaborator; others saw him as a sign of African dignity. For the latter, his efforts at defining the Shonas' ancestral deity, Mwari, as the Christian God became a symbol of his identification with African aspirations.

In South Africa, Anglican leaders founded a Bernard Mizeki Guild in 1973. Its purpose was to provide an Anglican meeting place for migrant workers coming into South Africa who found Anglican worship confining and so were drifting off to Methodist or African Independent Churches. The guild, with its lay-led, informal, worker-friendly environment, spread rapidly. After Zimbabwe gained its independence in 1980, the place of Mizeki's martyrdom became an increasingly popular pilgrimage site. African Anglicans now conducted a Eucharist on the weekend closest to June 18, and pilgrimages to the site were considered a continuation in Christian form of the ancient Shona practice of travel to sacred places.

Dana Robert has provided an account of what the annual commemoration was like by the early 2000s. Pilgrims arrived on the Thursday ahead of the Communion service; there was much singing and dancing, as well as many fires (to fend off the cold of the southern-hemisphere winter). On Friday a competition took place among church choirs. On Saturday, after a huge procession, local bishops and the archbishop of Central Africa celebrated a two-hour Communion service, with much singing. The liturgy was spoken in the many languages of the Church of the Province of South Africa. After the official service, Africans renowned for their charismatic gifts conducted healings. On Saturday night, bonfires once again encircled the hills. On Sunday, local Anglican priests led a final Eucharist. Throughout the weekend, pilgrims ascended to the spot from where Mizeki is said to have disappeared. The stand of trees surrounding the place had once again become a sacred grove, with Shona religious traditions taken up into Christian remembrance. When in recent celebrations, some participants have tried to make political statements about Zimbabwe's current situation, most of the other participants have turned aside. In 2005, despite Zimbabwe's internal political tensions, massive shortages of food and fuel, and an unemployment rate of 80 percent, almost twenty thousand pilgrims attended the annual festival.

SOURCES

The diligently researched book by Jean Farrant, *Mashonaland Martyr: Bernard Mizeki and the Pioneer Church* (Cape Town: Oxford University Press, 1966), is the basis for much of this chapter. The quotation from Mizeki is on p.208, and Farrant's account of what happened after his death is on pp.216-22. Material on the memory of Mizeki in this chapter is taken from Dana L. Robert, "St. Patrick and Bernard Mizeki: Missionary Saints and the Creation of Christian Communities" (Occasional Publication no.19, Yale Divinity School Library, 2005), which is also expanded in Dana Lee Robert, *Christian Mission: How Christianity Became a World Religion* (Malden, Mass.: Wiley-Blackwell, 2009), pp.167-70. Information about the first record from 1909 of the great light and sound of birds at Mizeki's death is found on p.177 of Terrence Ranger, "Taking Hold of the Land: Holy Places and Pilgrimages in Twentieth-Century Zimbabwe," *Past and Present* 117 (1987):158-94.

2

JOHN CHILEMBWE c.1870-1915

HOLISTIC CHRISTIAN AND ACCIDENTAL REBEL

January 15 is John Chilembwe Day in the landlocked central African country of Malawi, which lies between Mozambique on the east, south and west; Tanzania on the northeast; and Zambia on the northwest. The long Lake Malawi (or Lake Nyasa) makes up much of the country's eastern border with Tanzania and Mozambique. Most of its southern border is formed by the Zambezi River, which Europeans read much about in books written by the pioneering explorer and missionary David Livingstone. Malawi, formerly the British colony of Nyasaland, became independent in 1964; as one of its first official acts the newly independent nation issued a stamp in memory of John Chilembwe and the revolt he had led against British imperial oppression fifty years before.

John Chilembwe (seated) with wife Ida and daughter Emma

That revolt was one of several African reactions at about the same time to the tide of European colonialism that swept over the continent from the 1880s onward. In South Africa, for example, the African National Congress, which decades later became that country's ruling political party after the overthrow of apartheid, was established in 1912. The revolt under Chilembwe in Nyasaland shared much with these other initiatives, including its desire to establish "Africa for the Africans" and escape subservience to Europeans. But there is much in the Nyasaland story that also makes it important as a Christian story.

One of the three Europeans killed in the short-lived 1915 revolt was William Jervis

Livingstone, a distant relative of David Livingstone. The famous Livingstone, David, had worked near the site of John Chilembwe's revolt, as he evangelized and tried to provide economic alternatives to slavery. Moreover, William Jervis Livingstone was employed on an estate owned by a wealthy Scotsman, Alexander Low Bruce, who was married to David Livingstone's daughter. Most strikingly, the father of the murdered plantation overseer had long served in his native Scotland as a missionary on the Isle of Skye and then as a Baptist pastor. The irony is that John Chilembwe, leader of the 1915 revolt, was also a Baptist pastor and missionary who like David Livingstone had given himself to evangelizing and providing economic self-sufficiency for Africans. The bloody events of early 1915 were unusual in themselves. They were also the culmination of a story filled with complex interpersonal relations, worldwide geographical connections and memorable initiatives on behalf of new African believers.

JOSEPH BOOTH COMES TO NYASALAND

A fateful meeting in 1892 between a strong-minded British missionary and an unusually capable native serving "boy" constitutes the first act of this dramatic story. Early that year Joseph Booth had arrived in the Zambezi region as a mature forty-one-year-old dissenting Protestant of decidedly independent convictions. The area was only just being defined as a British Protectorate, soon to be called Nyasa-land, in the wake of competition among Britain, Germany, Portugal, Belgium and France for colonies throughout the continent.

Booth had been raised in an English home where Christian ethics enjoyed great respect but also where unorthodox opinions prevailed (Booth's father was a Unitarian). At an early age Booth indicated his contrarian course by posing questions to his father about the military service of Booth's grandfather and uncles. These relatives often boasted of the number of enemy troops they had killed in battle. The young Booth challenged his father to explain how the biblical commandment, "Thou shalt not kill," could be squared with that boasting. His father, who had insisted that young Booth memorize and regularly repeat the command-ments, floundered in providing an answer. In response, Joseph Booth abandoned Christianity and set off on a course of religious searching.

Again to indicate the singular course of Booth's spiritual journey, he was set back on the path of more orthodox Christianity by reading the religious writings of Thomas Paine.

Paine at the time was reviled as one of the great infidels of his age; what Booth took from him was not infidelity, however, but Paine's confession that it was impossible to deny that Jesus of Nazareth actually lived. From that starting point, Booth moved on to embrace standard Christian teachings, though always with his own distinctive emphases. For instance, from his earliest days as a convinced believer, Booth was a consistent pacifist—his early doubts about the use of deadly force in battle led on to a deep aversion to any use of violence. Booth was always an independent operator who set up his own organizations and who remained very much his own man as he tried to change the world for Christ.

Booth's route to the mission field was circuitous. Before his own faith stabilized he migrated in 1880 to New Zealand, where he showed his practical abilities by becoming a successful sheep farmer. In 1886 he joined the Tabernacle in Auckland, a church pastored by Thomas Spurgeon, son of the famous London minister Charles Haddon Spurgeon. Under Thomas Spurgeon's guidance, Booth made a firm commitment to Christ and took part in a range of Christian ministries. Then Booth moved to Australia, where he established successful restaurants in Melbourne and became a deacon in a local Baptist church. When in Melbourne he experienced a call to missionary service and tried to enlist in the China Inland Mission of J. Hudson Taylor but was told he was already too old. Undaunted, Booth organized his own supporters in Australia, Scotland, and England and set off for Africa. His models were David Livingstone and the first British missionary to India, the Baptist William Carey. Booth found both Livingstone and Carey particularly inspiring because they combined a strong commitment to evangelism with an equal commitment to the economic development of the evangelized.

Booth arrived in Nyasaland at a time of colonial ferment. The new British administration was trying to sort out land claims involving colonial settlers and the many African tribes of the region. British officials were also struggling to outlaw the slave trade that Arab merchants and powerful African chiefs had no intention of giving up without a fight. The British colonial administration was being helped (and critiqued) by the Scottish and English missionaries who had worked in the region for a generation. Missionary labor near Lake Nyasa had begun at the instigation of David Livingstone in the late 1850s, but spectacular failures had occurred before church planting got underway in the 1870s. Progress remained slow as colonial-African, Arab-African, and intra-African tribal conflicts all contributed to tumult and disorder.

Booth came to Nyasaland with a teenage son and a young daughter. Their mother, who had encouraged Booth's move to missionary service, died in Australia shortly before they embarked for Africa. The motherless family struggled in its first weeks on the field. They were not at all helped by their first house servants, whose skills were much more advanced in pilfering and malingering than in cooking, translating or foraging. Into this discouraging situation came a young man, perhaps twenty years old, who spoke only a few words of English but who told the Booths he had heard they were looking for reliable help.

A FATEFUL MEETING

Little hard information survives about John Chilembwe's early life. His father was of the Yao people, who had won a reputation for fierce resistance to the European colonizers, and his mother was a member of the Mang'anja tribe, who were said to be marked by softer human virtues. A period of instruction at a Church of Scotland mission school had introduced him to the English language. That school was in Blantyre, which was becoming a center of British administration in the area between the southern end of Lake Nyasa and the Zambezi River. (Blantyre took its name from the Scottish birthplace of David Livingstone.)

Immediately the new houseboy won the respect of the Booth family, then their admiration and soon their love. He was honest, meticulous, caring and self-giving. The depth of affection between the Booths and John Chilembwe is indicated by what the two surviving members wrote after the tragic events of 1915. (The teenaged son had died as a youth in Nyasaland.) The young daughter, Emily Booth, whom Chilembwe nursed through several life-threatening illnesses, later returned to Britain, married and years later published a memoir about her experiences in Africa—in it she had only kind things to say about Chilembwe. For his part Joseph Booth, though he repudiated Chilembwe's turn toward violence, was even more deeply attached. After Chilembwe was killed and he himself had been expelled from Africa because British authorities connected him (without cause) to the Chilembwe revolt, Booth wrote these tender words:

> Poor kindhearted Chilembwe, who wept with and for the writer's feverstricken and apparently dying child; nursed and fed the father with a woman's kindness during 10 months of utter prostration; wept, laboured with and soothed the dying hours of my

> sweet son John Edward [18 years old] at the close of a 2 month's toilsome journey to the ocean post, for food and goods, in flood time of rainy season, 1894.... Yes, dear Chilembwe, gladly would I have died[,] by my own countrymen shot, to have kept thee from the false path of slaying.

With Chilembwe's help, Booth's labors in Nyasaland bore fruit in converts and in the establishment of the Zambezi Industrial Mission, located in Mitsidi, just west of Blantyre. Chilembwe was a critical part of that success as steward of the household, translator for the Africans and also Booth's star pupil. Anglican and Church of Scotland missionaries distrusted Booth because his Baptist faith was so single-mindedly biblical and so independent. Colonial officials were nervous because he promoted African economic self-sufficiency so vigorously. Through his Zambezi Industrial Mission, Booth taught primarily agricultural skills aimed at preparing natives to sell homegrown coffee and other products in the emerging market towns of the region. But the mission also trained workers in crafts and small-scale manufacturing with the intent of providing economic foundations for community self-development and self-organization. And all within the context of conservative, Bible-driven, Baptist piety.

Booth explicitly spelled out his vision for Christian mission in Africa on several occasions. One of these occasions was the formation of an "African Christian Union" in Blantyre in January 1897. Included in the twenty "objectives" of this union was, first, "to unite together in the name of Jesus Christ such persons as desire to see full justice done to the African race and are resolved to work towards and pray for the day when the African people shall become an African Nation." Other objectives included equal legal treatment for Africans and Europeans, repentance for "the great wrongs inflicted upon the African race in the past and in the present," establishment of profitable agricultural and industrial operations run by Africans, education for training Africans in liberal arts and practical subjects, and restitution of African lands appropriated by the European colonial powers. It also called on black Americans and Caribbeans of African descent to come to Africa as workers for the reconstruction of the continent, and it asked the United States government to "make a substantial monetary grant to each adult Afro-American desiring to be restored to African soil, as some recognition of the 250 years of unpaid slave labor and the violent abduction of millions of Africans from their native land."

Four individuals—Booth, another English missionary, Morrison Malinka from the Chipeta Tribe and Chilembwe—signed the document proclaiming this African Christian Union. The provisions of the document mentioning the United States were particularly significant for this story, since in 1897 Chilembwe was preparing for new ventures that would take him, with Booth, to America.

TO THE U.S.A.

The reasons why Chilembwe accompanied Booth to America are not entirely clear, but they seem to have come as much from Chilembwe's initiative as from Booth's. In 1895 Booth had made an earlier American journey with the goal of asking African Americans to support his industrial mission. That trip had not been successful, but it held out the possibility of better results at a later time. When Booth returned with Chilembwe to the U.S. in 1897, he once again tried to enlist American blacks in support of his holistic missionary vision.

For his part, Chilembwe seems to have wanted to show what Africans could do if they learned some European ways. In the early days of European colonization, the Arab slave traders had circulated several legendary accounts of Europeans in order to keep the trade for themselves. One of those legends was that the vast stream of Africans taken as slaves to the new world (none of whom were ever seen again) were captured, sold and transported vast distances—in order to be eaten! Joseph Booth's daughter once reported that she and her father had been accused of cannibalism after she had kissed an African baby. For Africans not accustomed to kissing, Emily Booth looked like she was savoring a meal. By going to the U.S. with Booth and then returning to report on how free blacks lived in the new world, John Chilembwe was confident he could provide convincing refutation of this malevolent legend.

It was a struggle for Chilembwe and Booth to raise money for the trip, which took them from the Zambezi River to London, Liverpool, New York and Washington, D.C., before finally arriving in Virginia, where Chilembwe spent more than two years. But survive they did, and shortly after their arrival in the U.S., Chilembwe began study at the Virginia Theological Seminary and College in Lynchburg, Virginia. This institution was still a relatively new foundation of local black Baptists, but it was linked to missionary efforts of the National Baptist Convention of the United States of America, which itself had only been organized in 1895. The school's student body of about two hundred provided a hospitable home for Chilembwe while Booth was off raising funds, working up support for African ventures and publishing a landmark book with a long, self-explanatory title: *Africa for the African. Dedicated First, to Victoria, Queen of Great Britain. Second, to the British and American Christian People. Third and Specially to the Afro-American people of the United States of America.—By Joseph Booth, Missionary, Nyasaland, East Central Africa.*

Chilembwe's journey and his life in Lynchburg provided more than enough firsthand knowledge to rebut rumors about European and American cannibalism. More importantly, his presence in the United States during a critical period of African American history eventually led to his friendly separation from Booth as well as to the principles he later implemented in Africa.

Chilembwe received wholehearted support in America from independent black churches that had successfully established independent educational institutions. Organization of the National Baptist Convention came late after several other black denominations had organized, the largest of which was the African Methodist Episcopal (AME) Church. These denominations and their schools provided Chilembwe with models of what he dreamed for Nyasaland. These same churches had also put a great deal of energy and raised considerable money for missionary ventures of their own in Africa. In fact, during Chilembwe's time in the United States, a leading bishop of the AME, Henry McNeal Turner, was making a tour of South Africa that was widely reported in the U.S. Turner was there not only to scout out prospects for black American missionaries but also to encourage African churches that were seeking a counterweight to European missionaries. To many African Christians, especially those who had founded what they called "Ethiopian" churches, contact with the well-organized black churches of North America provided a stimulating example of self-direction.

"Ethiopianism" was a young movement in the 1890s. But at several places on the continent, particularly in South Africa, different groups of Africans had grown dissatisfied, not with the Christian faith brought by Europeans, but with the Europeans who brought Christianity. That dissatisfaction led to black-organized movements splitting off from missionary control and setting up their own churches. Biblical inspiration came from Psalm 68:31, "Ethiopia shall soon stretch out her hands unto God" (KJV). Almost from the start, some of the leaders in these churches made contact with African Americans; some Americans like Henry McNeal Turner responded with open arms, even to the point of accepting African Ethiopian churches as branches of the AME church.

The convictions that supported African American eagerness to connect with Ethiopian churches had much to do with the disastrous American situation of the period. For black Americans, the 1890s represented an absolute low point after the heady promise of emancipation in the Civil War and the constitutional changes that promised full civil rights for former slaves. In the sad history of Reconstruction and its aftermath, however, most of those rights for African Americans in the South (and many in the North) had been systematically undermined. During Chilembwe's stay in Virginia, for example, the Virginia Democratic Party finalized its schemes for excluding blacks from the state's political life. Also during the 1890s, more than 150 blacks were lynched each year in the United States, with some of those illegal assaults perpetrated close to Lynchburg. One of Chilembwe's closest friends in the U.S. was the Reverend Charles Morris. As a minister in Wilmington, North Carolina, Morris witnessed the city's 1898 race riot, which left eleven blacks dead and many more injured. When Chilembwe returned to Africa, Reverend Morris accompanied him as an opponent of white supremacy as well as a representative of African American missions.

The details of Chilembwe's American education are not recorded, but his later career in Africa suggests the course of his study and the range of his American contacts. He certainly would have learned about Booker T. Washington, founder of the Tuskegee (Alabama) Normal and Industrial Institute, and Washington's much-admired plans for bettering the Negro race. From Washington, Chilembwe would have taken lessons about the importance of education, the wisdom of incremental change and the all-important practical achievement of self-respect. But Chilembwe would have also heard about W.E.B. DuBois and DuBois' more militant willingness to confront racist abuses of power. During Chilembwe's time in Virginia, DuBois denounced the Spanish-American War as imperialist aggression dooming Filipinos to the same second-class status long experienced by American blacks. Shortly after Chilembwe returned to Africa, DuBois helped found the National Association for the Advancement of Colored People. In America, Chilembwe would also have acquired some awareness of American slave revolts and the prime role Scripture had played in these revolts. He may have heard about Nat Turner's famous rebellion of 1831 in Southampton County, Virginia, which was inspired by Turner's particular focus on apocalyptic biblical texts. Chilembwe, in other words, learned at the Lynchburg school as much about black resistance to white oppression as he did about Baptist standards of Christian faith and practice.

Toward the end of his time in America, Chilembwe was formally taken under the wing of the National Baptist Convention. This sponsorship came about as Chilembwe was breaking his ties with Joseph Booth. The separation was amiable; both men retained a respectful affection for each other. But Booth's lack of funding had continued to put a strain on his activities, and with sponsorship from African American Baptists Chilembwe acted on his own initiative to relieve Booth of financial responsibility and of the need to pay his way back to Africa. For his part, Booth had taken up yet another radical Christian position by associating with the small Seventh Day Baptist movement. When he returned to Africa, Booth became an ambassador for the doctrine that the proper Christian day of worship was Saturday. Chilembwe did not share this conviction.

Yet although henceforth independent of Booth, Chilembwe's work continued to reflect Booth's influence. At Lynchburg, Chilembwe was the key figure in founding an African Development Society whose principles and procedures followed closely the ways in which Booth had tried to develop his own industrial missions. And much that Chilembwe attempted after his time in the United States represented a continuation of Booth's holistic Christian vision.

RETURNING TO AFRICA

Chilembwe returned to Nyasaland in 1900 as an ordained minister of the National Baptist Convention; in 1901 the Virginia Theological Seminary and College conferred A.B. and B.D. degrees on him in absentia. Chilembwe also returned dressed in formal European style as he had seen the ministers of black Methodist and Baptist attired in the United States.

One of the first things Chilembwe did upon his return was to purchase a plot of land in the Chiradzulu District northeast of Blantyre. On this land at Mbombwe he established the Providence Industrial Mission, patterned on Joseph Booth's Zambezi Industrial Mission. It soon provided a center of Christian instruction, basic liberal education and training in agriculture as well as the trades.

Through hard years of struggle, Chilembwe and his helpers succeeded in making a go of the effort. Some of the help came from the United States in the form of African American Baptists who served short terms of service. Americans also provided some financial and legal assistance. Within ten years, the Mission expanded to seven sites with well over one thousand younger pupils and six to eight hundred adults. It experimented in growing cotton, tea, pepper, rubber and coffee. And it provided the means for many Africans to move toward economic independence. It also remained consistently marked by conservative Christian ethics, dedicated study of the Bible and strong Baptist principles of congregational independence.

Great assistance in these efforts came from Chilembwe's wife, Ida, whom he married (probably) after returning from America. Ida Chilembwe was one of the head teachers at the main school in Chiradzulu. In the mission's early years Ida Chilembwe, assisted by an American, Emma DeLany, taught sewing and European manners to women who came to the Mbombwe school. She also traveled regularly into the villages, providing instruction in the Scriptures and encouraging native women to be more active in their religious, domestic and social lives. Ida Chilembwe spoke out against the practice of marrying girls early and in favor of providing education for female students as well as for boys. She was a hard-working, pious exemplar of what she hoped for in her female students. Reports of her work include the sad fact that she received no help from European women and so found herself isolated from Africans by her "advanced" ways and from Europeans by her race.

Chilembwe himself regularly preached orthodox Baptist sermons, helped Africans read the Scriptures in English as well as their own languages and maintained high standards of personal morality. He stressed abstinence from alcohol as a negative ethic; positively, he encouraged values of hard work, personal hygiene and self-help. In 1913 the Providence Industrial Mission completed a large, stately church building where worship in the Baptist style was sustained until, in the wake of the 1915 rebellion, it was razed by the colonial authorities.

More or less following the path set out by Booker T. Washington, Chilembwe urged Africans to develop stable habits as a way of securing their place in a world ruled by whites. Much of the Providence Industrial Mission's work looked anything but radical as it focused on basic literacy, numeracy and economic skills. At the same time, it was also obvious that Chilembwe had learned much from the more assertive, critical stance of W.E.B. DuBois. From the start, his mission was a thorn in the flesh to colonial administrators. In particular, he complained steadily about *thangata,* the oppressive practice by which European landowners extracted work from African dependents in lieu of rent.

In 1909 Chilembwe led in founding a Natives Industrial Union (later called the African Industrial Society). It sought an organized means to protect the interests of Africans in commerce, education and communication; it encouraged more Africans to become professionals; and it even lobbied for a court of arbitration where legal matters affecting Africans and the white population could be adjudicated. In his formal capacity as spokesman for the union, Chilembwe constantly berated colonial officials for keeping Africans dependent and poor. Eventually the African Industrial Society organized a war council and formed five separate battalions of an African quasi militia. Chilembwe was named the "field marshal" of this nascent self-protective organization.

THE RISING

Events surrounding the start of World War I led directly to Chilembwe's 1915 Rising. From 1911, he had suffered physical setbacks with increasing debility brought on by attacks of asthma. His mission was suffering financial reverses. He found himself powerless to prevent the colonial government from imposing harsher taxes and the colonial landowners from requiring more time-consuming, more demanding *thangata.* And from 1913 poor harvests led to near-famine conditions in the region.

When the European war broke out in the summer of 1914, Africa felt the effects almost immediately. By the tens of thousands, Africans were recruited as *tenga-tenga* (carriers, diggers, construction crews) to support the military operations aimed at German East Africa (Tanzania today). In September 1914, a battle at Karonga in the far north of Nyasaland led to dozens killed on both the German and British sides, with the majority of the dead in both armies African. Many more Africans died of malnutrition and disease while on military duty.

This combination of events moved Chilembwe to compose a public letter for the *Nyasaland Times.* Copies of the document are scarce since colonial authorities immediately destroyed issues of the newspaper where it appeared, and an incomplete run of this paper leaves some uncertainty as to its exact date. The careful research of historians George Shepperson and Thomas Price, however, has determined that the letter was published in late November 1914. It was a hard-hitting indictment. Chilembwe began by stating, "We understand that we have been invited to shed our innocent blood in this world's war which is now in progress throughout the wide world." He then posed, for Africa, the most serious question possible: "We ask the Honourable government of our country which is known as Nyasaland, Will there be any good prospects for the natives after the end of the war? Shall we be recognized as anybody in the best interests of civilization and Christianity after the great struggle is ended?" Chilembwe contended that Africans had always been loyal to the British, but with nothing to show for it: "in time of peace the Government failed to help the underdog.... And instead of honor we suffer humiliation with names contemptible. But in time of war it has been found that we are needed to share hardships and shed our blood in equality." If the conflict were an honorable war, Chilembwe asserted, it would have meant that "the rich men, bankers, titled men, store-keepers, farmers and landlords" would go into harm's way. Instead, "the poor Africans who have nothing to own in this world, who in death, leave only a long line of widows and orphans in utter want and dire distress are invited to die for a cause which is not theirs." He closed with, "Hope in the Mercy of Almighty God, that some day things will turn out well and that Government will recognize our indispensability and that justice will prevail."

The sequence of events surrounding the posting of this letter is contested. Chilembwe may have begun talking about an armed uprising against some of the most oppressive estates before he sent the letter, or perhaps only afterward. The colonial government may have made plans to expel Chilembwe before this letter, or only after it was sent. Regardless, relations deteriorated rapidly in late 1914 and early 1915. Chilembwe gathered about two hundred loosely organized "militia," while the government pushed forward with plans to send him into exile.

When rumors of imminent reprisal multiplied, Chilembwe called for concerted action on the night of January 23, 1915. It was the night of an annual party for Europeans at the Blantyre Sports Club, where it was assumed many guests would be away late and come home intoxicated. African militia loyal to Chilembwe advanced on several estates and also tried to take over a cache of weapons and ammunition. Shortly before, Chilembwe had told his followers about John Brown and the raid in 1859 on the arsenal at Harper's Ferry, Virginia, where Brown hoped a spontaneous slave revolt would result. Planning for the rising had been slipshod, and most of these efforts failed. At the Bruce Estate, however, Africans succeeded in overcoming the house; they killed William Jervis Livingstone; then they cut off his head and took it to the church of the Providence Industrial Mission, where it was displayed on the altar. Livingstone had been notorious for whipping African workers, cheating them of their wages, and burning down churches and schools they had built for their own self-improvement.

Two other European men were killed. At the same time, the African rebels scrupulously obeyed Chilembwe's orders not to harm women and children. As he was reported to have said, he did not want acts of righteousness soiled by "lechery." Although panic gripped the European communities in the Blantyre region, the rising was swiftly put down. Some of the rebels were apprehended immediately; those who were thought to have played any serious role were shot immediately or hung after summary legal proceedings.

It seems to have been Chilembwe's original intent to gather followers in his church and wait there for death from the expected counterattack. But when the rebels disbursed he fled this site and made for the Mozambique border. Rumors persisting in Malawi to this day suggest that he escaped over the border and made his way to America. But well-verified reports at the time, along with later historical research, confirm that he was shot to death on February 3 by African troops working with colonial officials.

In the wake of the rising, most of the Africans who cooperated with Chilembwe were apprehended and then executed or exiled after being flogged. Missionaries attached to churches whose members took part were expelled. Joseph Booth, then living in South Africa, was also exiled, though he had had little direct contact with Chilembwe for over a decade. A commission of inquiry was asked to investigate the causes of the revolt and recommend reforms, but when it finished its work in 1916 its suggestions were disregarded. Chilembwe's effort to hasten honorable treatment of Africans seemed to have run into the ground with his blood, leaving many questions unanswered. One of the most pressing has been well described by the historian Adrian Hastings: "What is very difficult is to understand how the rather mild-mannered Ethiopian churchman was transformed in his last weeks into the instigator of murder and anarchy. Perhaps the sheer awfulness of the prospect of war and his own deep isolation combined to craze the mind of a sensitive man long embittered by a colonial system which bore particularly painfully on the few who were as educated as he."

ASSESSMENT

As enthusiasm for Chilembwe in modern Malawi suggests, it is necessary to say something more. In fact, Chilembwe represented one of the most serious African attempts of the early twentieth century to extend what white missionary pioneers of the nineteenth century had attempted. Thomas Fowell Buxton was a British evangelical who succeeded William Wilberforce as leader of the forces in Parliament who opposed slavery and the slave trade. In 1839 he published a book titled *The African Slave Trade and Its Remedy,* in which he proposed "Christianity, Commerce, and Civilization" as a formula for reconstituting an Africa decimated by the ravages of slavery. The ideal was genuine Christian faith supported by the fruits of education (civilization) and economic alternatives to slave-trading (commerce). Buxton's own efforts at implementing this ideal were not successful, but they did inspire a young Scottish Congregationalist to devote himself to helping Africa by bringing the gospel and by finding alternatives to slavery. That individual was David Livingstone, who pioneered his holistic mission in John Chilembwe's home region. Joseph Booth took up the same holistic vision in his own idiosyncratic way. It became the key to John Chilembwe's personal attachment to Joseph Booth, to his education and relations with African Americans, and to his efforts with the Providence Industrial Mission. As a slogan, "Christianity, Commerce, and Civilization" may have an imperialistic ring. As a way of life, it was the path that John Chilembwe chose for himself and that remains to inspire a great number of the increasing throngs of Christian believers throughout the African continent to this day.

SOURCES

The source of quotations from Chilembwe and Booth and an outstanding study for all aspects of Chilembwe's life is George Shepperson and Thomas Price, *Independent African: John Chilembwe and the Origins, Setting and Significance of the Nyasaland Native Rising of 1915* (Edinburgh: Edinburgh University Press, 1958; a second edition was published in 1987), p.358 for Booth's comments on Chilembwe, pp.531-32 for quotations from Booth's Christian Union, and pp.234-35 for quotations from Chilembwe's 1914 letter. The last quotation about Chilembwe is from Adrian Hastings's splendid survey, *The Church in Africa, 1450-1950,* Oxford History of the Christian Church (New York: Oxford University Press, 1994), p.489. Good outlines of Chilembwe's life are found in the *Historical Dictionary of Malawi,* 3rd ed. (Lanham, Md.: Scarecrow, 2001); *Encyclopedia of African History* (New York: Fitzroy Dearborn, 2005); and the online *Dictionary of African Christian Biography* (www.dacb.org). The broader political context of the 1915 Rising is explored in Robert I. Rotberg, *The Rise of Nationalism in Central Africa: The Making of*

Malawi and Zambia, 1873-1964 (Cambridge, Mass.: Harvard University Press, 1965). Connections between African American churches and African churches are well explored in James T. Campbell, *Songs of Zion: The African Methodist Episcopal Church in the United States and South Africa* (New York: Oxford University Press, 1995). For contemporary interest in Malawi, see the articles by David T. Stuart-Mogg in *Society of Malawi Journal* 50, no.1 (1997):44-58; and 50, no.2 (1997):54-56. We offer special words of thanks to Wheaton College (Illinois) student Amy Rogers for her fine paper in 2005 on Booth and Chilembwe, and to George Shepperson for his personal help with this chapter.

3

ALBERT LUTHULI
1898-1967

GENTLEMAN OF JUSTICE

In his 1962 autobiography, *Let My People Go,* Albert Luthuli reminisced about his teenaged years,

Albert Luthuli

Many years ago, around about 1913, when first the significance of being landless pawns began to dawn, we sang a folk song:

Sikho siphi tina ma Afrika
Siyo zula, sizule, sizule...
Sakubona sakubaletha ma Afrika
Where are we Africans?
(We seem to be nowhere),
We shall wander and wander, and wander.
How far shall we go?

Behold, people of Africa, what a burden we bear!
We shall wander, and wander, and wander,
The Englishman this side, The Afrikaner this side,
The German this side, the German this side,
We shall wander, and wander, and wander.
How far shall we go?
Behold, people of Africa, what a burden we bear!"

In 1913 South Africa's parliament had just passed the "Native Land Act," which decreed that nonwhites would be allowed to live only on a designated 7 percent of South African land. An odd sort of kindness motivated this act. Prior to 1913 many native South Africans had not yet developed the concept of land ownership because they saw all land as communal. A family might claim a garden plot for one season and share the produce with others in the community but cultivate some other spot next season. Between seasons anyone could use any land for grazing. While the Native Land Act reserved a set amount of land, thus making ownership and permanence possible for native Africans, it also cemented great differences between the races. European colonists, having arrived less than three centuries earlier, were imposing their forms of law, land and legality on indigenous peoples who had lived there for more than two thousand years. The result in 1913 was systematized inequality.

By age sixty Albert Luthuli had lived all of his adult life under the Native Land Act and many subsequent rulings that created the system of apartheid in South Africa. If we were to enter the mature Luthuli's world we would see something like this:

> The year is 1958; you live in South Africa—and you are black. Your home is a two-room shanty on five acres of land in a rural area where in a good year, if you work hard, you can earn about 60 dollars. You may not buy this land, because you are among the 70% of the population assigned to 13% of the land; it is government land, not yours. You may be ordered to leave at any moment for any or no reason. You rarely see government currency; your wealth is cattle. But the land is overgrazed and so the government has "reduced" your cattle, with no compensation to you.
>
> You carry a pass which identifies you by name and race, and records every trip you have made more than a few miles from home. Your pass allows you to work, but only at the lowest types of physical labor. Jobs are assigned by race. You may marry but also only within your own race group.

If you find work in a city, you cannot bring your family with you; you eat and sleep with other workers in a fenced outdoor space on the edge of town. When you leave your work, after six months, to visit your family, you are quickly replaced and may not return. If you visit a town, you may stay only seventy-two hours. Your pass will note your entry and exit times. If you overstay, you may be arrested, questioned and beaten.

You may not vote. You may not speak to the press. Your tribe used to elect a chief who served as magistrate over local disputes. In the African reservation your "chief" is now a white government official, and you've never met him. Your children must leave your home on the day that they turn eighteen. Your younger children go to school, but it is a "Bantu school" where they learn to work, not read. Most classrooms have sixty or more children who attend school only half the day. The teacher takes another sixty children for the remainder of the day. You remember your own mission school which prepared you for University. Now you do not have enough to eat—ever. One out of three of your children die of malnutrition before they are a year old.

It was the burden of Albert Luthuli's life to change this situation.

EARLY YEARS

Albert Luthuli was born in 1898 near Bulawayo in what is now Zimbabwe, which lies north of modern South Africa. His mother, Mtonya Gumede, had lived in the household of Ceshwayo, the Zulu king. On his father's side, both his grandfather Ntaba and his uncle Martin Luthuli were tribal chiefs. John Luthuli, Albert's father, worked as an evangelist and interpreter for a Seventh-day Adventist mission near Bulawayo, but John died when the child was only six months old. When Albert was about age ten, the Adventists sent him and his older brother Alfred to assist with new mission work in South Africa not far from their father's ancestral home. Alfred would translate; the younger Albert would tend to the mission mules. "It was my mother who rescued me from my intimacy with mules," he later wrote. "She decided that I needed education and sent me back home to Groutville to get it." So Albert spent his teen years with his uncle's family in Groutville, a rural area in Natal near the city of Durban on South Africa's southeast coast. Later he told a story about how he began to learn the meaning of power. Luthuli's Uncle Harry, elected Chief of the Umvoti Mission

Reserve, had both civil and criminal jurisdiction over all African residents in that place. Albert remembered watching his uncle mediate a domestic dispute in which a man complained that his wife had deserted him, saying, "There she stands in the very clothes I have provided." This was the last straw for the deserting woman, so "she stripped herself completely naked, rolled her clothing into a bundle, and threw it at the man. To cap it all, my uncle and his *indum* bolted from the scene like terrified horses. It was a revelation to us children—that a woman could make a chief run."

By 1918, Albert Luthuli had completed his formal education, which consisted of the Groutville Mission day school followed by two terms of boarding school at Ohlange Institute and a two-year teacher's course at Edendale about fifty miles west of Durbin. He then took his first job as principal and solo teacher of an intermediate school in Blaauwbosch in the Natal uplands. Throughout these first twenty years, Luthuli experienced his life and education within an African context shaped by European and British missionaries. Yet at his first teaching post "my religion received the jog that it needed" through the influence of "an old and very conscientious African minister, the Rev. Mtembu." Also important was the host family with whom he lodged, "an evangelist of the

Methodist Church, named Xaba, the devout and peaceful atmosphere of whose home echoed my own." Luthuli refused to pinpoint a date for his own conversion, but it was there that he was confirmed in the Methodist Church and became a lay preacher. Luthuli hated the term "Black Englishman," which many nationalists used to described graduates of mission-connected schools like himself. In Luthuli's thinking, "Two cultures met, and both Africans and Europeans were affected by the meeting. Both profited, and both survived enriched." This ideal of mutual help would become a prime theme of his life's work.

In 1920, Luthuli received a scholarship for another two years of teacher training at Adams College, also in the Durban area. He studied, lived and subsequently taught there (specializing as college choirmaster) for a happy and peaceful fifteen years. During this period he became secretary and then president of the African Teachers Association; he also founded the Zulu Language and Cultural Society. These activities soon brought his name to the attention of South African authorities. He also enjoyed friendship with the only other black teacher at the school, Z.K. Mathews. Luthuli and Mathews, two natural leaders, would spend much of their adulthood side by side, including a later trial for treason.

Beyond the college walls, those fifteen years were far from peaceful in South Africa as a whole. Between 1920 and 1935, racial segregation became the norm and apartheid loomed in the wings. In 1922, the army quelled a miners' strike, killing 214, mostly blacks. In 1923, the Native Urban Areas Act segregated many urban areas; by 1927, segregation became compulsory in 26 cities. Native Africans stirred toward action.

Meanwhile, in his relatively peaceful academic setting, Albert Luthuli married Nokukhanya Bhengu in 1927, after suitable family negotiations. Because blacks could not purchase land near Adams College, his wife lived in Groutville some eighty miles distant. "Behind our decision to live apart right from the first year of our marriage lay the spectre which haunts all Africans ... the spectre of impermanence and insecurity.... For all we knew at the time, this separation might have to persist throughout our lives.... As it was we lived away from each other for only eight years." Eventually the couple had seven children, about whom Luthuli later recalled, "We pray very hard about our children, most of all because of the South Africa in which they are growing up."

THE LEADER EMERGES

Luthuli's teaching career came to an end in 1935, when the tribal elders concluded that they needed his leadership at home and his people elected him the third-generation Luthuli to be named "Chief of the Umvoti Mission Reserve." On this reserve he could finally live with his wife. For the next sixteen years he served as tribal magistrate, mediator, advisor and connecting link with the outer world for the five thousand people living on the ten thousand acres of the reserve. The experience was a revelation: "Now I saw, almost as though for the first time, the naked poverty of my people, the daily hurt of human beings." In Luthuli's culture, the position of "Chief" was a lifetime commitment. It was a title he bore with honor, even when it was stripped away, until his death.

During those same sixteen years, South Africa moved step by step from segregation to apartheid. Black voting rights were revoked in the Cape (1936); the colony rejected UN oversight (1947); the Afrikaner Nationalist party came to power determined to enforce apartheid (1948); mixed marriages were forbidden (1949); pass laws, which limited where black South Africans could travel, became stricter (1950); public protests against apartheid were forbidden (1950); the United Nations criticized apartheid, but the criticism was rejected (1950); and separate voting lists made it impossible for "nonwhites" to exercise the franchise (1951).

The African National Congress (ANC) had been founded in 1912 as an organization working for the betterment of Africans in the face of restrictions and oppression like the Land Act of the following year. By 1952, its membership had grown to more than 100,000. In this year it also joined with the South African Indian Congress in a passive resistance effort called the "Campaign for the Defiance of Unjust Laws." This defiance consisted of mass meetings of up to 10,000 people (giving police notice ahead of time and directing traffic themselves if necessary); its supporters attempted to use white-only public facilities; they stayed out past curfews declared for Africans; and they publicly disobeyed pass laws. In response, the government arrested more than eight thousand resisters—including Albert Luthuli. That same year, 1952, Luthuli was elected president general of the ANC.

At this time in its history, the ANC had become the clearinghouse for a number of resistance groups with differing ideologies. A Youth League, the subsection with which Luthuli most closely identified, had been part of the organization since 1944. This segment of the

ANC worked in orderly, businesslike fashion to implement action plans aimed at making a public impact, but without violence. A second group was the Old Guard, led by Albert Bitina Xuma, former president general of the ANC: it generated resolutions, telegrams and interviews from cozy but sometimes ineffective business meetings; occasionally this body was accused of "dirty political washing." A third group was made up of political moderates, led by Luthuli's friend Z.K. Mathews; it worked at drawing together disparate parts of the organization, a service for which it was sometimes criticized as "fence sitters" by more actionminded delegates. Communists made up the fourth wing of the ANC. The presence of Communists worried all of the others, particularly members of the Youth League, who thought of Communists as "double-dealers" whom they feared might try to use the ANC to attack capitalists for their own purposes. From 1949 to 1952 the ANC boiled with internal debates among these four segments, meanwhile carrying out the public task of mostly nonviolent resistance to apartheid. It was almost happenstance that during this confusion over leadership, when it came time to elect a new president general in 1952, Albert John Luthuli of the Youth League rose to the top. Luthuli would hold that position the rest of his life. Historian Eric Feit has described Luthuli as "a man of high ideals, impressive personality, great courage, and singular political naiveté."

STRUGGLE

Immediately upon Luthuli's election, the South African Department of Native Affairs insisted that Luthuli either resign as president general of the ANC or give up his position as tribal chief at Groutville. Even though his own people elected him, the government would not allow a chief to sanction disobedience of any law. Luthuli chose the ANC. In a public statement of November 1952, titled "The Road to Freedom is Via the Cross," Luthuli explained the reasoning behind his decision:

> I have embraced the non-violent passive resistance technique in fighting for freedom because I am convinced it is the only non-revolutionary, legitimate and humane way that could be used by people denied, as we are, effective constitutional means to further aspirations. The wisdom or foolishness of this decision I place in the hands of the Almighty. What the future has in store for me I do not know. It might be ridicule, imprisonment, concentration camp, flogging, banishment, and even death. I only pray to the Almighty to strengthen my resolve so that none of these grim possibili-

> ties may deter me from striving, for the sake of the good name of our beloved country, the Union of South Africa, to make it a true democracy and a true union in form and spirit of all the communities in the land.

During the remaining fifteen years of his life, Luthuli did indeed endure many of the hardships he envisioned. For most of that time the condition of nonwhites in South Africa steadily worsened. From 1958 to 1966 Hendrik Frensch Verwoerd governed as the nation's prime minister with the express goal "to maintain white supremacy for all time to come over our own people and our own country, by force if necessary." To sustain this purpose, Verwoerd stated publicly that nonwhites should be taught from their earliest years that they could not be the equals of Europeans.

Verwoerd enforced supremacy of the white minority by trying to restrain all nonwhite "troublemakers," including the president general of the ANC. Almost as soon as he assumed his new position, Luthuli was placed under the first of what would eventually be four successive bans. The bans limited his travel to a fifteen-mile radius of his home, screened visitors and barred him from all public gatherings. These restrictions meant that when he suffered a stroke in 1955 he could not be taken immediately to a hospital for treatment, though eventually he did receive good medical care, for which he was deeply thankful. The ban also created some difficulties in worship. Under its provisions, Luthuli continued to attend Communion services because they were restricted to "communicants" and therefore not "public." But often he preached and prayed at home, where others came to join him because, as he wrote, "I do not ever intend to ask permission to worship God with my fellow-Christians—I do not concede that any man has the right either to grant or to withhold this 'privilege.'"

When his first two-year ban expired in 1954 Luthuli reported, "I immediately misbehaved. I went to Uitenhage, near Port Elizabeth, where I addressed the Cape Provincial Annual Conference." His next speaking assignment was to be in Johannesburg for an address to the three thousand delegates of the Congress of the People, who had gathered to create what would become the famous Freedom Charter. Luthuli was met at his local airport by police who presented him with papers and demanded, "Do you understand English?" "Well," said the now-famous orator, "perhaps just a little bit." Not convinced, the police explained in broken Xhosa the content of the papers, "You understand, you can't go from here and address any meeting. You understand?" Luthuli acknowledged that he did. This was the beginning of his second two-year ban. It would be followed by later bans, arrests and much general harassment that lasted the rest of his life. Luthuli's friend and colleague from Adams College days, Professor Z.K. Mathews, shared his fate as an ANC member accused of treason.

Amazingly, Luthuli continued despite this persecution to function as an effective leader. From behind the scenes he carefully orchestrated largely peaceful resistance such as the ANC bus boycott in 1957, when virtually all of the workers among a hundred thousand Africans living in one square mile on the fringe of Johannesburg walked up to twenty miles to work each day in protest of increased bus fare. Other actions included workers' stay-at-home days for "appropriate expressions of mourning" and mass demonstrations by African women who publicly broke the pass laws. Through all of this activity Luthuli earned the respect of even hostile observers as an individual of personal integrity and moral power.

Yet the ANC's attempts at peaceful resistance did not always end peacefully. On March 21, 1960, the Pan African Conference (PAC), an activist spinoff of the ANC, requested a public meeting in the township of Sharpeville and was refused. The participants' goal was to protest the pass laws and then give themselves up for peaceful arrest. When the crowd grew to an intimidating thousands, police opened fire. Sixty-nine protesters died; 186, including eight children, were wounded. When newspapers reported that 80 percent of these wounds were in the back, the "Sharpeville Massacre" became a rallying cry for the oppressed. In response, the South African government exonerated the police, declared a national emergency, imprisoned hundreds of blacks, and banned both the ANC and the PAC from any further activity.

After this massacre, a shaken Albert Luthuli wrote, "The guns of Sharpeville echoed across the world, and nowhere except among totalitarians was there any doubt about the true nature of what had occurred." Luthuli asked his people to respond with a stay-at-home day of mourning on March 28 so that they could pray and grieve. Large-scale arrests ensued; Luthuli estimated 20,000. "My own arrest took place, like many others, in the small hours of the morning. I was staying in the home of white Pretoria friends.... My host entered my bedroom with the police in order to arouse me. He himself was already under arrest."

The specific cause of this arrest after Sharpeville was that Luthuli publicly burned his pass in protest. Because he was too ill to go to prison, his guilty sentence was suspended and he was fined before being returned to home detention in Groutville. His attorney for this trial was Nelson Mandela. The trial itself was well publicized and so served to expose South Africa's apartheid system to the world.

In the midst of all this turmoil at home, the 1960 Nobel Peace Prize was awarded to Albert Luthuli "in recognition of his nonviolent struggle against racial discrimination." Still banned to within fifteen miles of his home, and despite sullen protests from Prime Minister Verwoerd and other South African officials, the first African to receive this prize was granted grudging permission to travel to Oslo, Norway, to receive his award.

MOTIVES

In a setting where safety meant silence, what kept Luthuli speaking? Why did he resist and keep on resisting? The answer was his Christian faith and his belief in the ancient doctrine of the image of God (the *imago Dei)* —that he, Albert Mvumbi (Continuous Rain) Luthuli, a black Zulu, bore the stamp of God. When arriving back in South Africa from a mission visit to the United States in 1948, he learned that such travel would be prohibited in the future because "natives who travel get spoilt." Said Luthuli, "I can only reply that I was not spoilt abroad. I was spoilt by being made in the image of God." Remarkably, Luthuli extended that grace to opponents. In 1959 he was asked point blank a question that must have hovered in the minds of every black person in South Africa: "Should we get rid of the whites?" Luthuli replied, "The aim should be to get him to repent of his wrongdoings rather than to work for his forceful removal out of the country." When questioned about why he allowed Communists to participate in the resistance work of ANC, he replied with an indirect response indicating that even Communists were included in the *imago Dei:* "I am in Congress precisely *because* I am a Christian.... My own urge *because* I am a Christian, is to get into the thick of the struggle ... taking my Christianity with me and praying that it may be used to influence for good the character of the resistance.... I am confident enough in the Christian Faith to believe that I can serve my neighbour best by remaining in his company." When he received the Nobel Prize, Luthuli returned to this theme as a defense for his life's work: "To remain neutral in a situation where the laws of the land virtually criticized God for having created men of colour was the sort of thing I could not as a Christian tolerate."

Albert Luthuli would not live to see his cause triumph. The very year that he received the Nobel Peace Prize, his own African National

Congress created a military wing that became increasingly violent. For the next two decades the laws enforcing apartheid became ever more repressive. In 1967, the almost deaf Luthuli was knocked down by a train during a walk near his home. He died soon after. The struggle to which he contributed so much would continue for almost three more decades, until Nelson Mandela, leader of the ANC, was elected President of South Africa in 1994 in the country's first all-race national election.

For Albert Luthuli, piety and social justice were harmonious parts of the same gospel. His message for South Africa was a message of reform and hope, but also of warning: "It is not too late for white Christians to look at the Gospels and re-define their allegiance. But if I may presume to do so, I warn those who care for Christianity, to go into *all* the world and preach the Gospel. In South Africa the opportunity is three hundred years old. It will not last forever. The time is running out." Throughout his years of public leadership Luthuli spoke out forcefully against a form of Christianity that "estranges my people from Christ." In his vision of the gospel, "Hypocrisy, double standards, and the identification of white skins with Christianity, do the same" in obscuring the Christian message. Albert Luthuli was a gentleman of justice who spent his life trying to stay the hand of violence. As moral leader of his nation and Africa's first recipient of the Nobel Peace Prize, he proclaimed with all means possible that because people of all races were created in God's image, they could and should live in dignity with one another.

SOURCES

An earlier version of this chapter by Carolyn Nystrom and Gerald J. Pillay appeared as "God's Image in Color," *Christian History and Biography* 94 (Spring 2007):28-31. The chapter has benefited greatly from Dr. Pillay's insights as well as from his book *Voices of Liberation: Albert Lutuli* (Pretoria, South Africa: HRSC Publishers, 1993). The African National Congress maintains a website with electronic access to many of Luthuli's works. Quotations in this chapter from Luthuli are from his book, *Let My People Go* (New York: McGraw-Hill, 1962). The words about Luthuli from Edward Feit are from his article, "Generational Conflict and African Nationalism in South Africa; the African National Congress, 1949-1959," *The International Journal of African Historical Studies* 5, no.2 (1972):181-202 (quotation, p.191). Leonard Thompson's *A History of South Africa* (New Haven, Conn.: Yale University Press, 1990) is a reliable general history; the quotation from Prime Minister Verwoerd comes from p.216 of this volume. Other general works with helpful background include J.W. Hofmeyr and Gerald J. Pillay, eds., *A History of Christianity in South Africa,* Vol.1 (Pretoria, South Africa: Haum Tertiary, 1994). For more specific treatment of Luthuli, see Gay W. Seidman, "Blurred Lines: Nonviolence in South Africa," *Political Science and Politics* 33, no 2 (2000):161-67; Jaulani Sithole and Sibongiseni Mkhize, "Truth or Lies? Selective Memories, Imaginings, and Representations of Chief Albert John Luthuli in Recent Political Discourses," *History and Theory* 39, no.4 (2000):69-85; Dorothy C. Woodson, "Albert Luthuli and the African National Congress: A Bio-Bibliography," *History in Africa* 13 (1986):345-62; and the entry for Luthuli in the online *Dictionary of African Christian Biography* (www.dacb.org).

WEST AFRICA

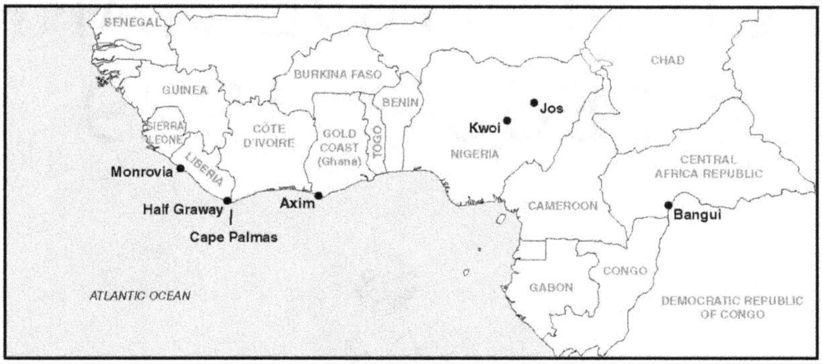
SENEGAL
GUINEA
SIERRA LEONE
LIBERIA
Monrovia
Half Graway
Cape Palmas
CÔTE D'IVOIRE
BURKINA FASO
GOLD COAST (Ghana)
Axim
TOGO
BENIN
NIGERIA
Kwoi
Jos
CHAD
CAMEROON
CENTRAL AFRICA REPUBLIC
Bangui
GABON
CONGO
DEMOCRATIC REPUBLIC OF CONGO
ATLANTIC OCEAN

4

WILLIAM WADÉ HARRIS c.1865–c.1929

William Wadé Harris with baptismal bowl, Bible, calabash gourd, and staff

PASSIONATE PROPHET

On February 13, 1909, a strange scene takes place on a beach in southern Liberia where a cluster of rivers meets Paduke Bay on its way to the Atlantic. An energetic black man in his mid-forties hoists a Union Jack on a flagpole. Not content with this mere gesture of British patriotism in support of a country he has never seen, the man mocks the Liberian flag that flies at the Liberian town of Harper across the bay, shouts invectives at the American-Liberians who guard it and tells them to get out of his country. Then he is put in jail, not for the first time, nor will it be the last. When questioned at his trial three months later, he will say that he had acted "in ignorance" and that he was "only playing."

William Wadé Harris, a son of the Grebo tribe in Liberia, had been born into a tumultuous place and time; for much of his life he would add to that tumult. Yet he began and ended his life in obscurity—so much so that both his birth and his death dates are uncertain. But for eighteen months spanning both sides of 1914, Harris had a dazzling public career as he traversed the three-hundred-mile coast of West Africa from Cape Palmas in southern Liberia through Côte d'Ivoire on to Axim, forty miles into the Gold Coast (now Ghana). Prior to this trip, eighty years of Protestant and Catholic mission work in Côte d'Ivoire had produced only several hundred converts. Ten years after Harris's momentous journey, with little intervening mission effort, estimates of Christians in that area ranged between two and three hundred thousand.

Who was William Wadé Harris? And what exactly did he do? As historians attempt to reconstruct his lifeline, important questions emerge: Was he Christian? Was he honest? Was he sane? (His wife thought not.) How did

African indigenous religion and culture shape the Christianity that Harris practiced and preached? What good did he accomplish? What evils resulted? How did his influence shape African and now global Christianity?

OBSCURE BEGININGS

William Wadé Harris was born in Half Graway, a small Liberian village on a coastal strip of land separated from the mainland by one of the many lagoons lacing Africa's western coast, about five miles east of Cape Palmas and a mere ten miles west from where Liberia borders Côte d'Ivoire. Uncertainty obscures the specific year of his birth as it does much of his life. His parents were from the Grebo tribe, his father a polygamist follower of local fetish religion and his mother an early Methodist convert. Harris had at least one brother.

The nation of Liberia, with its knuckle of Cape Palmas jutting into the Atlantic, was an unusual ethnic blend—even for Africa. The only West African nation not eventually subjected to European colonialism, Liberia began as an American settlement, or resettlement. In the early 1800s governmental and philanthropic groups in the United States began sending freed black slaves "home," often to Liberia, sometimes without consulting their desires in the matter. In 1824 these "settlers" drafted a constitution modeled after the U.S. government and established their capital city on the northwest coast, naming it Monrovia after James Monroe, president of the United States at the time. The Liberian flag, with its red and white bars reminiscent of "Old Glory," features a single white star in its blue field. Although heralded as a significant humanitarian project, the formation of Liberia almost completely bypassed indigenous peoples like the Grebo (sometimes termed Glebo). Indeed, the freedoms outlined in the new national constitution applied only to settlers, not to the Africans who already lived in the region.

After several generations in America, the returning settlers were lighter skinned than indigenous Liberians, and they were accustomed to Western culture. Many of them, having served in "the big house," now set up their own ethnic class system, this time with themselves at the top. They "bought" local property and constituted the Liberian government. The darker indigenous people became the despised working class, though usually not slaves. The Grebo and other coastal tribes became the crewmen whom European ship captains relied on as they navigated the treacherous waters hammering the ocean coast around Cape Palmas.

By the early twentieth century competing European powers were stirring Liberia's ethnic stew. Would the Grebo people be better off ruled by white European colonialists than the highhanded settlers from the United States? If so, should they keep their current language and align with England, which was already at work in Sierra Leone to the north? Or perhaps France, which controlled the Côte d'Ivoire just a few miles down the coast? How about Germany, with its ties to Togoland just beyond the Gold Coast and Namibia further south?

Harris knew of the high-stakes players in the global colonial game, and it seems likely he got caught in one of its secondary moves. By 1909 Harris had become a lead teacher and interpreter in his small coastal town. What happened next has been pieced together by the painstaking work of historian David Shank, who has traced Harris's travels, his meetings in Monrovia, the position of a British gunboat and the mobilization of British troops from Sierra Leone—Shank draws the conclusion that in 1909 an attempted coup d'état against the Liberian government was in process. The names of the plotters included Edward W. Blyden, Liberia's Secretary of the Interior and advocate for indigenous people; British Consul Braithwaite Wallis; British Major Cadell—and William Wadé Harris. What Harris could not know as he prepared for action on the beach was that 250 miles west along the coast in the capital of

Monrovia, the coup was thwarted. As a consequence, on February 13, 1909, Harris was left literally holding the flag. By the end of the day, he must have known the coup had failed. But undaunted and ever eager to make his own stand, Harris the next morning once again planted his British flag on the beach of Liberia's Cape Palmas. He was arrested and jailed for treason.

SPIRITUAL ROOTS

What happened next would shake his soul—and also the trajectory of Christianity in West Africa. But to understand these dramatic events, a little prehistory is required.

Harris spent his first twelve years near Cape Palmas in Half Graway, a collection of some forty huts rimmed by cocoa trees. We may assume that in addition to the social-political unrest around him he also absorbed the conflicting religious passions of his spiritist father and his Christian convert mother. One Catholic missionary of the time said that the local religion consisted of belief in a creator God who "would always come to any human who tried to live a good life, unless the plans of God were thwarted by lesser, evil spirits."

These evil spirits monopolized much of a Grebo's religious attention. An evil spirit might inhabit you even without your knowledge, turning you into a witch so that you would "eat the vital force of others," most likely close family members. Death of someone in the family engendered intense guilt in those who remained because they feared they might have indulged in "cannibalism at a distance." The spirits of witches hovered everywhere and only a fetish could keep them at bay. No Grebos who loved their families would go anywhere without a fetish charm, amulet or several of them to protect themselves and their families from witchcraft of their own doing. If witchcraft was suspected, spirit leaders would diagnose the truth through ordeal. The suspected witch had to drink a poisonous tea made from sassywood bark. If he or she lived, innocence was proclaimed. Most who underwent the ordeal did not live.

At about the age of twelve, perhaps because his mother had died, Harris along with his older brother moved to Sinoe County, a hundred miles northwest, to live with his mother's brother, Reverend John C. Lowrie, who was a Glebo Methodist pastor among the colonists. There Harris was baptized into the Methodist Church because as a Liberian witness later said, "Rev. Lowrie would not have kept him without baptizing him." Harris learned to read and write both in Grebo and English, and he became a student (perhaps unwillingly) of the Bible. In 1879, when Harris was about eighteen, the Methodists transferred his uncle back to the Cape Palmas area, where Harris said, "My father, a heathen, came and stole me before Rev. Lowrie's death."

This situation was soon remedied when Harris signed on to the rowdy life of a crewman ("kruboy") on a British ship, for which service his father received an advance on his son's wages. Harris probably made at least four trips along the African coast south of Cape Palmas, going as far as Lagos, Nigeria. Sometime in this period he spent a couple of days in jail; as he later told a missionary, "I was thrown into prison at Gaboon by the white Government man because I sang at night! ... No, it was not a hymn, but a popular song!" Harris returned to the Cape Palmas area sometime in 1880, attended the funeral of his Uncle Lowrie, and began a series of jobs on land.

ORDINARYAND EXTRAORDINARY

The next twenty-four years of Harris's adulthood saw him rise in the colonial culture. He worked as a carpenter, a brick mason, a headman of former kruboys employed in a goldmine inland from Axim. Eventually, drawing on language skills learned in Reverend Lowrie's household and then during his time on British cargo ships, Harris worked as a government interpreter for native-speaking Grebo people and the American Black settlers who made up the government.

In about 1885 he married Rose Bedo Wlede Farr, daughter of John Farr, a former catechist and head teacher at the Episcopal Spring Hill School. Her father had died, and so her brother Nathaniel Sie Farr assumed the schoolwork of his father and also arranged his sister's marriage. By 1888 Harris was an Episcopalian, confirmed by Bishop Ferguson at nearby Saint Mark's Church in Harper. When asked late in life why he made this denominational switch, Harris said simply, "For money."

The money at first wasn't much. His first salaried job for the Episcopalians was to work as assistant teacher and catechist at Half Graway village for five dollars a month. But his in-laws continued to provide employment, though often meager and sometimes tumultuous. Harris became a teacher in a day school "amongst the heathen" in an outlying village, and he taught Sunday school in the mission church. In 1897 he was licensed as a lay reader; in this capacity he used the Anglican Book of Common Prayer to lead the forty-six-member Episcopal congregation at Spring Hill mission village in weekly worship. When their pastor was transferred, Harris and his brother-in-law shared the preaching rotation at Half Graway with others and also at nearby Wolfe Memorial, a mission chapel. His job as an interpreter at two hundred dollars a year became his most dependable source of income when in 1899 he was appointed the official interpreter of Maryland County (887 square miles) and thereby occupied the difficult position of middleman between the Glebo people and their American-Liberian authorities.

Meanwhile, children arrived in his family at regular intervals so that by 1901 Harris and Rose had six children, the oldest of them age fifteen. Harris used his manual skills to build a two-story home of cement and stone with windows, shutters, a staircase and a hearth. That same year his brother-in-law, who was also his employer, died. For a couple of years Episcopal authorities tried various newcomers in the vacated position of school headmaster, then named Harris to the position in 1903, which provided a measure of job security and an additional two hundred dollars a year. But Harris soon got himself into trouble. In 1904, his bishop reported that two school employees had "fallen into [Satan's] snares." Harris was one of them. He was suspended for several months and the boarding school closed. The infraction must have been minor or mended because a few months later the school reopened with Harris once more as its head.

Harris's move from mission station headmaster to influential prophet took place against the background of political-religious uncertainty. Through his marriage into an Episcopal family and then his work in the church, Harris was aligned with the Liberian government, even though the local Grebo population much preferred the British in favor of the oppressive American-Liberians. Had he been a Catholic, he would have assumed French allegiance (and language), as did most Christians in the nearby Côte d'Ivoire. But he was what he was—a Grebo and an interpreter employed by the Liberian government. At a time of conflict between Liberia and Britain, with competition also involving France in the background, Harris's post placed him at the center of political tension.

His upbringing and life experiences also placed him at the center of religious tension. As the son of a mother converted by missionaries and an employee of the Episcopalians, he knew well the standard teachings of Western Christianity. Yet Harris also remained a Grebo whose faith was marked by the Grebo conception of a creator God and a Grebo sensibility about the evil power of the spirit world. He also had firsthand knowledge of Africans who were creating their own indigenous expressions of Christianity. His friend Edward Blyden, who may have been involved in the coup attempt of 1909, had been trained as a Presbyterian. But in 1887 he published a book, *Christianity, Islam and the Negro Race,* that outlined a new ideal for African religion. It would include ingredients of Islam and traditional indigenous religions along with some essentials of Christianity. "Let us make our own religion," Blyden decreed. Harris's job also exposed him to Samuel W. Seton, a Grebo Christian and ordained Episcopalian priest who in 1887 had been elected the first Grebo in the Liberian national legislature. Seton too underwent an adult reconsideration of faith, then left the Episcopalians and founded the African Evangelical Church of Christ. This new body also hosted meetings and distributed literature for the "Russellites," who later became known as Jehovah's Witnesses.

The combination of worlds in which Harris lived can be illustrated by an incident from 1907. It reveals how close he remained to the spiritism of his father's heritage. In that year a Liberian newspaper reported, "On the 4th of July ... the catechist W.W. Harris was seized by the Natives (heathen) at Graway and was compelled to drink sassywood." A fuller report revealed that Bhne, another Graway man, had been accused of witchery for allegedly casting a spell that reduced the local catch of fish. He was condemned to the ordeal of sassywood to establish his guilt or innocence. Harris intervened, but then he too was ordered to drink the sassywood. Only the further intervention of Liberian Episcopalian clergy and a local chief rescued Harris from the ordeal.

Harris's ordinary activities put him in touch with Episcopalians, Catholics, Presbyterians, Methodists, Muslims, Jehovah's Witness sympathizers, and various indigenous practices tied to fetishes and evil spirits. This spiritual mélange was complicated by tribal and colonial politics, since governmental authorities often aligned themselves with one or another of these religious movements. By 1909, when we see Harris on the beach with his British flag, he had lived within this mixture of national and indigenous religious and political loyalties all his life. What happened next brought these beliefs, practices and instincts into a combination that historians are still trying to figure out. But the result no one disputes. The face of faith on the coast of West Africa would be forever changed.

FAITH DEFINED

Harris was jailed in Cape Palmas in February of 1909 and spent most of the next four years in prison. He was given standard treatment: little ventilation, little food and possibly physical abuse. In the first half of 1910 the region's ethnic hostilities turned into civil war, with the Grebo moving to place their region under British jurisdiction and the British waiting patiently offshore while Liberian troops challenged the insurgents. Harris fully supported the insurgency. B.K. Speare, the Episcopal priest who had been Harris's supervisor at Half Graway, was among those killed. The outcome was a defeat for the Grebo that left Harris in total despair. This was the conflict-ridden situation when Harris's life was transformed. Though unusual, what happened next followed the pattern of his previous varied experiences.

Harris had received Christian baptism as a teenager, but he later spoke of his conversion as a series of decisive encounters with God. In 1926 a Methodist missionary, Pierre Benoit, recorded a conversation in which the aged Harris said, "The first I converted it was under Rev. Thompson—Liberian—in Methodist Church.... [He] was preaching on Revelation 2:5—I was twenty-one or twenty-two. Rev. Lowrie was dead.... The Holy Ghost come on me. The very year of my conversion I start[ed] preaching.... I was confirmed in 1888 by Bishop Ferguson in Cape Palmas."

The next encounter was much more decisive. Sometime in the first half of 1910 the angel Gabriel visited the imprisoned William Wadé Harris. What exactly happened is impossible to say, in part because Harris later used several different phrases to describe this event: "trance," "a light not with my eyes but spiritually," "the spirit descended three times like ice on my head." The commission Harris received from the angel was, if disjointed to Western ears, dramatically decisive: "burn the fetishes beginning with your own," "preach Christ everywhere," "Christian baptism," "abandon western clothes," "wife will die," "power upon you," "take a long cane," "give up money and drunkenness," "no adultery," "you are a prophet like Elijah, Daniel, Ezekiel, John," "Sabbath."

The day he received this vision, Harris told his wife what he had seen and heard and asked her to make him new clothing: a long white gown. Later scholars have described this apparel as reminiscent of the garb of priests who served a local river spirit named Tano. No one should ignore Harris's probable familiarity with these Tano priests, who wore white gowns and blessed people by sprinkling them with sacred water, or his likely knowledge of the Ebrié creator god Yankan, who governed his people by bestowing either hardship or prosperity. Yet Harris's teachings also clearly differed from those who followed these competing deities. His wife, who had been ill, delivered the gown he requested—and died shortly afterward, but not before announcing to their children that Harris had gone mad. When released from prison, he went about like a poor pilgrim telling people to "repent."

A PROPHET AT WORK

Harris next appears along the shoreline road of the Côte d'Ivoire in the fall of 1913. He has been released from prison. He is dressed in a simple long white gown, he is barefoot, and he carries four objects: a long staff topped by a cross, a beaded gourd calabash, a Bible (often in a sheepskin, on which he prays daily), and a small bowl filled with water. He wears a white turban and a slim stole of dark cloth that makes a cross over his chest. He is accompanied by two women also in white, Helen Valentine and Mary Pioka, who also carry calabashes: they are his singers, and possibly his wives. Before Harris speaks one word, he has already communicated symbolically much of his message, combining elements of Christianity, tribal culture, Islam and perhaps a few creative additions of his own. He is careful that no one mistakes his makeshift cross as a fetish. If it is broken or damaged, he simply throws it to the side of the road and crafts a replacement. Like a prophet, which he claims to be, his eyes and his voice command attention.

In the next eighteen months Harris traveled the coastline he once sailed as a kruboy. His message was direct: repent of your sins and burn your fetishes. He made stops at Fresco, Ebonou, Lozoua and Grand Lahou, where he spent a few days in jail for creating too much ruckus; but he left with the words, "Grand Lahou, I came in the name of God and you have not received me. But one day you will see the truth, for it was in the name of Christ that I came." Next he stopped at Kraffy, where a later historian has reconstructed his presence like this:

> He raised his cross to Heaven and said, "O God, if Thou hast sent me give me water, that I may baptize those who ask for it." Then he lowered the cross and as he tipped it, water ran out of the hollow top and filled his bowl. When he touched with his water anyone who was hiding fetish objects, or who was possessed by evil spirits, this person would become crazed

and rush off into the bush or struggle in the sand. Harris would drive the spirit out by putting his sheepskin scarf on the person's head and his Bible on top of that. By the same actions, Harris healed those who were sick.

From Kraffy he continued down the southeast coast, visiting Dabou, Jacqueville, Audouin and Grand Bassam, where he left a curse because he saw kruboys loading a freighter on Sunday. The ship was destroyed by fire a few days later. He crossed the border into what is now Ghana and traveled about fifty miles, stopping at Half Assine, Beyin, Ataubo and finally arrived at Axim, where there were established Orthodox and Catholic churches. He remained there for several weeks, gathering daily crowds numbering in the thousands.

Harris meetings were noisy, attention-grabbing affairs. They began with a great clatter from calabashes as he and the women sang and danced, "Come to God, come to God. Repent of all your sins!" He healed the sick, holding his Bible in front of their faces and shouting at God to make them well. Some said he even raised the dead. He demanded that they bring all fetishes to him, and he burned them.

Many coastal people already had a love/hate relationship with their fetishes. They feared the spirits and wanted to be liberated from the expense and restrictions the fetishes required to fend off evil spirits. But they also feared giving up fetishes without some new protection from evil. Harris supplied this protection with baptism. Drops flung from his bowl or even from the rain became baptism, their new protection from evil as he shouted over them, "I baptize you in the name of the Father and Son and Holy Spirit." Unlike the missionaries, who asked converts to wait for baptism until they had been instructed, Harris offered the protecting water immediately. When new converts asked what they should sing to worship their new God, he told them: "Sing the songs you know, but put God's name in them." If he had time, Harris taught his preliterate converts the Lord's Prayer, the Ten Commandments and sometimes the Apostles' Creed. Harris's form of Christianity had a simple moral code: burn your fetishes and never return to them. Do your work in six days but don't work on Sunday; it is the day for prayer. Don't commit adultery (although he did not consider polygamy adultery). Send your children to school. Go to church. When the crowds grew large and officials encouraged him to move on, he left new converts with a staff and a water bowl and told them to continue his work. Dozens, perhaps hundreds, of these evangelizing converts became known as "the water people."

Where no Christian churches existed, Harris instructed converts to construct a building; often he appointed "twelve apostles" from among the new converts at a locality, some of them former fetish witch doctors. He also told them, "Wait for a white man with a Bible." They did—by the thousands, some of them rebuilding their simple structures over and over as government officials, worried by unexplained large assemblies gathered for no discernable purpose, torched the buildings. The converts bought English Bibles (which they could not read) from local traders and placed them in the churches. When the French-speaking government (mistrustful of anything English) confiscated the Bibles, they bought more—in French, though few could read them either.

By the time Harris got to Axim, five women were traveling with him as singers. When questioned about polygamy, he shrugged and said, "God did not intend to make the same law for black and white people. Blacks can take as many wives as they can look after." He also prophesied seven years of upcoming hardship and then the coming of Christ's kingdom. His followers would soon shape this teaching into a promise of prosperity to those who remained faithful to God for seven years.

Harris began revisiting the areas he had cleared of fetish worship, but midway, in early 1915, he was stopped by French colonial authorities, jailed and severely beaten (Helen Valentine died from this mistreatment), and deported to Liberia. When near death many years later, he reported that he had walked to the border between Liberia and Côte d'Ivoire eight times and eight times had been turned back. With war in Europe, anyone who assembled hundreds of uncontrolled people in a high-pitched emotional state appeared threatening to colonial officials. Their simple solution was to get rid of the source of the excitement.

AFTERMATH

Methodist and Catholic churches in the areas Harris visited immediately outgrew their meeting spaces. They were also overwhelmed by the task of instructing Harris converts. One Catholic priest, disturbed by indiscriminate and uninstructed baptism, complained, "The trouble is his baptism is valid." Throughout the next ten years Protestant and Catholic mission churches saw unprecedented growth. But these were war years, and missions of European and American origin lost staff and could not bring in more. Most areas of the coast had no Christian church at all within walking distance. In those places Harris converts built rude church buildings, fronted by a pulpit with a Bible—and waited.

Ten years later British Methodist missionary W.J. Platt was among the early white arrivals on the scene. In town after town he found church structures full of people waiting for "teachers of the Book." In the meantime they had learned a few hymns from store clerks; some of their leaders had walked great distances to hear a Christian sermon, then walked back to repeat it as best they could to their own people. One of their few readers would select a single verse from the Bible and explain it over and over to those who listened. By 1924 thousands of people waited in and around these buildings for missionaries to continue the work that their Prophet Harris had begun.

About the time that W.J. Platt was discovering the preformed Christian congregations along the Côte d'Ivoire, other missionaries headed to Liberia in search of the person who had exerted such influence. In 1923 a colleague of W.J. Platt, Pierre Benoit, found him. Harris had returned to his home in Cape Palmas, now a crumble of ruins where he slept alone on a dirty cot, cooking his meager food over the smoke-stained hearth. He had just returned from the Liberian interior where he baptized some five hundred persons. He also had apparently suffered a stroke, and he spoke in jerky random fragments. Among them the repeated phrase, "Jesus Christ must reign; I am his prophet."

Today the countries of West Africa still feel the influence of William Wadé Harris. Harris's form of Christianity starts in the Old Testament that resembled his own culture in many ways. In the Old Testament Harris found no condemnation of leaders among God's people who took multiple wives. He also found a God who over and over promised to prosper those who pleased him by keeping his commandments. Harris preached Jesus; indeed he carried a cross and baptismal bowl with him everywhere he went. But he more closely resembled an Old Testament prophet than a New Testament apostle. He called himself the West African "Elijah." Even his command to "wait for the white man with a Bible" rings more of expectancy than fulfillment.

Though many of his immediate converts became members of local Methodist or Catholic churches, their practice of polygamy and other traditional practices kept other Harris converts from these Western, "European" denominations. During the years before missionaries arrived, many waiting converts developed a purely African expression of Christianity, which like the message of their prophet resembled more the book of Ezekiel than Paul's letter to the Romans.

Today some 200,000 people in Côte d'Ivoire worship in Harrist churches, but even these numbers minimize his effect. Africanist practices and ideals still color much of Christianity in contemporary West Africa. The emphasis on material objects of power, legalistic moral standards, the ruling name of Jesus and a gospel of prosperity—along with a lack of concern about polygamy and strict attention to the Bible—add up to a form of Christianity that Western Christians can find both attractive and disturbing. This situation repeats a regular feature in the long history of Christianity, as when in earlier centuries missionaries from the Mediterranean found practices of Gallic and Anglo-Saxon converts both attractive and disturbing. Time, and the gathered wisdom of local Christian movements, will doubtless sort out these matters as they did long before with the British, French and Americans (descendents of the Gauls and the Anglo-Saxons) who eventually brought a missionary gospel to the coasts of West Africa.

Today in Côte d'Ivoire and Ghana tourists can view hundreds of Harrist Christians parading in their white clothing through the streets on their way to worship. Their worship services consist of songs and dance, the Lord's Prayer, the Ten Commandments, Bible reading and commentary, and many statements of loyalty to the Prophet Harris and his God. Then the service ends as it begins, with a procession through the streets that commemorates their prophet who walked along the coast of West Africa for such a short time, with such a great effect.

SOURCES

Three books were especially helpful in preparing this chapter. In the mid-1920s, the missionary W.J. Platt worked in West Africa and collected many lively and engaging accounts of what had happened in the fifteen years or so before his arrival. They are found in his book, *An African Prophet: The Côte d'Ivoire Movement and What Came of It* (London: Student Christian Movement Press, 1934). Forty years later, Gordon MacKay Haliburton built on Platt's work in the book, *The Prophet Harris: A Study of an African Prophet and His Mass-Movement in the Côte d'Ivoire and the Gold Coast 1913-1915* (New York: Oxford University Press, 1973). Then after intensive research in written records, diligent interviews and very careful weighing of evidence as both a historian and a theologian, David A. Shank published what has become the definitive study, *Prophet Harris, The "Black Elijah" of West Africa* (Leiden: E.J. Brill, 1994).

Also helpful are other writings by David A. Shank, including his entry on Harris in the online *Dictionary of African Christian Biography* (www.dacb.org) and "The Prophet Harris: A Historiographical and Bibliographical Survey," *Journal of Religion in Africa* 14 (1983):130-60; John Pritchard, "The Prophet Harris and Côte d'Ivoire," *Journal of Religion in Africa* 5 (1973):23-31; Sheila S. Walker, *The Religious Revolution in the Côte d'Ivoire: the Prophet Harris and the Harrist Church* (Chapel Hill: University of North Carolina Press, 1983); and Elizabeth Isichei, "A Soul of Fire," *Christian History* 79 (2003):22-25. Late in the preparation of this chapter, it was a real treat to meet David and Wilma Shank and to have David offer editorial help for the chapter. We experienced a great sense of loss when learning of David's death in October 2010.

5

BYANG KATO1936-1975

THEOLOGICAL VISIONARY

The place: Jos, Nigeria. The time: early 1970s. Hammers, saws, drills, tape measures and sweat mingled as skilled Nigerian workmen and several white men obviously more familiar with books than hammers remodeled the Bingham Hospital into a new headquarters for the Evangelical Churches of West Africa (ECWA). Founded by missionaries, ECWA was now a denomination with 1200 congregations and some 300,000 people attending church each Sunday. As a hospital built and operated by Sudan Interior Mission (SIM) the Bingham had long served the sick and injured of its local community. Now with modernized transportation and an enlarged Evangel Hospital across town, the older hospital was being outfitted as administrative offices and publishing facilities for the ECWA, which SIM was handing over to African leadership. Appropriately, Nigerians and missionaries were working side by side.

Byang Kato

From behind a sheet of plastic marking off a makeshift office, a young black man with confident bearing and laugh creases at the corners of his eyes motioned to the workers. Byang Kato was calling a meeting. As they had many times before, four men gathered in Kato's office. They talked about families and schools but mostly about ways that the ECWA could continue to help those who had suffered in the Biafran Civil War by using ECWA's goals of reconciliation, rehabilitation and reconstruction. They also spoke of Kato's new responsibilities as continent-wide general secretary of the Association of Evangelicals in Africa and Madagascar (AEAM). It was a daunting job, never before held by an African. His assignment would mean constant travel not only across Africa but also throughout the world as the representative of African evangelicals to like-minded Christian groups elsewhere. Kato regularly asked these friends to pray for his wife, Jummai, and their three children in what would be his frequent absences from home.

At this particular meeting, Harold Fuller, SIM's deputy director for West Africa, sat on a stool in one corner. Fuller, just a few years older than Kato, was a colleague, friend and mentor. A typical letter from Kato opens, "Dear Harold, I cannot thank the Lord enough for knitting our hearts together." Bill Crouch, nearing retirement as field director for SIM, rested against a dusty wall, glad for a moment to be listening instead of hammering. Jim Plueddemann, SIM's director of Christian education, age thirty-one and now in his second term of mission work, sat back in a folding chair, hands clasped behind his head. After some fifty trips together visiting the churches of Nigeria during his first mission term, Jim could say of his boss, "Byang is my best friend." In easy conversation these four men resolved the particular issue (now forgotten) for which Kato had called them into his office. Then almost as an afterthought Jim Plueddemann asked a question about Kato's new responsibilities, "What do you hope for long-term in Africa, for the future of Christianity here?"

Kato paused, then launched ahead as if he had been preparing for just that question. "African Christianity is being consumed by a dreadful disease," he said. "We must find a cure for our *theological anemia."* In an impromptu address lasting a full hour, Kato spelled out four goals he believed would support the responsible development of genuine Christianity in Africa throughout the coming century. In a much abbreviated summary he said:

1. We need to have African scholars writing and publishing African theology. I picture a whole library full of books written by Africans who are evangelical in thought and in practice.
2. We need schools of higher education in theology so that our best students do not have to leave the continent in order to learn. We need one theological graduate school in French-speaking Africa for the West and another for English-speaking Africa for the East. Existing schools won't do; they are either too tied to European and American thinking or they are too influenced by African indigenous religions. We need two new uniquely Christian, uniquely African graduate schools of theology!
3. We need a journal. African theological scholars will seek a place to publish their ideas and read and see responses of their peers across the continent.
4. We need an accrediting agency. Anybody with enough money and energy can start a school in Africa. But we need some au-

thoritative group that will set standards of good education and monitor progress of schools to maintain those standards. African scholars should, with hard work, be able to earn respect so that scholars throughout the world will want to know what Africans think about Jesus.

Forty years later much of what Byang Kato envisioned that day in Jos, Nigeria, has become a part of Africa's landscape. The *African Bible Commentary,* published in 2006 with Temukbo Adeyemo as editor, contains contributions from seventy African scholars. Other published African theologians include Kwame Bediako, *Jesus in Africa: The Christian Gospel in African History and Experience* (2004); Ogbu Kalu, *African Pentecostalism* (2008); Samuel Ngewa, *The Gospel of John: For Pastors and Teachers* (2005); Jehu J. Hanciles, *Beyond Christendom: Globalization, African Migration, and the Transformation of the West* (2008); and also Kato's former rival, whom he considered far too liberal, John Mbiti, *African Religions and Philosophy* (1970, 1992).

Byang Kato himself played a critical role in achieving the other goals he outlined. In particular, in February 1974, he laid the groundwork for the second point of his vision, when he made an audacious visit to President Jean-Bédel Bokassa, head of state of the Central African

Republic. Bokassa, the self-proclaimed emperor of this former French colony, developed elaborate means to protect himself from visitors with hands extended for donations. Yet Kato got through, and Bokassa was impressed by Kato's vision of a Christian school of theology in French-speaking Africa. It would be located near his own capital of Bangui, centrally placed near the border with Zaire and less than a day's drive from the Congo, Chad, Cameroon and Nigeria. Kato left Bokassa with a gift of seven acres and permission to use the Central African Republic's university library.

In 1977 Bangui Evangelical School of Theology (BEST) opened its doors and has since graduated more than seven hundred students. The school presently offers both master's and doctoral programs in Bible, translation, theology and pastoral ministry. Many Africans with Ph.D.s make up the faculty. The library is one of the largest in French-speaking Africa, with over 20,000 volumes. In addition, BEST supports the community with a preschool and primary school for eight hundred children.

Kato's vision for an English-language institution like the BEST has also been fulfilled. In 1983 the Nairobi (Kenya) Evangelical Graduate School of Theology (NEGST) opened its doors with help from John Stott Ministries. It has recently expanded into the African International

University (AIU) as an indication of the growth of its programs. Already there are more than 1,000 alumni with 90 percent of them serving in Africa. In 2010-2011 the student body numbered 170 residential students and more than 200 extension students from twenty-five African countries, as well as a dozen or so countries outside of Africa. Many of the students pursue graduate degrees in Bible, Christian history, theology or translation. In 2005 the school launched a doctoral program in biblical and translation studies as part of its move toward university status. The AIU has become a gathering place for African Christians who seek graduate education and who want to use that education for ministry in their home continent.

The *African Journal of Evangelical Theology (AJET),* though not directly connected to Kato, fulfills much that he envisioned in his third goal. Launched in 1978 and published twice yearly by Scott Theological College in Kenya, it offers contributions from scholars throughout Africa as well as Western scholars experienced in Africa. *AJET* has published such articles as "Sacrifice in African Tradition and Biblical Perspective," by Cornelius Olowala (1991); "Biblical Basis for Some Healing Methods in African Traditional Society," by Udobata Onunwa (1993); "The Human Soul in Yoruba/Igbo Tradition and the Bible," by Peter Ogunboye (2000); and "The Human Condition through African Eyes," by Joe M. Kapolyo (2007).

Kato took a large part in reaching his fourth goal when in 1975 he convened the first meeting of the Accrediting Council for Theological Education in Africa (ACTEA) at Nairobi. Since then this organization has functioned as an evangelical accrediting agency for the continent. One of ACTEA's major steps was to determine what African schools of higher education needed and expected of their theological graduates; only after making that determination did they write the accrediting guidelines. Today's standards for a Ph.D. program reveal exacting requirements for students and faculty alike, including the standard of being funded by more than 50 percent from within Africa. Partly on the basis of these ACTEA standards, missiologist Keith Ferdinando in 2007 called Byang Kato "the founding father of African evangelical theology."

Kato's dreams were big dreams, and they triggered great accomplishments. Yet a mere two years after that meeting in Bingham Hospital, Byang Kato was dead at the age of thirty-nine. Who was he? And what kind of person could inspire a vision that survived so vigorously after his own lifetime?

EARLY YEARS

Byang Kato, son of Henri and Zawi of the Jaba tribe in Sabzuara near Kwoi in central Nigeria, was born on June 23, 1936. Henri was a tribal fetish priest who looked forward to his son succeeding him in that honored position. To that end, shortly after his birth, Henri dedicated his son to the juju priesthood. When six of their next seven babies died, local people assured Henri and Zawi that the devil was protecting this special child from competition in his designated life assignment.

At the age of ten Byang accompanied some three hundred other boys his age for the perilous weeklong Jaba initiation rites. Photos of Kato as an adult reveal two small slash marks on each side of his face, a memento of that week. Later, his training for the juju priesthood included bloody sacrifices, exorcisms, curses, trial by poison or smallpox pus (the innocent would survive), lessons on reincarnation, evil spirits and evil places, as well as occasional visions of "witches" who really did appear to see into the future. These were the ingredients of Byang's spiritual training throughout the early years of his childhood. But this was about to change.

By the 1940s, 50 percent of Jaba's 100,000 people had become Christians; soon the young

Byang would come into contact with this *other* local religion. Mary Haas, a SIM missionary, visited his neighborhood several days a month; from her "black box" (phonograph) Byang heard music and words in the Hausa language. Fascinated, Byang began to attend the Sunday school and then the SIM primary school. Christina Breman, who later wrote a Ph.D. dissertation on the AEAM, recounted what happened next in Kato's spiritual development. "Within the first month at school at the age of twelve Byang's Nigerian class teacher explained to the children the way of salvation, using the story of Noah and the ark. Byang realized that he needed to enter the boat of salvation just as Noah's family had done. So he stood up in front of the class to ask Jesus Christ to come into his heart. Although he had done this several times before, this was the time he could point out convincingly that he understood the Gospel enough for a conscientious decision."

In November 1948, after appropriate instruction by Reverend Raymond R. Veenkener, Byang Kato was baptized—along with three hundred others. Byang's life suddenly became much more difficult; he was twelve years old.

Byang's father, who was disappointed in his son's public rejection of his future as a juju priest, now refused to pay his school fees ($1.50 a year). Instead, he ordered him to a harsh regime of farm work. Sometimes Kato's father deprived him of food and clothing; sometimes he beat the lad. Byang lost about a year of school. Another missionary, Elsie Henderson, intervened with an elder from her church; they visited the father with a plea to allow Byang to continue his education. Eventually, his father made a grudging agreement: Byang would work the farm in the morning, go to school in the afternoon, then after classes work a part-time job provided by the school in order to pay for his fees, books and clothing. Although this arrangement still sometimes left him short of food, Byang also became an ardent student and careful steward of his time.

Byang's new life-course was further solidified in 1953 when revival came to Kwoi. Later he told what happened after a week of intense preaching:

> The Holy Spirit convicted us of our selfishness ... nearly a thousand men and women wept for their sins. Husbands and wives were confessing how they they'd sinned against each other.... With my heart breaking within me, and tears streaming down my face, I went forward to confess my sins before the Lord and His people. As a symbol of my sincerity, I took off my shirt and laid it alongside the other

gifts. Oblivious to everyone, I knelt in prayer.

"It's not only your shirt I want," Jesus said to me.

"What do you mean?"

"I want your life, son."

"Lord, I give You my life. I don't know what You want me to be, but I dedicate myself to You. Do whatever You want with me."

Byang Kato was now sixteen. He began to set aside his own interests in order to help neighborhood children who could not attend school. Later several of these testified that they could read and write Hausa and English only because of these efforts.

HIGHER LEARNING

In 1955, at the age of nineteen, Kato entered Igbaja Bible school, where he later became a teacher. He graduated in December 1957. Earlier that year he married Jummai Gundu, a childhood playmate. Jummai at age seventeen was not looking for an American type of romance. Kato proposed by mail, saying, "I've prayed a long time to know the Lord's choice for my wife. I'm certain you're the one." They were married in Kwoi over his winter break; the next day they traveled the three hundred miles south to school. Jummai, who did not know the local Yoruba language, spent most of those early days alone while Byang went to classes, studied, worked, sang in a quartet and helped publish the school magazine. Ten months later their first child, Deborah Bosede, was born at Igbaja; the presence of a baby gave Jummai a welcome chance for more contact with other families in the school community.

Immediately after graduating from Igbaja at the end of 1957 the Katos returned home to Kwoi, where Byang began to teach at Kwoi Bible Training School for a salary of fifteen dollars a month. Without food from Jummai's relatives, the little family, soon including their second child, Jonathan, would have often gone hungry. Meanwhile Byang began correspondence study for the English General Certificate of Education (GCE), a process that led on to further examinations, more study and teaching. The arrival of their third child, Paul Sanom, in October 1960, completed the family.

Byang Kato was sprinting through early adulthood. During the six years between 1957 and 1963—besides marrying, starting a family and using correspondence study to meet Western standards for theological education—he taught in several schools in Nigeria, enlarged and strengthened the ministry of Boys' Brigade and Youth for Christ throughout his country, worked in Jos as counseling staff for *African Challenge* magazine (which received about two thousand letters a month requesting spiritual counsel), and moved at least five times. In September 1963, Kato left his family in Nigeria and traveled to London to study for a bachelor of divinity degree from London Bible College. En route he stopped in Scotland to represent the Boys' Brigade of Northern Nigeria at an international camp. His children did not see him again for three years.

Midway in his three years, Jummai joined him in London where together they served as a host home for InterVarsity's international students, particularly Nigerians. In the spring of 1966, after three years of study at London Bible College, he received a diploma from that institution and the bachelor of divinity from London University. On their return journey to Nigeria, Byang and Jummai spent three months in France at the European Bible Institute, where they studied Christian education with Child Evangelism Fellowship through scholarship funding by SIM. This study revolutionized their sense of parental responsibility and also their thinking about appropriate spiritual care of children within the church.

The Kato family spent the next four years in Africa, during which time each of the children professed Christ as personal Savior and, more surprising, Byang's father also came to faith. Again Kato quickly assumed leadership among Nigerian evangelicals. He was teaching at Igbaja Seminary when in September 1967, he was named general secretary (the highest office) of the ECWA, with responsibility for its 1200 churches and 300,000 adherents. On January 28, 1968, he was ordained as pastor of Bishara Church in Jos, with both of his parents in happy attendance. The next year in February he was a featured speaker in Kenya at the triennial conference of the AEAM. For the delegates from nineteen countries he provided a challenge about the importance of children and youth in the African church; this message struck a responsive chord among the delegates who embraced a heightened responsibility for the future of African Christianity through early discipleship of its future leaders.

From 1967 to 1970 Nigeria suffered grievously during the Biafran Civil War, which led to millions of casualties, graphic scenes of starvation and much local destruction. The war resulted from an effort by the largely Igbo people of southeast Nigeria to form an independent state, Biafra. The mostly Muslim Hausa people of the north as well as some of the Yoruba of the southwest, who like the Igbo were mostly Christian, opposed them. Some of the war's intense fighting took place near Kato's home territory in Kwoi. In response, Kato focused on mobilizing ECWA churches to provide relief for the war's victims. For a couple of months the Kato living room hummed with the activity of eight tailors producing clothing that Bible school students then hauled along with truckloads of grain into the devastated areas, preaching the gospel at every stop. Kato sometimes joined the preaching teams, at one point speaking to two thousand troops. When the war ended, Kato created a national "Operation Blacksmith" movement with local blacksmiths making hoes and shovels and ECWA-SIM providing yams and seeds so that war-ravaged people could once again begin to grow their own food.

After these tense years, Kato journeyed to the United States for more education. From 1970 to 1973 he studied for master's and doctoral degrees at Dallas Theological Seminary. Once again Jummai and this time the children joined him midway through the program. And once again Kato excelled in learning, his own teaching and energetic ministry. The seminary gave him its Four-Way Test Award that paid for tuition in recognition of scholarship, Christian character, human relationships and trustworthiness. An interesting sidelight of this period was the summer of 1970, when Byang did mission work with Lake Spenard Baptist

Church in Anchorage, Alaska. Ministry in Alaska represented a vast cultural leap for a black man from Nigeria, but Byang enjoyed the challenge; the fifty-some talks and sermons he delivered that summer were well received. "I am sure the Lord brought me to North America to teach me more than academic knowledge. He also sent me as a messenger of good tidings." Byang Kato was becoming a world Christian.

The broad reach of Kato's ministry extended further, when in December 1970, he addressed 12,300 students gathered at InterVarsity's triennial missions conference in Urbana, Illinois. When Jummai joined him in Dallas, they also hosted Good News club meetings for neighborhood children. Kato received a Master of Sacred Theology from Dallas, then completed his doctorate with a dissertation later published as *Theological Pitfalls in Africa.* In this book he contended that African Christianity by its own nature and history was rooted in Holy Scripture, but he also argued that the Bible prohibited acceptance of traditional African religious practices, as if all religious routes led to one God. At the time of its publication this was Kato's only full-length book. It received both accolades and criticism. Critics viewed it as an African example of undue influence by

Western and fundamentalist themes that lacked the theological sophistication necessary to guide Africa into an honest balance of culture and faith. Supporters viewed the book as a maiden voyage by a young man who could become a great scholar. They approved his efforts to maintain the basic truths of Christianity despite fierce pressure to make theology conform to the particulars of an African cultural heritage.

Completion of the dissertation that became *Theological Pitfalls in Africa* marked the end of Byang Kato's twelve years of higher education. During these same twelve years he had also taken on a host of other major responsibilities. Few Africans had been better prepared by training, spirituality and personality to lead a new era of African evangelical Christianity. The future seemed very bright, but Byang Kato had a mere two and one half years left to live.

THEOLOGICAL CONTRIBUTIONS

Byang Kato was the first evangelical African to earn a Th.D. and a pacesetter in promoting theological higher education for other Africans. To grasp his significance it is important to understand the African theological milieu of his era. By the 1970s all of sub-Saharan Africa had been missionized and Christianized for more than a century. The continent had endured three generations of colonial imperialism, during which European powers divided up the continent according to European priorities. Colonialism meant that the European overlords combined government and Christianity in a way they would have hardly tolerated at home. While many Western missionaries were wise, compassionate, godly and fair-minded, others treated Africans as almost sub-human. As an example, C.T. Studd, one of the famed "Cambridge Seven" volunteers of the late nineteenth century and a much lionized symbol of evangelical missionary success, spoke in 1927 with extraordinary paternalism about all of the non-Western world, including Africa:

> To send blacks out as evangelists who have merely a smattering of the Gospel ... is murder ... and suicide as regards the work of God in our hands.... One can get them to hold up their hands and stand on their feet to declare they are going to quit sin and follow Jesus ... but it is another thing for them to be converted.... The Chinese are liars, that I know. The Indians are ditto—that also I know. But they are babes in the wood in comparison to these people.... The only thing to be estimated in

their opinion is, "What gain is going to come to me?"

Byang Kato was a living refutation of C.T. Studd's racist opinions, yet Kato would have agreed with Studd on one particular. Studd, the demeaning outsider, and Kato, the experienced insider, concurred that African Christian leaders needed to be educated for the task they faced. For Kato, theological higher education was a must. But he insisted that it had to be for Africans, in Africa, by Africans.

By the 1970s most missionaries had also come to share this conviction, at least in theory. But theological education for Africans, particularly among evangelicals, had not kept pace. Part of the problem was that Africa's emerging theological education had inherited many of the problems of nineteenth-century liberal theology, which called into question Scripture's accuracy and authority, doubted the deity of Christ, denied the existence of sin and the need for personal salvation, and in general saw mission work primarily as Christlike compassion in meeting the many physical, psychological and social needs pervasive throughout Africa. In Africa this humanistic expression of theology turned toward syncretism and universalism, with some Western missionaries even encouraging Africans to return to their traditional religions in order to preserve what was valuable in their own culture. The underlying theological assumption was that all religions led toward one god and that all religious believers belonged to Christ—whether or not they knew him. Kato's goal shared some features with the purposes of liberal theologians, but he also sought a more distinctly Christian theology for Africa that was freed from European and merely humanitarian constraints.

Another aspect of the problem came from the other end of the theological spectrum. For a vital theological education to emerge in Africa, it was also necessary to overcome what Africans had been taught by some forms of Western fundamentalism—that higher learning was inherently dangerous, that crude notions of biblical literalism were sufficient for understanding the will of God, that ignorance was as pleasing to God as disciplined study or that moral codes developed to serve Europe and America could be applied without adjustment in Africa.

Byang Kato, in other words, faced a stiff challenge. While disproving the kind of prejudice about African abilities expressed by C.T. Studd, he had to fend off what Africans had learned from theologically lax liberalism and theologically ignorant fundamentalism. His solution, which he proclaimed in print, and at several notable gatherings of African church leaders, was to "let African Christians be Christian Africans."

By this aphorism Kato did not mean that African Christians should strip themselves of African cultural practices and adopt Western culture along with Christian faith. Nor did he mean that Africans should simply remain where they had been culturally and spiritually with the addition of small bits of Christian ritual and verbiage. Instead, he searched the Scriptures to find authoritative guidance between these two extremes.

In an article written just prior to his death and published posthumously in *Bibliotheca Sacra,* Kato wrote:

> It is God's will that Africans, on accepting Christ as their Savior, become Christian Africans. Africans who become Christians should therefore remain Africans wherever their culture does not conflict with the Bible. It is the Bible that must judge the culture. Where a conflict results, the cultural element must give way.

Kato's strategy rested on his belief that Christianity was itself rooted deeply in African history, that Africa had contributed to the shape of Christianity from the outset. His basis for this claim was the African theologians who had provided leadership for the Christian church in its first centuries, including Origen, Athanasius, Tertullian and Augustine. Christian theology as a whole was almost entirely dependent on these

African fathers of the faith. He observed that Africa's indigenous religious practices originated at a much later date than the Christianity practiced by these early framers of the faith. When dealing with such African concerns as polygamy, family life, the spirit world, tribes and communities, Kato advised a thorough study of early Christianity and biblical texts instead of reflexive reactions based only in more recent Western or African cultures.

In recognition of Africa's role in shaping Christian theology in the early centuries, Kato appealed for a stronger African role in theological education in his own century. As he put it, Africa must rid herself of "theological anemia." He meant a theological anemia that diluted Christianity with harmful cultural customs and beliefs wherever they came from: from African indigenous practice, Western liberalism or Western fundamentalism. In particular, he warned against the theological anemia caused by fright at the stern discipline of study. Instead, he envisioned a continent where believers would learn and study and teach and write so that Africa would once again take her place as a theological leader in the entire Christian world.

Controversy, which continues to this day, was the result of Kato's proposals. To some fellow Africans who defended indigenous religion without qualification, he sounded far too Western. To other Africans who had adopted Western humanistic approaches, he was far too indebted to American conservative theology. To still other Africans who embraced fundamentalist approaches, he was far too open to traditional African influence. Even some among his strongest admirers have expressed the opinion that Kato published these ideas as a young man whose thinking was only just developing. All agree, however, that for the broad world of evangelical and theologically conservative Africa, Kato had made a most important beginning.

THE END AND THE BEGINNING

It was a sunny day on the beach near Mobassa, Kenya, in December, 1975. The Kato family was celebrating son Jonathan's seventeenth birthday. In the previous months his father had zigzagged across the globe in his role as general secretary of AEAM preaching, speaking, teaching, listening and conferring at every stop. At the Lausanne Conference on World Evangelization in May of 1974, he presented two papers and then six months later traveled to Mexico for a Lausanne follow-up, then to Moody Bible Institute in Chicago and nearby Trinity Evangelical Divinity School in Deerfield, Illinois, followed by visits to eight countries throughout West Africa, then South Africa, back to Nigeria, north to London, then South Africa again and Zimbabwe, and finally back to Nairobi.

Exhausted, Byang needed a break, and the whole family needed time together before they separated again for various schools and ministries. They rented a thatch-roofed cottage at Mizpah, about twenty miles from the coastal vacation city of Mombasa. Even on this weeklong break Byang was writing a report and preparing a series of newspaper articles that criticized actions at the recent gathering in Nairobi of the World Council of Churches, which he believed were harmful to true African Christianity. He was looking ahead to a trip to Switzerland and another three months of international travel.

On the first morning of the family vacation, Byang arose at six thirty, worked on his report and then enjoyed a leisurely family breakfast followed by the family's customary devotions—Scripture reading, discussion and prayer. Then he went for a swim with his boys in warm, chest-deep ocean waters surrounded by coral reefs. When Jonathan and Paul eventually got hungry, their father sent them to the cottage to help Jummai prepare lunch. He'd be there soon, he told them. He was not. The next morning the police found his body.

They placed him in a barge and rowed the body back to Mobassa, where the coroner pronounced Byang Kato dead by drowning. The controversies that surrounded Kato's life were mirrored in controversy about his death. In his hometown of Kwoi, the opinion grew that he must have been attacked. Others thought that he was felled by witchcraft, still others that he died of exhaustion.

Death at age thirty-nine could have meant a premature and permanent end to Kato's vision. Yet the strength of his personality, the breadth of his influence, the intensity of his learning, the passion of his faith, the resources of his networking and the persistence of his many friends sustained the vision he inspired. The four goals that he outlined in a dusty construction site in Jos, Nigeria, continued with hundreds of hands and minds and donations (both Western and African) to make it happen. Today evangelical theological higher education is alive and well in Africa. Throughout the continent, God-honoring students of the Bible and theology learn from one another. More than a few are being invited to the cities of Europe and America, where they are asked to share before respectful Western audiences what they have learned. The legacy of Byang Kato continues to expand.

SOURCES

This chapter depends heavily on Sophie De La Haye, *Byang Kato: Ambassador for Christ* (Achimoto, Ghana: African Christian Press, 1986), a book written by a retired SIM missionary who was active in Niger and Liberia during Kato's lifetime. The quotation about the 1953 revival is from pp.21-22, and about Kato's time in Alaska, p.63. The chapter has also benefited from personal conversation about Kato with several individuals who knew him and whose insights have been deeply appreciated. They include Jim and Carol Plueddemann and Jack and Theo Robinson. Byang Kato's own writings include *Theological Pitfalls in Africa* (Kisumu, Kenya: Evangel Publishing House, 1975); "The Christian Surge in Africa," *Christianity Today,* September 25, 1975, pp.4-7; "Africa's Christian Future," *Christianity Today,* October 10, 1975, pp.10-16; *African Cultural Revolution and the Christian Faith* (Jos, Nigeria: Challenge Publications, 1976); and "Theological Issues in Africa," *Bibliotheca Sacra* 133 (April-June 1976):142-52 (Kato's quotation about "God's will for Africa" is from p.146 of this essay). The quotation from C.T. Studd is from his article, "On Advance," *The Keswick Week, Fifty-Second Convention, 1927* (London: 1927), p.171.

A number of helpful articles have addressed Kato's theology and his legacy, including Paul Bowers, "Evangelical Theology in Africa: Byang Kato's Legacy" [a review of Kato's *Theological Pitfalls in Africa], Themelios* 5, no.3 (1980):33-34; Christina M. Breman, "A Portrait of Dr. Byang H. Kato," *Africa Journal of Evangelical Theology* 15 (1996):135-51; and Keith Ferdinando, "The Legacy of Byang Kato," *International Bulletin of Missionary Research* 28 (October 2004):169-74. Ferdinando's article is also reprinted on the website of the *Dictionary of African Christian Biography* (www.dacb.org), a site that also includes two other articles, Francis Manana, "Byang Henry Kato, 1936-1975," and Emele Mba Uka, "From Juju to Jesus Christ" (reports of the controversy over Kato's death are from this last article). Other important background information is found in Steven Paas, *The Faith Moves South: A History of the Church in Africa* (Zomba, Malawi: Kachere Series, 2006); Mark Shaw, *The Kingdom of God in Africa: A Short History of African Christianity* (Grand Rapids: Baker Books, 1996); and Tite Tienou, *The Theological Task of the Church in Africa* (Achimota, Ghana: African Christian Press, 1982).

An abridged version of this chapter appeared as an online article for *Christian History and Biography,* May 2, 2009.

EAST AFRICA

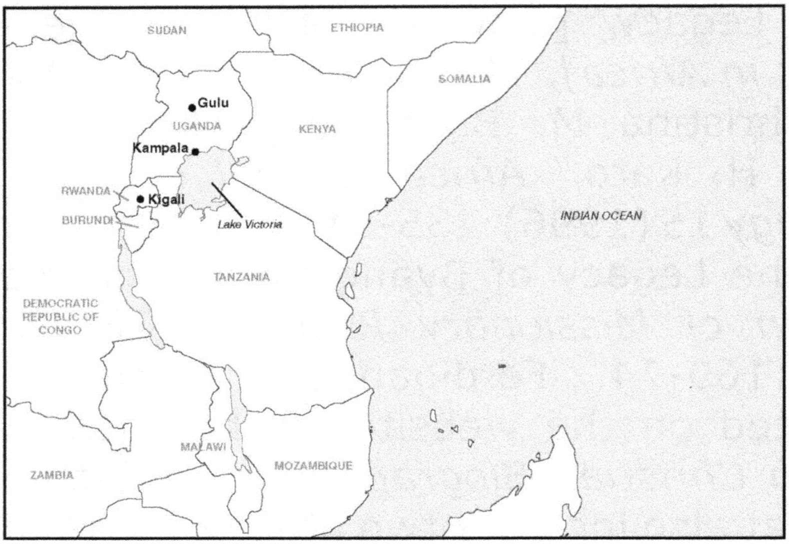
SUDAN
ETHIOPIA
SOMALIA
Gulu
UGANDA
KENYA
Kampala
RWANDA
Kigali
BURUNDI
Lake Victoria
INDIAN OCEAN
TANZANIA
DEMOCRATIC
REPUBLIC OF
CONGO
MALAWI
MOZAMBIQUE
ZAMBIA

6

SIMEON NSIBAMBI 1897-1978

Simeon Nsibambi

REVIVAL ANCHOR

The scene is a meeting room in Kampala, Uganda, November 1927. A "formidable Irish woman" named Mabel Ensor is leading a Bible class, an add-on to her primary work as a missionary nurse at Mengo Hospital. She has invited as guest speaker a recently arrived young medical doctor from England, Dr. Joe Church. Among others sitting in this class is a dignified young landowner named Simeon Nsibambi. Unknown to either of them, this first almost accidental meeting will bring into contact two streams of global Christianity and thereby influence the shape of Christianity in East Africa for decades to come.

Nsibambi and Church are, on the surface, quite an unlikely pair. Church runs at a frenetic pace of words and action; Nsibambi is calm and thoughtful. Church brings the revivalist heritage of John Wesley and George Whitefield; Nsibambi has generations of African spiritism in his blood. Church is white; Nsibambi is black. Both are Anglicans. These two men will offer both fire and stability to the "East African Revival." And they will somehow manage to keep the Ugandan portion of that revival largely within the Anglican Church.

Mabel Ensor, however, is on her way out. Within a year she will leave the Anglicans, calling them backsliders, polygamists, worshipers of witches and evil spirits who cover the whole facade with a wash of baptism and a Christian name. She won't have much use for revivalists either:

> The Pharasaism and insolence with which they parade their works of repentance are painful. Rudeness, coarseness, bawling outside places of worship, clawing one another as a sign of fellowship, literally bellowing sacred hymns as though it were a drunken carousel, to the great distress

of some godly souls who are scoffed at—what is this?

Decrying errors on every side, Ensor would form her own fellowship, the Mengo Gospel Church. But cutting herself off from Anglicanism's revival, she would leave scant room for her own church, about which little would be heard. Simeon Nsibambi, however, would choose another course. With Ensor, he too saw problems in Anglicanism, but even more possibilities if he would stay with "my brothers" and work to change from within.

The East African Revival was born amid such conflicts and choices. As unlikely as a partnership between Nsibambi and Church might seem, the different perspectives, histories and cultures that they and their colleagues melded together would revitalize the Anglican Church in Uganda and Rwanda and moderate the excesses of revivalism. The resulting impact exerted a tremendous influence in East Africa (see the chapter on Janani Luwum, which follows) and, before too many years had passed, the world as a whole.

REVIVAL ROOTS

Revival was not new to East Africa in the 1920s and 1930s. In 1893, just four years prior to Nsibambi's birth, George Pilkington of the Church Missionary Society (CMS) grieved over the lack of moral change in Africans who converted to Christianity. Seeking personal spiritual renewal, Pilkington retreated to Kome, an island in Lake Victoria. There he prayed all night and by morning was transformed by a joyful experience of the presence and power of God. Upon his return to Kampala, in the British colony of Uganda, his renewed zeal proved infectious for other missionaries who also came to see that their own sins hindered the cause of Christ. Upon confession, they too experienced a similar transformation that soon spread to African believers as well.

In this early Ugandan revival, outpourings of the Spirit seemed to begin with an overwhelming awareness of sin, leading to confession, resulting in reconciliation and forgiveness, which in turn produced great joy and enthusiasm for sharing the gospel of Christ with others who did not yet know him or had not made a "total surrender" to Christian moral values. To be sure, Pilkington's spiritual renewal did not trigger widespread revival, though episodes of confession and renewal peppered the next three decades among believers living in areas of East Africa that would become Uganda, Rwanda and Burundi. Nsibambi pushed much further what began with Pilkington.

BEGINNINGS

Simeon Nsibambi was born in 1897 to a tribal chief named Sezi Walusimbi Kimanje and his wife Tezira Wampanyo. His birth into a privileged Ugandan family led to financial, cultural and educational advantages, which he used wisely. His father must have discovered early on unique personal qualities in Simeon because, even though Simeon was not the oldest son, he became the designated inheritor of family property, with its accompanying responsibility. He studied at Mengo High School and served during World War I in the African Native Medical Corps, where he was promoted to the senior rank of sergeant and decorated for his efforts. After the war he attended King's College in Budo and became head prefect his senior year with written commendations describing him as "just, faithful, strict, highly disciplined, and generous." Nsibambi finished his schooling at King's College in 1920. At age twenty-three he was made chief health officer in the Bugandan king's government. The young man was known as an accomplished singer, footballer, wrestler, artist and hunter.

On August 25, 1925, Simeon married Eva Bakaluba, daughter of Erasto Bakaluba, a Christian and one of the first African professors at the British-style King's College, who would contribute to the East African revival in an unusual and perhaps inadvertent way. Future leaders of the revival tended to marry his daughters. William Nagenda married Sala Bakaluba; Blasio Kigozi (Simeon's younger half-brother) married Katherine Bakaluba, but Simeon led the way. He and Eva had twelve children. They became a respected family in their community, welcoming frequent guests into what was described as a peaceful and productive home.

SPIRITUAL FORMATION

Nsibambi was a second-generation Christian whose parents had responded to the first wave of Protestant mission work in Uganda, which began in 1877. At the age of five Simeon was baptized at Namirembe Anglican Cathedral in Kampala and by the age of fifteen had shown his seriousness in a pledge to renounce alcohol. Drinking was an established element of both traditional tribal and colonial British culture. Personal understanding of salvation took more time. He later reported that he was "saved" only at age twenty-two, near the end of his college years. The use of the term "saved" was especially important for what would come later. In the East African Revival, *balokole* ("the saved ones") was a term that both friends and foes of the movement used to identify its adherents. About the time of his marriage to Eva, Nsibambi became increasingly conscious of "irregularities" in the lives of church leaders; his response was to pray earnestly for them.

Always a voracious reader in both English and Luganda, Nsibambi began to consume a wide variety of Christian literature, from tracts to classics to commentaries and most of all the Bible itself. This led him to fervent prayer, and in due course he recorded a spiritual vow on a page of his Bible: "I have committed myself to God the Father. As from today I desire to be genuinely holy and never unintentionally do anything unguided by Jesus." Shortly thereafter, Nsibambi experienced what he described as a special work of the Holy Spirit: "I was filled with the power of the Holy Spirit of an unusual kind. I felt overwhelmed in my body and especially my head." He retreated to the nearby Rwenzori mountains for quiet prayer and reflection. What came next seems incongruous for a man who would become a stabilizing anchor for revivalist excesses. Nsibambi said that during that mountain retreat he experienced God's presence in such an intimate way that he sensed God telling him as he had told Moses to take off his shoes because the place where he was standing was holy ground. Nsibambi obeyed, left his shoes off and rarely wore them the rest of his life, which would become an embarrassment to his children.

Shortly afterward in 1926, Bishop John Willis, Anglican bishop of Uganda, invited Nsibambi to lead a weekly prayer service at Hannington Chapel. Sometimes few attended these meetings, but they still deepened his own spiritual life. Later Nsibambi's church work grew into an intense commitment to Namirembe Cathedral, where he served as warden, choir singer, offering receiver, evening preacher and all around good Samaritan to the sick and the needy.

A SECOND MEETING

From his late twenties it is possible to observe the life of Simeon Nsibambi through the eyes of British physician-evangelist Joe Church, who records much of what is known of Nsibambi's adulthood in a vivid autobiographical account, *Quest for the Highest.* In late summer of 1929, Church, himself a young CMS worker, was exhausted. Famine at the CMS Gahini Hospital some twenty miles east of Kigali, Rwanda, distress about the ill health of his fiancée back in England and the relentless pressure of fundraising had brought him low. Feeling spiritually drained, he visited friends in Kampala, Uganda, so that he could "think, pray, get some rest and sleep." What happened next on September 23, 1929, is recorded in nearly every account of the life of either Joe Church or Simeon Nsibambi. This is Church's account:

> On Sunday morning I joined the Africans going up to the cathedral for the morning service. I walked through the old sun-dried brick archway at the top of the hill and there, opposite the entrance of the Synod hall, was a man in a dark suit standing beside his motor bike. He spotted me and ran out to greet me.... I had been praying for a long time that God would lead me to one really saved African with whom I could have deep fellowship. God was answering that prayer that Sunday morning, when something happened that changed the course of my missionary career.

Simeon Nsibambi and Joe Church spent the next two days together on the grounds of the cathedral quietly studying Scofield Bible notes regarding the work of the Holy Spirit and what it might mean to live a "victorious, Spirit-filled life." Church later wrote, "I have often referred to this time in my preaching ... as the time God in his sovereign grace met with me and brought me to the end of my self and thought fit to give me a share of the power of Pentecost. There was nothing very spectacular, nothing ecstatic.... The only special gift is the experience of the transforming vision, of the risen Jesus himself." At one point Nsibambi left his own chair and knelt beside Church. In Nsibambi's words: "Kneeling down as the Bagando do, ... we took each other's hands and prayed for the fullness of His Spirit, and God answered that prayer."

Church then returned to Rwanda, driving a Rugby Plymouth Chrysler with its long, open body and side flaps that someone had donated for hospital work. Nsibambi went back to his public health job, but not for long. Soon he resigned that position in order to work side by side with Church, which he did for the next decade. The East African Revival was on its way.

REVIVAL

In Joe Church's account of the next ten or fifteen years Nsibambi plays a secondary role, although hints in his book suggest that more was going on. In May 1930, for example, we read that Nsibambi gathered a core of thirty-five Africans who met with him at Namirembe Cathedral on Friday evenings. These were meetings of prayer and fellowship for men whom Church's account recognized as leaders whom God had touched and who were active in preaching and personal evangelism. One of these Namirembe men, Yusufu Mukasa, worked as a hospital orderly at Mengo Hospital and joined Nsibambi in marketplace preaching while Nsibambi partnered with him in caring for famine refugees. In September 1931, Church brought his wife, Decie, and their infant son John to Kampala; while others were off for meetings at Mukono Theological College, Nsibambi cared expertly for their baby.

In September 1935, Church put together a ten-person revival team to work in western Uganda, where their ministry included service at a leper colony near Kabale. Soon the group felt the need for Nsibambi; he responded immediately, bringing a musician with him on the three-hundred-mile trip. Two years later, in February 1937, Nsibambi preached the first service of a revival week in and around Kabale with a "strong insistent voice" and a cry that was long remembered, *"Ekibi kibi nyo!"* ("Sin is sin!")

This particular mission began a two-month trip for the revival team that stretched through several sections of Uganda and Rwanda and even as far east as Nairobi, Kenya. Since much of the trip was by car, the revivalists often ministered to each other, reading and discussing books, singing, or problem solving. Once a fellow worker noted how much he had been blessed from "that little sermon of Nsibambi's in the car." This one-on-one listening, caring and praying was where Nsibambi was most effective. At best his preaching was careful and edifying. But his brother-in-law William Nagenda or his half-brother Blasio Kigozi were the preachers people came to hear, along with any number of other eloquent and passionate Africans who spearheaded the work of revival.

Nsibambi's gifts of discernment were well displayed at a Keswick conference in Kenya during September 1938. Joe Church's report on the meeting provides a tantalizingly brief account of Nsibambi's effectiveness:

> They wanted to talk over some problems that had arisen.... It was very interesting to listen to the two sides ... the elders, some doubtful, some opposing, produced many of the old arguments. How we praised God as Nsibambi and Balaba dealt sympathetically but firmly with these things and then there seemed to be joy and laughter again.

Meanwhile at home during the late thirties, Nsibambi had to deal with a situation that tested his discernment even more sharply. A small group of the *balokole* ("saved ones") used the grounds of his home as a gathering place where they put into practice what seemed to them a logical conclusion. This particular group had become convinced that their rigorous disciplines in holy living had finally freed them of all temptation to sin. As proof of their new freedom, these men and women began to worship together—completely naked! They could hardly have picked a better spot to have their craziness corrected.

But if this incident was quickly remedied, it brought considerable embarrassment to the revivalists, particularly Nsibambi. One of the results led African *balokole* to publicly reject the doctrine of *okufuba* ("striving"). Striving toward sinlessness, with the expectation of success, had been promoted by adherents of the Keswick movement and also in certain Scofield Bible notes. The incident on Nsibambi's property prompted the leadership of the East African Revival to reconsider this teaching. They reasoned that if human sinlessness were a possibility, striving toward that goal would obscure the work of Christ on the cross and also obscure the believer's constant need to be washed clean by the blood of Christ. Nsibambi and other mainstream *balokole* leaders concluded that the Christian must constantly resist sin but also accept that resistance to sin would be a lifelong struggle. Only by the cross of Christ, not endless striving, might sinful humans be redeemed.

At the end of the decade we find Nsibambi in a photo as one of the featured speakers at the first Balokole Convention at Namirembe. In August of 1940, African and mission leaders held a Keswick-style weeklong conference in his home territory of the cathedral, where five hundred people spent a week of spiritual invigoration around the subject of the "Victorious Life." This revivalist conference, with the bishop's backing, had been announced in Anglican churches throughout Uganda. The event marked the public acceptance of the revival movement, but by then Nsibambi's public ministry was nearing an end.

In May 1941, Church described a convention in Toro, on Uganda's western border, at a large church that later became a cathedral. The revival team consisted of two European clergy and seventeen senior Africans. Joe Church then adds, "This was the last convention that Nsibambi took part in." Though Simeon Nsibambi lived another thirty-seven years, after 1941 "ill health" and "weakness" kept him home near Namirembe Cathedral, and he never again entered public life. Yet he was far from idle.

A LONG RETIREMENT

Over the years Nsibambi had suffered a number of painful losses, among them the death of his younger brother and fellow revivalist, Reverend Blasio Kigozi, who was married to his wife's younger sister Katherine. Blasio had been a brilliant evangelist. Church later spoke of him as exemplifying the African proverb, "He who leads the attack against the leopard gets the wounds." In other words, the pioneer was the first to fall. In January of 1935 Blasio became ill with tick-borne relapsing fever and died within five days. Nsibambi stood with Katherine at his bedside singing hymns until his breathing stopped.

The "Mukono Incident" of 1941 also caused Nsibambi considerable grief and must have made him wonder if revival could really secure a long-term place within African Anglicanism. The incident pitted bishops against revivalists—both friends of Nsibambi—who were in conflict at a nearby theological school. His brother-in-law William Nagenda was among twenty-six students dismissed from theological studies at Bishop Tucker Theological College because of their constant denunciation of "liberal" teachers and students. Revival leaders at the time described the earnest *balokole* as without fault. Later historians have recorded an enormous amount of patience and compromise offered by Anglican officials in an attempt to keep these promising students in school—and no small haughty defiance on the part of the students. One of these historians, Adrian Hastings, described the grief of the teachers who were charged with "liberalism": "One old clergyman who had been through Mwagna's persecution testified in Synod to how hard it was to have a lifetime's faith so cursorily dismissed." Nsibambi must have seen with painful clarity the wrongs of both sides.

Nsibambi's infirmities—described as "weakness," "heart trouble" and later "diabetes"—kept him near his home but deepened a ministry in which he had already been active. People in need of spiritual refreshment came to him. Some rested and read and prayed on his spacious grounds. Others came for counsel. Whole groups came for retreats.

Visitors noted, in particular, the peacefulness of the home. The historian of the East African Revival, H.H. Osborn, provides hints about what lay behind this peacefulness in the words of Nsibambi's children:

> My parents taught us how to pray every morning and evening and how to read the Bible every day. As we sang together with my father, we learned how to sing songs I still sing today.
>
> Our parents loved each other so much that I learned that I should follow their example by loving my children, my brothers, sisters and other people.
>
> He was actually in the home more than my mother. If we were hungry or thirsty he would go and find something nice for us to eat or drink.

> He was particular about discipline. Whenever we brought our reports from the school he would first read the section dealing with character.
>
> He used to apologize as soon as he was aware that he had been wrong.... He used to say, "Forgive me, and God forgive me too."
>
> He allowed us a lot of freedom of discussion.
>
> My father quietly said, "Mama, God has a reason." Now these words have become our family motto.

One of Nsibambi's sons, Apolo Robin, born in 1938, became in 1999 the prime minister of Uganda, an office he continues to hold. Apolo learned some of his diplomatic skills from his father: "Whenever there were disputes in the family, he used to listen carefully to both sides and invoke his highly developed sense of procedure and justice to resolve the problems. He would, of course, always urge us to refer all problems to Jesus in the first instance."

Many people came to Simeon Nsibambi's door for spiritual guidance. His wide reputation told them what to expect. Nsibambi would greet them barefooted, seat them comfortably, then say, "Excuse me," and disappear. He might be gone ten minutes or an hour. It was his time to pray for the person he had just seated in the outer room. Then he would return and open with a single question, "Are you saved?" If he received an affirmative answer, then next question was, "Since when?" This would lead to a life story and eventually some current spiritual need. Often Nsibambi, true to his *balokole* heritage, diagnosed confession as the most immediate need, whereupon he might ease the way by confessing his own need for forgiveness. At the close of their time together Nsibambi would read aloud from his Bible "a word from the Lord," which almost always sent his guest forward with renewed hope and vigor. African leaders, Western missionaries and quite ordinary people all came to his door. He welcomed each of them in much the same way.

Doctor Harold Adeney was one of the many Western missionaries who followed that path to Nsibambi's door. The "Excuse me" prayer time seemed particularly long to him while he fidgeted in his chair and imagined different directions the conversation might take. Adeney began to wonder if perhaps the old man might have fallen asleep over his prayers. Finally Nsibambi returned and skipped immediately to the confession section. "Doctor, I have a problem," he said. "Can you help me?" Adeney prepared his rehearsed script of spiritual exercises, but then heard Nsibambi's hesitant, "It's my constipation." H.H. Osborn, who relates this story, leaves it there.

ANCHOR WORK

What did Simeon Nsibambi accomplish in his dozen years on the road as a revivalist and then through the longer years at home as a family man, community servant and spiritual counselor? Why is he so often called the "patriarch" of the East African Revival? In the first place, Nsibambi brought wealth, education and respectability to the movement. His financial generosity might account in part for his wide acceptance among church and revivalist leaders. Yet, probed at a deeper level, it is clear that more was involved. He also cultivated a generosity of thought and motive that allowed him to bridge the gap between formal Anglican churches and activist revivalists. On the one side he could challenge Anglican churchmen to practice holy lives, study their Bibles, confess and forsake their sins, and accept Christ's redeeming grace. At the same time, he was at home among a raucous crowd of revivalists who sang and prayed through the night, fell into trembling trances and thought that all prescribed liturgy was a sign of spiritual death. Somehow he became an anchor to both groups, tempering the excesses of the revivalists and revitalizing the churchmen. His was an unfinished and perhaps unfinishable task. But for his lifetime, revival and church held together and both were better for it.

SOURCES

Two works were indispensable for the preparation of this chapter. Joseph E. Church, *Quest for the Highest: An Autobiographical Account of the East African Revival* (Cape Town, South Africa: Oxford University Press, 1981) was drawn from journal notes that Church made during his years as an evangelist in East Africa from the 1920s into the 1970s. The account of his fateful meeting with Nsibambi in 1929 is quoted from p.66 and of Nsibambi's effectiveness at the 1938 meeting from p.157. The second essential book was H.H. Osborn's *Pioneers in the East African Revival* (Winchester, U.K.: Apologia, 2000), which brings together dozens of stories from those who knew Nsibambi throughout his life. The quotations about Nsibambi's private and family life are from this book. The much-discussed "Mukono Incident" has received careful attention from Kevin Ward, "Obedient Rebels: The Relationship between the Early 'Balokole' and the Church of Uganda: The Mukono Crisis of 1941," *Journal of Religion in Africa* 19 (October 1989):194-227; and also Adrian Hastings, *The Church in Africa: 1450-*

1950 (New York: Oxford University Press, 1994), with his quotation about this incident from p.598. A fine, brief introduction to Nsibambi and the East African Revival is provided by Mark Shaw, "A Hunger for Holiness," *Christian History* 79 (2003):28-31. Shaw provides more helpful context in *The Kingdom of God in Africa: A Short History of African Christianity* (Grand Rapids: Baker, 1996). Other useful background material is found in William B. Anderson, *The Church in East Africa 1840-1974* (Dodoma: Central Tanganyika Press, 1977); Jocelyn Murray, "Simeon Nsibambi," *Biographical Dictionary of Christian Missions,* ed. Gerald H. Anderson (New York: Macmillan, 1998), 501; and E.S. Odhiambo, T.I. Ouso and J.F.M. Williams, *A History of East Africa* (Essex, U.K.: Longman, 1977). Especially good on broader effects is Richard K. MacMaster and Donald R. Jacobs, *A Gentle Wind of God: The Influence of the East Africa Revival* (Scottdale, Penn.: Herald Press, 2006).

7

JANANI LUWUM 1922-1977

MARTYR OF "THE SECOND CENTURY"

On the night of Wednesday, February 16, 1977, Janani Luwum, the Anglican archbishop of Uganda, Rwanda, Burundi and Boga-Zaire, was murdered by security operatives of the Ugandan dictator Idi Amin. Some reports have it that Amin shot the archbishop himself. On the next Sunday, February 20, thousands of Ugandans gathered at the Namirembe Cathedral in Uganda's capital city of Kampala to honor the slain leader. A grave was dug and a large gathering of Anglican notables from throughout East Africa and beyond had assembled in near-by Kenya to attend. But the Ugandan army prevented this delegation from crossing the border, and despite pleas by Uganda's other Anglican bishops, they could not obtain Luwum's body. Nonetheless, the service proceeded under the direction of Luwum's predecessor, the retired archbishop Erica Sabiti. Sabiti was the first native Ugandan Anglican archbishop but had been able to exercise his office only with difficulty because of intense intertribal conflicts that continued, with much greater violence, during the regime of Idi Amin.

Archbishop Janani Luwum

Sabiti preached that Sunday about the reality of the resurrection, a theme the mourners took up as they moved out of the cathedral and past the open but unfilled grave. "Christ is risen!" they shouted to each other. "He is risen indeed!" was the response. Then, spontaneously, a song sprang up from the crowd:

Daily, daily sing the praises
Of the City God hath made;
In the beauteous Field of Eden
Its foundation-stones are laid.

O, that I had wings of angels
Here to spread and heavenward fly;
I would seek the gates of Sion
Far beyond the starry sky!

Grant, O Lord, our eyes be open
Here to see our Saviour King,
And our hearts be ever eager
Him to hear, His praise to sing.

This hymn had been written in 1865 by the English polymath Sabine Baring-Gould, who is better known in British and American Christian circles for "Onward Christian Soldiers" and "Now the Day is Over." In its early days "Daily, Daily Sing the Praises" had accompanied members of the Anglican Church Missionary Society as they began their pioneering evangelistic work on the north shores of Lake Victoria in the kingdom of Buganda. That work, alongside similar labors by pioneering Catholic missionaries, preceded by some years the colonization of Africa by European powers. It eventually bore fruit with the first Baganda converts in 1877. In the year before he was murdered, Archbishop Luwum had helped coordinate elaborate plans to celebrate the "first century" of Christianity in Uganda, which incorporated the ancient Buganda kingdom as well as the lands of several other tribes. As he did so, however, Luwum insisted that he would not devote too much time to these observances, since, as he said, "I do not want to be the Archbishop of a dead church, but of a live one." Part of what Luwum hoped to inspire for the living Ugandan church in its "second century" was energetic missionary work, including Ugandans willing to volunteer as missionaries to Britain and the other increasingly secular lands from which he and his people had received the gospel.

Despite the archbishop's injunctions to think ahead, mourners on February 20, 1977, had their minds fixed on the most dramatic moments in their church's past. In Uganda, a slightly modified version of Baring-Gould's composition was known as "The Martyrs' Hymn." In 1884, the old Baganda king who had skillfully guided his people's fortunes in increasingly complicated dealings with Anglican and Catholic missionaries, Arab Muslims and encroaching European states, passed away. His son and successor, Mwanga, possessed little of his father's skill. As pressures mounted on Mwanga from older tribal disputes and newer conflicts with outsiders, he lashed out violently. In January 1885, three young pages at his court were killed because of their Christian profession. Later that year a missionary bishop, James Hannington, was murdered. Then followed a reign of terror that led to the execution of perhaps two hundred mostly young Baganda who willingly chose loyalty to their new faith, and martyrdom, over the reversion to tribal religion that Mwanga demanded. The names of forty-five of these martyrs are known; Catholics in this group have been canonized, while the Anglicans are memorialized in the Book of Common Prayer. Baring-Gould's hymn was luminous on the day of Archbishop Luwum's nonfuneral because those who sang it knew that some of the early Ugandan martyrs—beheaded, burned alive, dismembered, speared, castrated, ravaged by wild dogs—had sung those same words as they went willingly to their deaths.

A CHILD OF THE REVIVAL

Janani Luwum was born in 1922 at Pajong, near the town of Mucwini, which lies in the northern part of modern Uganda, close to the border with Sudan. He was a member of the Acholi tribe, which had long experienced tension with the Baganda who inhabit the south of modern Uganda. Luwum's parents were Christian converts, his father a peasant farmer who gained renown as a Christian teacher. When he was a lad Janani developed skills as a marksman while herding the family's cattle, goats and sheep. The family's economic situation did not permit schooling until Janani was ten years old, at which time he began attending a secondary school in Gulu, where years later he would exercise leadership as an Anglican bishop. He then attended a teacher-training institute conducted by the Church Missionary Society before becoming a primary school teacher himself. In 1947 he married Mary Lawil, who would be an active supporter of his pastoral work and who, with several of their children, was able to leave Uganda after Luwum's murder.

In early January 1948, Luwum experienced a conversion under the influence of Justo and Josephine Otunno, evangelists who were part of the great East African Revival. As related in the chapter on Simeon Nsibambi, this revival had begun in the early 1930s with the cooperation of a British physician and a Ugandan preacher. Its message of repentance, confession and rebirth had spread powerfully through many countries of East Africa. Now Luwum also was joining the *balokole,* or "saved ones."

Almost immediately he began to preach. Many years later, when he had gained some perspective on his own Christian experience, he related the earnestness of those early efforts:

> When I was converted, after realizing that my sins were forgiven and the implications of Jesus' death and resurrection, I was overwhelmed by a sense of joy and peace. I suddenly found myself climbing a tree to tell those in the school compound to repent and turn to Jesus Christ. From time to time I spoke in tongues. I stayed up that tree for a long time. Later on I

> discovered that some boys were converted due to a sermon I preached up that tree. The reality of Jesus overwhelmed me—and it still does. But I would be wrong to demand that those who are converted should climb a tree and speak in tongues.

In December of 1948, still less than a year after his conversion, Luwum responded to another sermon by Justo Otunno and surrendered himself for service to the church. He exchanged his goal of becoming a chief among his people for the goal of serving Christ. Yet, significantly, Luwum differed then and later from many of the *balokole* who spoke of the Christian life as a complete separation from the world. Instead, to Luwum Christianity meant the sanctification of power, not its renunciation. During his service as bishop and archbishop he reflected on the difficulties the churches of Uganda encountered because they had opted out of the public and political sphere in order to pursue religious work. Not power abdicated but power purified and used responsibly was the path he pursued to the day of his death.

ANGLICAN LEADER

From 1949 through the early 1960s there followed a series of educational opportunities intermixed with rapid advancement in the Ugandan Anglican Church. He trained first as a lay reader, then worked as a catechist in Gulu, returned to study for his ordination and eventually became a priest in 1956. As a parish pastor he served a poor district in the Upper Nile region of northern Uganda, where his responsibilities included oversight (with only a bicycle for getting around) of twenty-four separate congregations across a parish forty miles wide. From the start he was an indefatigable worker who won the loyalty of parishioners through his openness to all comers, his wide-ranging energy and his fearless gospel preaching.

In 1958 he spent a year at Saint Augustine's College in Cambridge, England, and then once again was in England during the period 1963 to 1965 at the London College of Divinity. Between these educational forays abroad he was successively the vice principal and then principal of the same training school in which he had earlier studied.

Luwum became vice principal of Buwalasi Theological College in 1962, the year that Uganda gained its independence from Great Britain. Great celebrations heralded the new nation as Uganda joined much of sub-Saharan Africa in moving beyond the colonial era. The Uganda People's Congress Party under Dr. Milton Obote won control of the new government and set about a program of social development that drew on Anglican leaders as well as Catholics and Muslims. Obote was from the Lango people, also from the north of Uganda, with whom the Baganda of the south did not enjoy warm relations.

Janani Luwum's rise to leadership in the Anglican Church corresponded closely with the development of his new country. He was appointed provincial secretary of the Church of Uganda, Rwanda, Burundi and Boga-Zaire in 1966, whereupon he, Mary and their numerous children moved to the capital city of Kampala. In Kampala, Luwum worked to smooth the way for Archbishop Sabiti, whose election had been contested by Baganda Anglicans who were promoting their own candidate. Luwum regarded his main task as implementing the Bikangaga Report, a ten-year plan drawn up to guide Ugandan Anglicans through the first phase of their country's independence. This report updated the visionary goals that had been outlined for the Church Missionary Society by its influential nineteenth-century director, Henry Venn. Venn, along with Rufus Anderson of the American Board of Commissioners for Foreign Missions, had outlined a mission strategy aimed at creating local indigenous churches that, as soon as possible, would become self-governing, self-multiplying and self-financing. During the African colonial period, this farsighted goal was substantially undermined because Europeans and Americans took for granted that they should be directing the younger churches. With the end of colonial rule, the ideal of local churches directed by local Christians came surging back.

Luwum was one of the Ugandan leaders who gave this goal legs. Yet the going was not always smooth. Overcoming difficulties in moving out from under British rule was one thing. Overcoming ancestral differences among African tribal peoples was another. In sad but telling anticipation of much worse strife to come, Luwum as the Anglicans' provincial secretary was forced to work overtime to defuse tensions between the Lango people and the Baganda, between the Acholi and other peoples in the north, and between still other tribal groups divided by ancestral animosities. Multiplied several times over, the ancient tribal antagonisms inspired the coup that ended Milton Obote's rule in 1971, that sparked the death and destruction under Idi Amin and later rulers, and that fueled the violent rebellion of Uganda's Lord's Resistance Army through much of the first decade of the twenty-first century.

BISHOP LUWUM

In 1969 Janani Luwum was named the bishop of a newly formed province for northern Uganda. Again, as a sign of difficulties to come, his service of consecration was held, not in a church, but at the insistence of Obote's government in Gulu's large open-air stadium. Both Milton Obote and his army chief of staff, Idi Amin, were in attendance. But Luwum worked hard at keeping politics at bay, particularly by having Handel's "Hallelujah Chorus" sung as part of the festivities.

As the first Acholi bishop, who was being given spiritual direction over an area with many Acholi, Luwum had to respond to incessant demands from members of his own tribe while also trying to serve all the peoples of his charge. From the start he traveled tirelessly to preach, listen, counsel and assist.

As a preacher, Luwum regularly told stories from everyday life as a way of promoting Christian living. One of them concerned a man who invited a friend to his home. The man made extensive preparations that included a thorough housecleaning, invitations sent to many others and preparations for a great feast. On the appointed day when the friend arrived, the man welcomed him warmly and invited him for a day of festivities. But when mealtime came, the visitor received only the head of a chicken. That inhospitable act, according to Luwum, showed the visitor that despite all the show, the man did not really love him as he should. "We are like that unloving friend," Janani explained. "We give God just a little. Yet we buy new clothes, meat and other things. Our hearts are far away from him. We love ourselves more than we love God." This kind of preaching led naturally to efforts at encouraging his people to become active evangelists. An outreach planned for April 1970 began slowly but eventually involved a successful mission that reached many in Gulu.

Luwum also cooperated with other willing hands in reaching out to those in greatest need. Relations between Anglicans and Catholics had warmed up considerably since the competition of Uganda's earliest Christian years. Yet distrust and alienation remained very much alive, especially in local areas where Catholics and Anglicans competed with each other. For his part, Luwum cooperated on many occasions with Catholic leaders, including the efforts he made in Gulu to help the unfortunates suffering with leprosy. Together with the local Catholic bishop, Luwum established a special clinic for leprosy victims. It was an anticipation of more collaboration later.

IN TO A POLITICAL MAELSTROM

On January 25, 1971, Idi Amin seized power from Milton Obote while the latter was attending a conference outside of the country. Bad blood between the two had been building for some time. Amin, a Muslim from a smaller tribal group associated with the Baganda, had risen through the ranks of the British army and then, with great speed, in the military of independent Uganda. Intermittent spasms of local violence, including assassination of political leaders, led the way to this coup d'état. Amin immediately set out to suppress Obote's followers, many of whom were Protestants. Because of support that the Acholi had given to Obote, they too felt the heavy hand of oppression. From early 1971 Bishop Luwum in his travels encountered more and more Acholi who mourned those killed by Amin's security squads, or who had simply disappeared.

In 1972 Amin issued a decree that expelled the fifty thousand or more Asians (Pakistanis and Indians) who lived in Uganda, many who were merchants. When the decree came out, Luwum was attending a meeting of the World Council of Churches (WCC) in Utrecht, Holland; with several others he immediately drafted a strongly worded protest. It was not Luwum's first, and it would be far from his last attempt to bring Christian influence to bear on Uganda's public life.

The next year Amin ordered public executions of young men rounded up indiscriminately for unspecified subversive activities. In Gulu, these executions took place in the same stadium where Luwum had been consecrated as bishop. Shortly thereafter, one of Luwum's daughters died of a lingering illness. The combination of death by violence and death by disease gave special urgency to the bishop's preaching. His stress on the urgent need to repent grew stronger. Frequently he turned to Isaiah 1:18: "Come now, let us reason together, says the Lord ... though your sins are like scarlet, they shall be as white as snow; though they are red like crimson, they shall become like wool" (RSV). In the words of Luwum's longtime secretary, Margaret Ford, who would later write his biography: "The Lord was recruiting for himself a mighty army to combat the evil which was beginning to take root in Uganda."

In 1974 Luwum was elected as the archbishop of Uganda and surrounding regions, as the successor of Erica Sabiti. By the time he and his family moved to the capital, Kampala, economic collapse was adding to the fear of random violence. Uganda was entering into the valley of shadow; before 1979, when Amin was ousted in another coup (led by the exiled Milton Obote), something like 300,000 Ugandans would be killed.

Luwum was consecrated as archbishop on June 9, 1974. Only a month later he traveled to Switzerland for the landmark First International Congress on World Evangelization at Lausanne. The meeting is justifiably renowned for its sponsorship by the Billy Graham Evangelistic Association and for the Lausanne Covenant, drafted by John Stott. But it also offered an opportunity for Christian leaders from the non-Western world to become acquainted with each other. During his stay at the Lausanne Conference, the new Archbishop Luwum asked to room with Stephen Mungoma, the head of Uganda's Deliverance Church, a new charismatic fellowship. His intent was to hear from the young leader about the aspirations of this new church.

Soon, however, Luwum was back in the much more difficult circumstances of Kampala. He tried to carry out the demanding duties of his multifaceted spiritual responsibilities while increasingly called on to negotiate with Amin and his regime. In fact, so frequently did the archbishop and the dictator confer that some Anglicans began to accuse Luwum of falling too much under Amin's influence.

CRISIS AND DEATH

The crises that culminated in Luwum's murder began in the summer of 1976. In late June, an Air France flight from Tel Aviv to Paris was hijacked by Palestinian terrorists and diverted to Uganda's Entebbe airport. On Sunday, the Fourth of July, while Americans celebrated the two hundredth anniversary of their nation's independence, a team of Israeli commandos carried out a daring raid that liberated the Jewish passengers whom Amin was holding as virtual hostages. Amin then accused Kenya of helping the Israeli commandos; in response Kenya closed its border with Uganda, which meant that gasoline supplies were cut off. Amin directed attacks on Kenyans living in his country and cracked down even harder on all threats to his regime, real and imagined.

Luwum became directly involved in this increasingly chaotic picture when, in early August, students at the University of Makerere in Kampala returned to classes and protested the murder of a much-loved administrator who had been killed by government thugs. The protests were met with a rampage authorized by Amin in which students were beaten, raped and brutalized. When an official report blamed student religious groups for the riot and for harboring revolutionaries, Luwum and the local Catholic bishop convened a meeting of Protestant, Catholic and Muslim leaders to compose a formal response. At this meeting, on August 26, 1976, Janani took the chair. The minutes spelled out not only Uganda's economic and social problems but also in specific detail the fear that gripped the country because of security forces running wild. They requested a meeting with Amin, a request that was ignored.

From this time onward, Archbishop Luwum's days were numbered, a fact he recognized clearly. Some, nonetheless, continued to criticize his willingness to treat with the government. He replied to one such critic in December 1976: "I do not know for how long I shall be occupying this chair. I live as though there will be no tomorrow. I face daily being picked up by the soldiers. While the opportunity is there, I preach the gospel with all my might, and my conscience is clear before God that I have not sided with the present government, which is utterly self-seeking. I have been threatened many times. Whenever I have the opportunity I have told the President the things the churches disapprove of. God is my witness." On Christmas Day a radio address by Archbishop Luwum was cut off when it began to criticize the atrocities of the regime.

The end came in February. On the fifth a raid took place on Luwum's house; security forces broke down the fence surrounding the dwelling and then ransacked the premises looking for weapons. They accused him of hiding arms as part of an Acholi plot against the government. None were there.

On February 8 Anglican bishops met to discuss the growing threat and drafted a letter to Amin with copies sent later, on February 14, to other government ministers, other church leaders and the All Africa Conference of Churches headquartered in Nairobi, Kenya. The letter read in part, "We have buried many who have died as a result of being shot and there are many more whose bodies have not been found. The gun which was meant to protect Uganda as a nation, the Ugandan citizen and his property, is increasingly being used against the Ugandan to take away his life and property." The letter was delivered to Amin on February 12, in some accounts by Luwum himself.

Two days later, on February 14, Luwum was summoned for a personal meeting with Amin, where the dictator accused him of plotting with Milton Obote to overthrow the government. Simultaneously this charge was broadcast over Radio Uganda and printed in Kampala's controlled press. When Luwum denied any such activity, Amin warned him to stick strictly to religious matters.

On February 16, Idi Amin called for a mass meeting of government officials, church leaders, army personnel and foreign ambassadors. When the crowd had assembled, it quickly turned into a kangaroo court. Amin's vice president read out a document purportedly written by Milton Obote that implicated Luwum among many others. Luwum was standing next to a fellow Anglican bishop, Festo Kivengere, and whispered, "They are going to kill me. I am not afraid." The vice president appealed to the crowd for a decision about the traitors, whereupon the soldiers present shouted, "Kill them, kill them now." Then some of the assembled crowd, including the Anglican bishops, were invited inside. They received a tongue-lashing and were told to go home. The archbishop, however, was called back: "You, Luwum are wanted in that room by the president." Janani turned to his fellow bishops and said, "I can see the hand of the Lord in this." It was the last words they heard. He was never seen again.

Festo Kivengere and another bishop waited for Luwum in searing heat for the rest of the day before they were driven away by armed guards. When they returned to the Luwum home without Janani, a frantic Mary Luwum insisted on driving to the conference grounds, but she too was repelled by troops. That night Luwum's arrest was announced, along with the arrest of two Christian cabinet ministers. The next day Radio Uganda broadcast a report that the three had been killed in a car accident when they tried to commandeer the vehicle. No body was ever displayed. No one ever believed this report.

Later, Festo Kivengere wrote: "There was a rumor ... that they were trying to make him sign a confession, which he would not do. We were also told that he was praying aloud for his captors when he died. We have talked with eyewitnesses who claim they saw him shot, and to others who saw the bodies in the morgue with bullet wounds. Evidence suggests that he was shot at six o'clock [on February 16]."

ONE PART OF THE REST OF THE STORY

In 1998, Cassell Publishers in London brought out a book titled *The Terrible Alternative.* Publication of this volume coincided with a project that Westminster Abbey brought to completion that year. As part of an extensive renovation, the abbey commissioned ten new statues to be placed in niches in the exterior wall. Each commemorated a Christian martyr in the twentieth century. Among the ten were well-known witnesses like Dietrich Bonhoeffer of Germany and Bishop Oscar Romero of El Salvador, as well as lesser-known figures from China, Russia, Papua New Guinea and, from Uganda, Janani Luwum. The book devoted one chapter to each martyr.

The chapter, called "Tribalism, Religion and Despotism in Uganda: Archbishop Janani Luwum," was written by John Sentamu, who as a young man first met Luwum in 1973. Sentamu had been sent by the Supreme Justice of the High Court in Kampala to serve as a magistrate in Gulu. Luwum welcomed the young lawyer eagerly and then expressed the hope that Sentamu might help the bishop care for those who had been orphaned and widowed in the violence that was descending on the country. He said, "We must be Christ to these people: be our advocate and take up their cases. The local prison is filled to capacity with innocent people suspected of opposing the government."

John Sentamu had occasion to work with Luwum on several projects over the next years until in 1974 Sentamu was forced to leave the country and settled in the United Kingdom.

Sentamu's chapter on Archbishop Luwum draws on his own personal experiences, interviews with many who had known the archbishop and books that had been written about him. This is how he ends his account:

> Janani Luwum gave to the Church of Uganda, Rwanda, Burundi and Boga-Zaire a new spirit and vitality. His wise leadership had encouraged Christians not to disregard, but to confront issues of church and state in Uganda. That he challenged the authorities of his day publicly, like the prophet Nathan, set him apart from other bishops of the church, whose relations with the state had often been confined to the private sphere. His contribution was also characterized by the confidence of his faith; that the gospel of Jesus Christ could offer eternal values to a violent, unjust and deceitful political power. He sought to shape his province into a distinctive Christian body that cherished its past and its diversity, but one that reached out to what was universal in the gospel. For me, his martyrdom was a defining moment. The day he died I resolved to be ordained.

John Sentamu, who intended to return to Uganda, was prevented from doing so by the unsettled conditions prevailing in his native land when he finished his theological training. Instead, he remained in the United Kingdom to serve the Church of England there. In 2002 he became the archbishop of York, next to the archbishop of Canterbury the foremost Anglican leader in the world.

SOURCES

Most of the details and quotations in this chapter are from a biography written by Luwum's friend and administrative assistant, Margaret Ford, in a book she dedicated to Mary Luwum, *Janani: The Making of a Martyr* (London: Marshall, Morgan and Scott, 1978). John Sentamu's essay is in *The Terrible Alternative: Christian Martyrdom in the Twentieth Century,* ed. Andrew Chandler (London: Cassell, 1998), pp.144-58. The online *Dictionary of African Christian Biography* (www.dacb.org) includes useful introductory articles on all of the church figures mentioned in this chapter. Helpful background is found in M. Louise Pirouet, "Religion in Uganda Under Amin," *Journal of Religion in Africa* 11 (1980):13-29, and on the website of the Archbishop Janani Luwum Trust (www.jananiluwumtrust.com). For Festo Kivengere's story, see his *I Love Idi Amin* (London: Marshall, Morgan and Scott, 1977).

INDIA

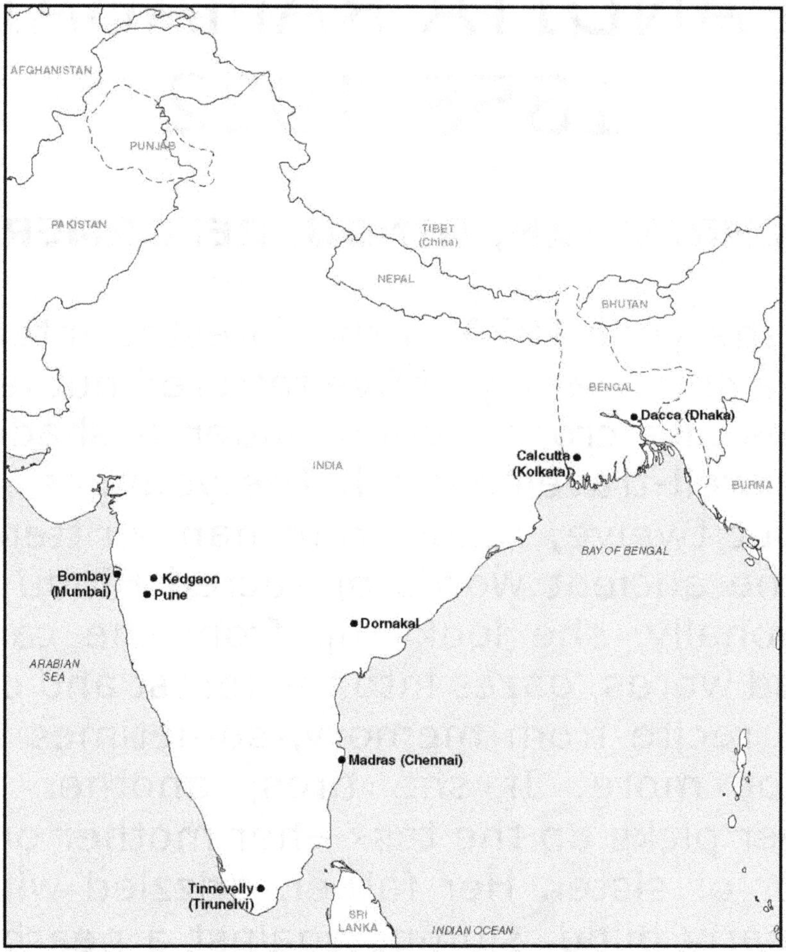
AFGHANISTAN
PUNJAB
PAKISTAN
TIBET
(China)
NEPAL
BHUTAN
BENGAL
Dacca (Dhaka)
Calcutta
(Kolkata)
INDIA
BURMA
BAY OF BENGAL
Bombay
(Mumbai)
Kedgaon
Pune
Dornakal
ARABIAN
SEA
Madras (Chennai)
Tinnevelly
(Tirunelvi)
SRI
LANKA
INDIAN OCEAN

8

PANDITA RAMABAI 1858-1922

CHRISTIAN, HINDU, REFORMER

In the year 1870 in the forested interior of India, a small family of five tattered but learned pilgrims sits cross-legged under a shade tree near a well-traveled road. The youngest, a girl of about twelve, reads from handwritten Sanskrit the ancient words of sacred Hindu texts. Occasionally, she looks up from the carefully lettered words, gazes into the forest and continues to recite from memory, sometimes for an hour or more. If she tires, another family member picks up the task—her mother or older brother or sister. Her father, grizzled with age and nearly blind, slumps against a nearby wall and listens. Hundreds of people pass without a glance. A few stop and listen for a moment, then place a small gift on the ground: a pretty stone, a flower petal, perhaps a few precious grains of rice. Late in the day, the family picks up these offerings, their only earnings, and walks to some other sacred spot. The recitation and reading continues there. The family has lived this way since their youngest was six months old.

Pandita Ramabai

In 1892 a small Hindu woman in her mid-thirties sits at a table in the front room of a large honeycombed building called Sharada Sadan, in Pune, India. Her door is open. She reads aloud to her eleven-year-old daughter, who sits next to her. Students, workers and children pass by outside the doorway. Some stop to listen. A few step inside for a moment. Some come back the next day and listen again to words read—without comment or explanation—from a Christian Bible. The child of the forest and the woman of the home are the same: Pandita Ramabai, one of India's most influential Christians of the twentieth century.

Why would a Hindu woman, highly skilled in her own ancient texts, take up the Christian Bible? Ramabai's story provides the answer, but a few words on Hinduism and Christianity show why this tale is so significant. Hinduism, the third most practiced world religion after Christianity and Islam, contrasts sharply with

Christianity. While the Hindu religion (or life view) is *in*clusive, Christianity is *ex*clusive. Christianity, on the one hand, says there is only one God and that the single way to salvation is through Jesus Christ his Son, thus creating a moral imperative to share the good news of Jesus Christ with those who do not yet know him. Hinduism, on the other hand, is henotheistic; it assumes that individuals may devote themselves to one god while at the same time acknowledging the existence of many others. One consequence of these differences is that Christians view evangelism as a gift offered to nonbelievers, but to Hindus evangelism often looks like an insult and a potential limitation on their freedom of conscience. Pandita Ramabai walked this tight rope all of her adult life. A Christian by belief and a Hindu by culture, she sometimes gathered the best of both, but at other times found herself caught in between by religious crossfire.

CHILDREN OF THE FOREST

Life began for Pandita Ramabai on April 23, 1858, near Karkal, in the southwest coastal area of India. She was the sixth child of her father Anant Shastri's second family. His first wife had died, so at age forty-six, when Anant noticed a nine-year-old child traveling with her family on pilgrimage, he struck a bargain with her father, married this girl the next day, changed her name to Lakshmibai and took her to his home some nine hundred miles away. Anant treated his new possession well. This child-bride was Ramabai's mother. A marriage transaction of this sort sounds shocking, even criminal, to Western ears, but in nineteenth-century Indian Brahman families, child marriages were routine. In fact, Lakshmibai's father had shown unusual care for his daughter by choosing a husband who offered kindness, economic stability and education—even for a girl, which was still rare in the India of that day. Ramabai later wrote that her father "found an apt pupil in my mother, who fell in line with his plan, and became an excellent Sanskrit scholar."

But teaching his child-bride to read generated opposition. Brahman pandits (or teachers) warned Anant, "The language of the gods is not for women." Seeking to avoid a battle for himself and his family, Anant Shastri retreated. He and Lakshmibai, now age fifteen and ready to become a mother, traveled deep into the forests of Gangamal, built a retreat home there, and cleared enough space to cultivate an orchard and vegetable garden. Pilgrims and students made their way to this new home, so Anant was able to continue instruction of his family along with the others who came to learn from him. Six children were born in this forest home. Ramabai was the youngest of three survivors. But teaching in a forest had its difficulties. Hindu religious pilgrims expected food, and the Hindu value system prescribed hospitality as a sacred duty. Thirteen years into his forest retreat, Anant ran out of money. So in 1858, he, with his wife and their three children, walked out of the forest and joined the throngs of India's religious pilgrims. Anant would become a *puranika,* a reader, reciter, preacher, of Puranas, the eighteen volumes of sacred Hindu texts. As the family walked they carried six-month-old Ramabai in a basket.

The first twenty years of her life were spent as a pilgrim wandering from one shrine to another throughout the length and breadth of India.

By the time Ramabai was old enough to learn Sanskrit, the beautiful and complex "language of the gods," her father was nearly blind and too old to instruct her. So her mother picked up the task. Each morning at first light they began the day's work of reading and memorization. Ramabai learned a word, then a phrase, then a sentence spoken first by her mother, then recited back by the child, once, twice, five, and then ten times, line by line committed to visual and auditory memory. By the time she was twenty, Ramabai could recite eighteen thousand verses of these sacred texts. She could also reason her way through the texts with the logical expertise of a scholar.

REDUCTIONS AND ADDITIONS

Tragedy struck when Pandita was sixteen. The family's journeys had taken them to the Madras Presidency, a region in the southern tip of India, where in the early 1870s famine gripped the land. No food was left for pilgrims. Her father, now eighty years old, could walk no farther. At one point the family prayed for a snake or a tiger to come out of the forest and devour them. Instead her father died of starvation in July of 1874. It took six weeks longer for her mother to die. Then, just over a year later, Ramabai's older sister met the same fate.

Ramabai and her older brother, Shrinivas Shastri, were now alone, yet they continued the only life they had known, as wandering readers/reciters of the sacred Puranas. Now traveling at a faster pace, the brother and sister traversed India from 1875 to 1878: the Punjab, Rajputana, Central Provinces, Assam, Bengal and Madras, covering more than four thousand miles, and eventually reaching Calcutta in India's far east. There a surprise awaited them: Ramabai became a celebrity. Her massive learning and understanding of ancient Sanskrit texts earned newspaper headlines, invitations to speak and two titles bestowed by scholars: "Pandita" (a wise person) and "Saraswati" (goddess of learning). Although she at first declined these titles, she would later be known as "the Pandita" or simply "Pandita."

For the next two years Ramabai and Shrinivas continued their travels, but now Ramabai was receiving invitations to teach and lecture. She took advantage of her newfound fame to mount a special campaign on behalf of Indian women. It was still a time when most Indian women were forbidden to learn to read, regularly forced into child marriages, often enslaved by in-law families, sometimes beaten into submission by husbands and generally treated as subhuman. As she carried out this campaign, Ramabai began to lose faith in the religious aspect of Hinduism for permitting such injustice, even though she could argue persuasively that mistreatment of women required a misreading of Hindu sacred texts. Then tragedy struck again.

While returning from a speaking trip in Assam in the far northeast of India, her brother, Shrinivas, became ill with cholera, a waterborne bacterial disease that can kill from dehydration in hours. Shrinivas died on May 8, 1880, in Dacca, now part of Bangladesh. Six months later, to fulfill his dying wish, and perhaps even out of love, Ramabai married her brother's friend Babu Bepin Behari Das Medhavi, an attorney, a Bengali of the Shudra caste, and also a teacher of chemistry. Because this was an intercaste marriage and also because they had both lost confidence in the Hindu faith, Bepin and Ramabai were wed in a civil ceremony. Women of her Brahman community responded with harsh warnings, "This wretch married a Bengali Baboo and polluted herself," and "Don't touch anything in our house after touching her." Not daunted by such rejection, just ten months after her marriage Ramabai gave birth to a daughter, Manorama, in April 1881. Unlike many firstborn females, this child was lovingly nurtured, but soon thereafter tragedy struck yet again. On February 4, 1882, Bepin died—also of cholera. Ramabai was now a twenty-three-year-old widow with a child ten months old.

FAITH EXPLORATIONS

Before her brother died, Ramabai had been introduced to Christianity during a visit to Calcutta. Her first impressions were not altogether favorable. She later wrote, "There were chairs and sofas, tables, lamps—all very new to us. Indian people curiously dressed like English men and women.... They ate bread and biscuits and drank tea with the English people and shocked us by asking us to partake of the refreshment.... They prayed to God ... but it seemed as though they were paying homage to the chairs before which they knelt.... We thought Kali Yuga, that is, the last age of quarrels, darkness, and irreligion, had fully established its reign in Calcutta." But Christianity, this strange foreign religion, soon became a major force in Pandita Ramabai's life.

Even during her brief marriage, while living in Silchar, near Dacca, Ramabai and her husband had participated in conversations with a Baptist missionary, Isaac Allen, and had begun to explore the Christian faith. For her husband, some of the conversations were a review, since he had attended mission schools before deciding against Christianity. But Ramabai found the biblical account in Genesis particularly appealing, with its creation account so different from the Puranas texts: "It stuck me as being a true story, but I could not give any reason for thinking so or believing in it." Bepin, not wanting to be isolated in the "despised Christian community," objected to her being baptized a Christian.

A month after Bepin's death, Ramabai traversed the country once more from northeast to southwest and returned to Pune with her baby. There she was soon in demand by activist groups working for the liberation of Indian women. In June 1882, for example, she addressed the 150 prominent women who made up the first meeting of Arya Mahila Samaj, an organization devoted to women's emancipation. She called on these leaders to free themselves from the oppression of child marriage, illiteracy, denial of basic education and the sufferings of high-caste child widows.

Of even greater significance during her one-year stay in Pune was contact with Anglican missionaries of the Community of Saint Mary the Virgin. During this period she met regularly with the Reverend Father Nehemiah Goreh, a Brahman convert to Anglicanism, who "used to come and explain the difference between the Hindu and Christian religions." The community of sisters soon encouraged her to go to England, where she could continue exploration of Christianity at their sister community at Wantage and also take up studies to become a medical doctor. The plan appealed to Ramabai, so in 1882 she wrote and published her first book, *Stree Dharma-Neeti (Morals for Women)* in order to earn passage to England for herself and her daughter.

ENGLAND AND BEYOND

Life in England proved to be a trial. Even though Ramabai was now a twenty-five-year-old widow and mother, the sisters at Wantage acted in loco parentis. As they taught her the fine points of Christian doctrine, they limited her travel and prescribed training also in the fine points of Victorian decorum. Most disappointing, Ramabai was not accepted for medical study because of problems with her hearing. To add to her woes, Ramabai's traveling companion, Anandibai Bhagat, became mentally unhinged and so frightened at the prospect of forcible conversion that she once tried to strangle Ramabai in order to save her from this fate. When that attempt failed, Anandibai poisoned herself and died in agony some twelve hours later. Understandably, Ramabai needed a servant to sleep in the same room with her for some nights thereafter.

Despite these difficulties, Ramabai did convert voluntarily while in England. She and her daughter, Manorama, received the sacrament of Christian baptism on September 29, 1883. On that occasion she was assigned a godmother and spiritual guide, Sister Geraldine, with whom she had a long and sometimes contentious relationship. It was a mix of not-so-patient teaching meeting not-so-cooperative learning. Sometimes in person, but mostly in letters covering many years, they argued about many things: the authority of the church, the nature of the universal church, whether Ramabai would be allowed to teach Sanskrit to boys (Sister

Geraldine deemed this an inappropriate activity for women), and how Mano would be taught to pray. When they discussed the Trinity, Sister Geraldine accused Ramabai of being an Arian heretic and expressed a fear that she might become a Unitarian or a Baptist. At one point Miss Beale, principal of the ladies' college in Cheltenham, attempted to quiet the storm, admonishing Sister Geraldine that Ramabai must "study Christianity as a philosophy. She cannot receive it merely as an historical revelation." For her part Ramabai once told Sister Geraldine, "As long as I am led to think that my asking questions to you leads you to misunderstand me, I shall not say one single word to you about it, but shall read the Bible by myself, and follow the teaching of Christ." Not surprisingly Ramabai soon left England for the United States. Yet she and Sister Geraldine continued their correspondence for the next two decades, though usually fondly and in more gentle tones.

In the heat of this battle with Sister Geraldine, two English observers made perceptive predictions about Ramabai's future. Bishop Thomas Lahore wrote to Miss Beale, "If [Ramabai] has not the heroic courage I take her to have, she will of course gladly settle down and become an English lady; but my impression is that the wail of her Indian sisters will not suffer her to rest, till she has mingled her tears with theirs, not in the way of sympathy at a distance, but where they can trickle from face to face." To which Dorthea Beale replied, also prophetically, "I think we must remember that God seems to have anointed her with power to throw down the pernicious caste restrictions and those barriers which wrongly separate men and women."

On March 6, 1886, Ramabai and her daughter arrived by ship in the U.S., where they were met by her cousin Anandibai Joshi, who was soon to graduate from medical school and become the first Indian woman to earn an M.D. in the United States. After Anandibai's graduation, Ramabai began a speaking and study tour throughout the United States that over the next two years would take her to hundreds of meetings spanning thousands of miles and raise substantial donations and pledges. During that time she also established local branches of the American Ramabai Association, which would continue as a communication and financial support link to the work she proposed to do in India.

Unlike Ramabai, who later enjoyed great success in India, Anandibai did not fare so well. Upon returning to India, she provided much needed medical care for women who were prohibited by law or by modesty from seeing male physicians. But already ill with tuberculosis while studying in Philadelphia, Dr. Anandibai Joshi died of the disease on February 26, 1887, less than a year after returning home.

PREPARTIONS

In spite of incessant travel Ramabai managed to complete a full year of study in the U.S., during which she concentrated on educational techniques introduced by German educator Friedrich Froebel earlier in the century. The knowledge of early childhood education that Ramabai took back to India included Froebel's concept of informal education through play. Ramabai's school in India encouraged children to build with geometric blocks, sing, dance and create gardens intermingled with their study of mathematics, reading and writing. While still in the United States, Ramabai translated Froebel's teaching materials and compatible curriculum into the Marathi language and provided her own explanations for adapting these methods to Hindu culture. Froebel's form of education fit well into Ramabai's developing Christian philosophy of life, which included respect for both genders, freedom of the will and liberty of conscience.

While in America, Ramabai also wrote a book, *The High-Caste Hindu Woman,* which included a great deal of introductory biographical material. The book grew from Ramabai's lectures and speeches as she traversed the American continent; it would become her most widely read work. Here readers saw the plight of Hindu women whom Ramabai hoped to rescue along with the religious-social structure that dictated these conditions. The book offered a full catalog of abuses:

- When the Rajputs gather with neighbors and friends waiting for announcement of a birth, if a boy is born they celebrate, but if the baby is a girl, "the father coolly announces that 'nothing' has been born," and "the friends go home grave and quiet."
- Infanticide of girl babies is the responsibility of the father: accomplished by a little opium to keep the child quiet, then "a skillful pressure upon the neck, which is known as 'putting nail to the throat.'"
- A child bride of age nine or younger is sent to the house of her father-in-law, where "breaking the young bride's spirit is an essential part of the discipline."
- A girl is normally "married" (by irrevocable betrothal) sometime between birth and age nine and may then become a lifelong "widow" if her husband dies, or refuses to take her, or makes her a slave to his parents, or marries a dozen or a hundred other wives.

- At the time the book was written India had more than half a million "widows" under the age of twenty, 79,000 of these under the age of nine.
- When a girl becomes a widow, it is assumed that she has committed horrible crimes in a former existence and she must now be punished.
- If she becomes a widow without giving birth to a son, she must be punished "as the greatest criminal upon whom Heaven's judgment has been pronounced."
- The most honorable way that she can redeem herself (and escape further punishment) is to throw herself on her husband's funeral pyre.
- If she lacks the courage to do this, wise men from her husband's family may help her accomplish this final act.
- If she lives after her husband's death, she receives direction to "emaciate her body by living on pure flowers, roots and fruit."
- If a widow has a son, all of her property belongs to him.
- There is "no place for a man (in heaven) who is destitute of male offspring."
- A woman's only hope of entering eternal bliss is to one day become reincarnated as a Brahman man.

Ramabai's book was, however, more than just sensationalism for American readers. It also described the world that Pandita Ramabai hoped to reenter, bringing help for the women of India. Proceeds from her book and gifts from new American friends moved to generosity by the plight of women half a world away would fund her work.

INDIA YEARS

Ramabai returned to India in February 1889, at the age of thirty. Except for a brief visit to the United States in 1898 to connect with her supporters, she spent the remainder of her life in India. Her daughter, Mano, by then nine, lived with her or near her during much of her growing up years but returned to England and the United States for her schooling.

Getting started was hard. In March 1889 Ramabai opened Sharada Sadan ("home of learning") in Bombay, a home and school for high-caste child widows. In line with Hindu culture, this dwelling would be "non-sectarian" inasmuch as children would be free to choose any religion and would not be coerced into any one faith system. Ramabai did, however, insist on her own religious liberty to act, read and worship as she chose. Hence, reading the Christian Scriptures aloud to her daughter with her door open was a right she reserved for herself and one she would give to any resident regardless of the spiritual text they chose to read. This was the pattern she maintained when in 1890 she moved the school one hundred miles from Bombay to Pune.

By the turn of the new century, Ramabai had bought a large farm near Pune and was cultivating food for hundreds of residents. She also opened a home for rescuing mistreated and homeless Brahman child widows while protecting their caste by the customary purification and separation from other castes. She also created an educational system that would enable them to enter college. The work expanded until by 1900 she employed eighty-five teachers and staff to operate several schools and group homes for twelve hundred residents. In addition to caring for child widows of all castes, Ramabai's institutions came to include a home for boys, an asylum for prostitutes, a refuge and workshop for the blind, even a home for the aged. When famine made its periodic visit to her region of India, Ramabai and her forces helped to feed and shelter the community.

Despite her tolerant approach to religious differences, conversions to Christianity regularly took place. Rumors about conversions and conversions themselves raised serious difficulties. In 1893 her local board of Hindu advisors protested and then resigned, and relatives of students began to remove students. For ten years she worked to keep Sharada Sadan as nonsectarian as possible, accepting funding as she did so from both Hindus and Christians. In the late 1890s she allowed this Sharada Sadan to become the "Hindu Widows' Home," which was later transformed into Women's University. Yet eventually, with some reluctance, Ramabai gave up the strategy of religious neutrality and turned her full attention to the newly constructed Mukti Mission in a village called Kedgaon, forty miles from Pune. This mission opened its doors on September 24, 1898. There she proclaimed the Christian gospel to thousands who would seek its refuge. The school's logo was an image of the Liberty Bell, which had caught Ramabai's eye in Philadelphia. It symbolized liberation to all people, including destitute little girls. The name Mukti itself means "freedom."

Ramabai's own experience strongly influenced the shape of the Mukti Mission. In 1897, at the age of thirty-seven, Ramabai returned for a brief period to the wanderings of her childhood. She donned the robes of a mendicant, carried a small bundle of belongings on her head and struck out to discover for herself what girls and women experienced when they wandered India without resources. The results were appalling. Not only did she nearly lose her life; but she also returned horrified by witnessing castaway wife-children suffocating in dark basement dungeons of expensive homes and encountering predatory men along the roads seeking young girls to enslave as sex objects and then beggars. With these experiences freshly before her, Ramabai returned to Pune ever more determined to create a refuge for any girl or woman in need.

CONVERSIONS

Christian conversion seemed to come in steps at several pivotal points throughout Ramabai's life. Although she had committed herself to Christianity under Isaac Allen's tutelage in 1881 and confirmed that commitment by her baptism in England in 1883, in 1891 she experienced a personal self-relinquishment to Jesus Christ. She later wrote,

> It was nobody's fault that I had not found Christ. He must have been preached to me from the beginning.... One thing I knew by this time, that I needed Christ, and not merely his religion.... I had failed to see the need of placing my implicit faith in Christ and His atonement in order to become a child of God by being born again of the Holy Spirit, and justified by faith in the Son of God.... I had at last come to the end of myself and unconditionally surren-

> dered myself to the Saviour; and asked him to be merciful to me, and to become my Righteousness and Redemption, and to take away all my sin.... The Holy Spirit made it clear to me from the Word of God, that the salvation which God gives through Christ is present and not something future. I believed it, I received it, and I was filled with joy.

PEACE AND PROGRESS

In 1905 Pandita's Christian journey took another step when a Pentecostal-type revival swept through Mukti Mission with accompanying fervent prayer, healings, glossolalia and the exorcising of demons. Yet despite these new experiences, historian Robert E. Frykenberg has described the Pandita Ramabai of this revival era as maintaining a sane attitude, avoiding extremes and sensation, but now more commonly expressing her praise of God by quoting a psalm or prophecy or prayer from the Old Testament. In Frykenberg's account, Ramabai "attained a remarkable depth of peace and tranquility, both within herself and with regard to forces arrayed against her." Even as the complexity of her institutions grew and local opposition increased, the inner peace that matured after the 1905 revival allowed her and her schools to flourish.

Throughout the final two decades of her life Ramabai returned to the discipline of her childhood, word-by-word study of sacred texts. As part of this discipline she translated the entire Bible into Marathi, the local language. But even as she carried out this work one final tragedy occurred: Manorama—her only child, her assistant in translation and her probable successor—died suddenly at age forty, on July 24, 1921. Pandita Ramabai finished the translation, then died herself eight months later, on April 2, 1922, at the age of sixty-three.

The significance of Ramabai's dedication to the sacred text of Scripture is suggested by an incident in England that seemed to influence the rest of her life. As part of her training she visited homes for the poor where Anglican Sisters of the Cross carried out their work. This ministry prompted a crucial conversation.

> I began to think that there was a real difference between Hinduism and Christianity. I asked the Sister who instructed me to tell me what it was that made the Christians care for, and reclaim "fallen" women. [The Sister] read the story of Christ meeting the Samaritan woman, and His wonderful discourse on the nature of true worship.... I had never read or heard anything like this in the religious books of the Hindus; I realized, after reading the

> 4th Chapter of St. John's Gospel, that Christ was truly the Divine Saviour He claimed to be, and no one but He could transform and uplift the downtrodden womanhood of India.

The education begun by the careful instruction of her Indian mother reached its culmination in instruction that took her back to serve India's daughters. More than a hundred years after Pandita Ramabai founded Mukti Mission, thousands of former recipients of its care have become capable nurses, doctors, teachers, homemakers, laborers, professionals, craftworkers, even politicians. Today Mukti continues not only to provide housing for needy women and girls but also includes a hospital, chapel, on-site job training, nursery, adoption agency (for Indian parents only), Braille instruction, and education from preschool through junior college. As a fulfillment of Pandita Ramabai's dreams, its doors remain open.

SOURCES

Christian History and Biography 87 (summer 2005) devoted a full issue to India, with a helpful introductory article on Ramabai by Keith J. White titled "Jesus Was Her Guru." For a fuller treatment, Robert Eric Frykenberg's biographical introduction, *Pandita Ramabai's America* (Grand Rapids: Eerdmans, 2003) was indispensable for this chapter. Frykenberg's larger work, *Christianity in India* (New York: Oxford University Press, 2008), provides deeper context. Anglican Sister Geraldine's collection of two decades of letters with Ramabai offers unusual insight into the development of Ramabai's mind and spirit. Ramabai's autobiography, *A Testimony* (Kedgaon, India: Ramabai Mukti Mission, c.1968) was also very useful. Much insight also is found in the book that Ramabai published in the United States, *The High-Caste Hindu Woman* (Philadelphia: J.B. Rodgers, 1888). Other useful materials include Meera Kosambi, ed., *Pandita Ramabai through Her Own Words: Selected Works* (New Delhi: Oxford University Press, 2000); Pandita Ramabai Sarasvati, *Pandita Ramabai* (Madras: Christian Literature Society, 1979); and Padmini Sengupta, *Pandita Ramabai Saraswati: Her Life and Work.* (London: Asia Publishing House, 1970). The work of the Mukti Mission today can be explored at www.mukti-mission.org.

9

V.S. AZARIAH 1874-1945

BISHOP, STATESMAN, PASTOR

Vedanayagam Samuel Azariah was the first Indian and second non-Briton to become a bishop of the Anglican Church. His 32-year tenure as bishop of Dornakal, in India's south-east (then part of the Madras Presidency, now in the state of Andhra Pradesh), began during the heyday of the British imperial *Raj* (1912) and ended shortly before India gained its independence from Britain (1946). Azariah participated in the complicated maneuvering and tense ideological debates that led to Indian independence, but he gave much closer attention to and expended much more energy on his duties as bishop. The approximately 30,000 Indian Christians in the Anglican Church of Dornakal in 1910 had grown to over 250,000 by the time of Azariah's death. Yet if he was one of the great evangelists in modern church history, he was even more notable for the consistency, humility and faithfulness of his own Christian life. For many of the figures profiled in this book, prominence as a Christian leader was no guarantee of balance, prudence or simple consideration of others; for Azariah, the renown he won as one of the foremost Indian Christians of his era was matched by the godliness he manifested in all of his many contacts, especially with India's rural poor.

Bishop Vedanayagam Samuel Azariah

EARLY LIFE

Azariah was born on August 17, 1874, into a Christian family in the village of Vellalanvilai, which is located in the Tinnevelly region (now Tirunelveli) of India's far southeast, across the Gulf of Mannar from Ceylon (now Sri Lanka). His parents were Nadars, one of the lower castes, but still clearly superior to the untouchables (or Dalits), who in every way lay beneath the members of India's elaborate caste system. Their native language was Tamil. They had been converted through the labors of a Welsh missionary from the Church Missionary Society, the evangelical Anglican body that pioneered principles of self-government, self-support and self-propagation for indigenous churches in its African and Asian missions. (The first non-British Anglican bishop was Samuel Ajayi Crowther, who served in what is now Nigeria from 1864 to 1891 after his appointment through the efforts of Henry Venn, director of the Church Missionary Society.) Azariah's father took the name Vedanayagam, which combined a Hindu word for "Bible" with another for "master." He served for many years as a teacher and deacon before being ordained as an Anglican minister shortly before his son's birth. Azariah's mother, Ellen, taught the young Azariah to sing Christian songs and practice disciplines of prayer and Bible reading that the son maintained through his life.

The young lad was educated at schools established by the Church of England and then the Church of Scotland, where he proved himself to be a diligent scholar. During secondary school at the Church Missionary College in Tinnevelly, it was significant that Azariah helped establish a Christian Brotherhood Association whose main objective was to resist the spirit of caste that bound Indians so tightly to the social and economic stations in which they were born.

Although Azariah never lost a deep love for the rural village culture of his youth, his three years (1893-1896) at the Madras Christian College brought significant changes. In the large cosmopolitan city of Madras he expanded his intellectual outlook with studies in Tamil, English and mathematics; he also deepened his experience with India's incredible diversity of languages, castes, religions and political ideologies. But most important was his introduction to the YMCA and its international connections.

THE YMCA AND THE ANGLICAN CHURCH

The Young Men's Christian Association had been founded in Britain in 1844 with the particular goal of helping young men face the multiplying pressures of urban, industrial life. It sought to support this target group in four areas: physical, intellectual, social and spiritual. The YMCA had been introduced into India only in 1890, yet even by the time Azariah arrived in Madras it had begun to make an impact. Azariah was drawn especially to the YMCA's emphasis on prayer, Bible study, street preaching and evangelism. In fact, Azariah became so caught up in YMCA activities that, when illness prevented him from taking his final university examinations in mathematics, an earlier commitment to join the YMCA prevented him from finishing his degree. (Years later, he did receive an honorary degree from Cambridge University.) The entrance of the YMCA into India soon generated competing organizations for young men that were established by Hindus, Jains, Theosophists and Sikhs. Azariah worked in various capacities for the YMCA from 1895 to 1909.

His labors from the start were extensive. As an example, in 1897 he journeyed 3,465 miles and gave 126 addresses to Christian and non-Christian groups. Much of his travel was in carts drawn by bullocks, which would be a mode of transport he used intermittently for the rest of his life. Susan Billington Harper, whose exhaustive study of Azariah is the basis for this chapter, has outlined the scope of his activities: "He delivered speeches and sermons, conducted Bible studies and prayer meetings, and arranged literary meetings, debates, lectures, concerts, social gatherings, and sporting events in YMCA branches throughout South India. In some locations he established YMCA reading rooms and libraries for which he also purchased books on a wide range of religious and secular topics."

In his work with the YMCA, Azariah pursued what became the central goals of his life. He was above all a patient, thoughtful, but tireless evangelist who gave himself without stinting to spreading the message of salvation in Christ. He was also a constant advocate against caste; to Azariah, the universal character of Christian faith rendered India's hereditary castebound social order defunct. And he was a firm believer in the benefits of Christianity for "civilization," by which he meant social uplift, education, employment and economic development. Unlike many of his contemporaries on the religious right and the religious left, Azariah maintained these objectives *together* throughout the long years of his ministry.

Through the YMCA, he was also drawn into a lively circle of internationally minded Christians who had taken the entire world as their mission field. Already in 1896, for example, Azariah met John R. Mott in Calcutta, where Mott had come in his position as college secretary of the YMCA and director of the Student Volunteer Movement (its motto: "the evangelization of the world in this generation"). Even more important was teamwork, and then friendship, with Sherwood Eddy, who arrived in India as a YMCA worker in 1896. Later in his life, Eddy moved away from evangelical convictions, but as a young man this graduate of Yale University and Princeton Seminary was greatly inspired by the missionary vision of Dwight L.

Moody's Northfield Conferences in Massachusetts; for a quarter of a century, he was one of the YMCA's most effective international evangelists.

Azariah and Eddy soon established a relationship that left a deep impression on both men. For Eddy, Azariah was a powerful example of Christianity flourishing beyond the boundaries of the Western world; in 1902 he described Azariah as "full of the Holy Ghost and of wisdom, and a man of much prayer," and then he added this significant comparison: "I never met an American student at Northfield or in the colleges who has so deep a Christian life." For Azariah, Eddy was a non-Indian with whom genuine bonds of friendship could be established. Years later, Eddy reported that Azariah once said to him that he supposed they were as close friends as an Indian and a foreigner could ever be. When Eddy replied that he was distressed to hear such a statement ("his attitude struck me like a blow") because of the presumed "racial barrier" that Azariah seemed to think required a "second-class friendship," Azariah reported his amazement that a non-Indian would want to stand on the level of complete friendship with himself. "From that frank moment," Eddy concluded, "Azariah and I became close and equal friends." Decades later, after Azariah had died, Eddy wrote that he "was the greatest man whose life I was very privileged to share." Significantly, Eddy expressed this judgment long after he had abandoned the evangelical convictions that Azariah never gave up.

Together, Azariah and Eddy preached countless street missions, they evangelized in villages, they read books together, they wrote a biography of Charles G. Finney in Tamil, they translated some of Finney's *Lectures on Revivals* and other English books into Tamil, and they traveled to meetings in other lands. For Azariah, whose life had been lived with the instinctive Indian awareness of caste and castedivisions, to enter into a deep, personal friendship with YMCA workers like Eddy was a transformative experience.

Azariah's years with the YMCA were important for several other reasons. With other Indians, he witnessed some of the tensions generated when Americans and Britons tried to cooperate as missionaries. Azariah's angle in viewing those tensions was unusual: even as he became active in the YMCA and established excellent working relationships with Americans like Eddy and John R. Mott, he also maintained close connections with Anglican officials representing the faith in which he had been raised. In general, his American colleagues were more flexible, less tied to institutions, more innovative and less bound by tradition. Some of these traits rubbed off on Azariah.

His stance toward Anglicanism was more complicated. Many leaders of the Church of England in India had worked hard to distance themselves and their Christian work from entanglement with the British empire. Yet the *Raj*—the name given to Britain's colonial rule—was a constant presence. That presence could help, since it created space for the Anglican Church to do its work. But it also often hurt Anglican church work because of heavy-handed British dealings with Indians. In addition, colonial officials sometimes hampered Anglican and other Christian efforts in order to keep peace with India's Hindu and Muslim political elites. Yet even when Anglican leaders worked hard to disassociate themselves from the *Raj,* they remained strongly identified with the British imperial presence. So too did Azariah simultaneously embrace and temper the British imperial presence.

Azariah's ability to work well with both American evangelists and British Anglicans left him in an unusual position.

- He was much readier than Americans to take advantage of the institutions that Anglicans had built because of their place in the British empire.

- He was much less bound than British Anglicans to the fine points of colonial protocol.
- He was much more willing than the growing number of Indian nationalists to express his gratitude for some of what Britain had brought to the Indian subcontinent—like attacks on the caste system, provision of education and, most of all, the missionary communication of Christianity.
- He was quicker than the Indians who were completely loyal to Britain to chart an independent course away from colonial rule.

As a parachurch organization the YMCA undercut Western sectarianism (that is, denominational competition), and as a broad-based Indian movement it also undercut the Indian caste system. Some historians have even viewed the YMCA as an important agency preparing the way for the Church of South India. This ecumenical union of Anglican, Methodist, Presbyterian and Congregational Indian churches was completed in 1947, two years after Azariah's death, but he played a key role in the long negotiations that eventually led to church union.

INDIAN WORK BY AN INDIAN

Through all his years of ministry, Azariah displayed an unusual ability to work cooperatively with international Christian organizations while also promoting Indian work as primarily an Indian responsibility. His basic attitude was to regard Christianity not as a Western religion but as a universal religion. As a consequence, his idea was to nurture vigorous local religion, connected to but not dependent on the Christianity of the West. He expressed an early version of these opinions at a conference of the World Christian Student Federation held in Tokyo in 1907: "No country can be fully evangelized except by its own sons.... The nineteenth century can well be called the missionary century of the Occident. Fellow-students of Asia, shall we make the twentieth century the missionary century of the Orient? ... Drawing our inspiration from the cross, let us go forth to make Jesus King of Asia!"

Practically, to make Jesus "King of Asia" required Indian organizations for Indians. So it was that, even as Azariah became increasingly active on the international stage (as a delegate to international meetings of the YMCA and the World Student Christian Federation), he led in establishing the Indian Missionary Society of Tinnevelly (1903) and the National Missionary Society (1905). The motto of the latter group was "Indian money, Indian men and Indian management." In promoting Indian organizations for Indians, Azariah's primary goal remained the salvation of Indians in village, town and city. The Indian mission societies he guided were never anti-British; indeed, both groups maintained warm relations with several Western missionary societies, including the Church Missionary Society.

The early years of Azariah's intense activity on behalf of the YMCA also witnessed the blessing of his marriage to Anbu Mariammal Samuel, a well-educated young woman who would later became an active promoter of women's education in the Dornakal Anglican diocese. Together she and V.S. Azariah raised six children. They began their married life by organizing a wedding that cost only forty rupees, which expressed their own modesty but also represented a protest against the practice of extravagant village weddings that often left lower-caste families buried in permanent debt.

In 1909 Azariah resigned from the YMCA and the National Missionary Society in order to take up a position as superintending missionary of the Indian Missionary Society in Dornakal. Dornakal, which lay to the north of Tinnevelly, was a Telugu-speaking region of great poverty. It included only small Christian communities, and these communities had made little of the educational and economic progress that marked the rising Christian population of Tinnevelly. In conjunction with this geographical move, he was also ordained to the Anglican ministry by the bishop of Madras, Henry Whitehead.

Whitehead was a brother of the famous philosopher Alfred North Whitehead and a formidable player in church and imperial politics. Himself a high-church Anglican, Bishop Whitehead had learned to cooperate with evangelicals of the Church Missionary Society and other denominations in order to advance the general cause of Christianity in India. He was particularly interested in advancing Indians to positions of leadership in his church. His wife, Isabel, was perhaps even more formidable than the bishop. Sometime earlier she had spotted Azariah as an Indian with unusual promise and so was an enthusiastic supporter of her husband when he ordained Azariah for the new work in Dornakal.

A MAN IN THE MIDDLE

The range of Azariah's duties during his early days in this new position underscored his place as "a man in the middle." From the beginning he was committed to intensely local work in an Indian backwater. The city of Dornakal as described by Susan Billington Harper was "surrounded on all sides by tiger-infested jungles and tracts of dry land without access to roads." Harper goes on to outline what Azariah did when he took up his new post:

Here he lived first in a tent, unprotected from dangerous wildlife, and began the strenuous work of evangelizing non-Christian Telugu villages and supervising new Christian congregations. Traveling by foot, bullock cart, and bicycle, with his food and Bible tracts hanging in a bag suspended from the handlebars, Azariah visited families in their simple houses, talked to small groups of men sitting in the shade of trees, preached to crowds gathering in the evenings to hear him, and, on Sundays, performed priestly duties for nascent congregations.

Sherwood Eddy had counseled Azariah not to take this new position because he feared it would leave his many gifts simply wasted on a backwards people. As it turned out, Eddy was wrong about what would happen in Dornakal, but also wrong about Azariah's service to a wider world. For even as Azariah got to work in Dornakal, he also continued to enjoy opportunities from the worldwide connections of the YMCA and the Anglican Church.

Most notably, in 1910 Isabel Whitehead secured an invitation for Azariah to attend the great missionary convention held that year in Edinburgh, Scotland. Traveling with the strong-minded Mrs. Whitehead proved to be a challenge, since she pushed Azariah to present himself as an Asian exotic outfitted with a turban and other "native" dress. Azariah resisted and continued to dress in the ordinary Western garb he had long worn in India.

At Edinburgh, Azariah was one of the very few non-Westerners invited to address the gathering. His memorable speech, which may have reflected his sense of being patronized by Isabel Whitehead, urged missionaries to abandon paternalism for partnership in their relations with the newly Christianized portions of the world. At great length he began by thanking Western Christians for communicating the gift of Christian faith: "Through all the ages to come the Indian Church will rise up in gratitude to attest the heroism and self-denying labours of the missionary body. You have given your goods to feed the poor. You have given your bodies to be burned." But then he went on to ask for yet a higher gift: "We ask also for love. Give us FRIENDS!"

The energizing vision behind this speech was of Christ, "the great Unifier of mankind." With that ideal placed in front of the delegates, Azariah pled for a new approach to missions and a new conception of world Christianity: "The exceeding riches of the glory of Christ can be fully realized not by the Englishman, the American, and the Continental alone, nor by the Japanese, the Chinese, and the Indian by themselves—but by all working together, worshipping together, and learning together the Perfect Image of our Lord and Christ.... This will be possible only from spiritual friendships between the two races. We ought to be willing to learn from one another and to help one another." From addressing the world's largest-ever gathering of Protestant missionaries, Azariah returned to his work of evangelization by bullock cart in dirt-poor Dornakal.

Azariah's stance toward "native dress" continued to illustrate his sensitivity to the perils of crosscultural communication and cooperation. With only a few exceptions, he dressed himself as much in the stereotype of a middle-class Briton as in the stereotype of a native Indian. His point in doing so was to thank the British for introducing a common style of dress to replace the various Indian styles that so closely (and oppressively) marked the strata of Indian caste divisions. The British churchman, historian and Bible scholar Stephen Neill, who knew Azariah during his tenure as bishop of Dornakal, reported with some amusement the times when he went to church with Azariah—Neill would go barefoot to express his identification with the Indians; Azariah would wear ordinary shoes to express his thanks for how the colonial power had opened dignity and sanitation to all! Especially for the lower castes and Dalits,

Western dress represented a much-sought liberation from an oppressive social system.

AN INDIAN BISHOP

Shortly after Azariah's return from Edinburgh, Bishop Whitehead succeeded in pushing forward his long-germinating plan for having an Indian Anglican priest ordained as a bishop. The first Anglican bishop had come out to India in 1814. Since that time a growing number of often capable bishops had served the church there, including Reginald Heber, who served as bishop of Calcutta (then the only Indian bishopric) from 1823 to his early death in 1826. Heber, who is known as the author of "From Greenland's Icy Mountains" and "Holy, Holy, Holy," had orchestrated the ordinations of a converted Muslim and a converted Hindu to the Anglican priesthood. But it had been a struggle to cede more authority in the church to Indians, especially as imperial rule grew stronger toward the end of the nineteenth century.

Whitehead exploited the fact that his diocese of Madras was way too large and far too unwieldy; he could also argue that the large untouchable and lower-caste population of the Dornakal region desperately needed a proven evangelist like Azariah. Whitehead was also knowledgeable about the complex ways that the Anglican Church in India was funded and so could show that appointing Azariah to the newly created diocese of Dornakal could be managed financially.

The upshot was a decision to create a new diocese and to ordain Azariah as its bishop. That ordination took place on December 29, 1912, at Saint Paul's Cathedral in Calcutta before the Governor of Bengal and the eleven other Anglican bishops of India. It was the first such ordination of an Indian to high office in any considerable body of believers within any Christian denomination in India.

But it did not happen without opposition. In England, some, including voices raised in Parliament, opposed the idea of giving an Indian any jurisdiction that included Europeans. Among the Telugu-speaking people of Dornakal there was some resentment about heeding a Tamil-speaking bishop (though Azariah was already on the way to becoming fully fluent in Telugu). Non-Anglican Dissenting Protestants worried that Azariah was part of a plot to increase Anglican dominance. High-caste Brahmans disapproved of elevating a low-caste Nadar to such a high position. And critics of the Church Missionary Society brought up the difficulties that had beset Samuel Ajayi Crowther's tenure as a bishop in Nigeria (which had, in truth, been caused more by runaway missionary imperialism than by Crowther's own missteps).

Yet before long, Azariah silenced all but the most determined of his critics. He did so mostly through a life of consistent, disciplined faithfulness. For most of his years as bishop, Azariah began the day at five o'clock in the morning. with two or two and a half hours of Bible reading and prayer; he ended most days by withdrawing from society in order to read theological books. In between he traveled constantly, partly to oversee various diocesan organizations, but mostly into the villages to evangelize and to encourage believing communities. He also led in setting up schools, from primary instruction in the villages to a Diocesan theological seminary—and for these institutions he wrote many of the textbooks himself. His ministry bore special fruit among the Dalits and lower castes; large family groups and sometimes entire villages responded to the message he and a growing cadre of Indian associates proclaimed. Confidence in what Azariah accomplished was expressed tangibly with regular additions to his diocese, until it eventually grew larger geographically than all England.

Mass conversions were controversial (and remain so) since they were interwoven with the special tensions of Indian political life. One of the great conflicts in recent Indian history has simmered over how best to practice democracy—by community or by individual. To those who wanted India to maintain its historic religious communities, mass conversions moved citizens from one voting bloc to another (in the Dornakal case, from Hindu to Christian) and thereby weakened the political power of the Hindu communities. Azariah tried to argue that true liberty had to include the right for individuals to change religion. The evangelistic campaigns he conducted were done with such integrity that these arguments were often convincing, though never with all audiences.

Azariah devoted himself especially to making the sacraments of his church come alive for the poor and often illiterate villagers who made up most Anglican adherents. When he carried out confirmations, he engaged patiently in lengthy sessions of questions and answers with those who were to be confirmed. Such ones, especially if they were illiterate, often replied by singing the simple songs that Azariah and his associates taught. As had early leaders of the Protestant Reformation like Martin Luther, Azariah put the Lord's Prayer, the Ten Commandments, and the Apostles' Creed into simple verse to be sung as a teaching aid.

The baptisms of families and individuals who had turned to Christ were often intensely emotional times. Since most baptisms were conducted in rivers and streams near the villages, they were also powerful ceremonies of social rupture and social renewal. Here is how a Western observer described one such event, after Azariah had examined the candidates. With the bishop standing waist-deep in the stream, "there is a solemn hush while the Creed is recited, and the promises are made. Then all are called in turn by their new names, family by family. Abraham, his wife Sarah, his children Peace, Hope and Joy. John, his wife Mary, his children Jewel-of-the-Lord, Servant-of-Jesus, and God's Beloved. Gone are the old, ugly outcaste names and gone is the old life of degradation and fear. As they step down into the clear running water under the blue eastern sky, and come up again with shining faces and joyful hearts, they know that they are indeed children of the Father of all Who has loved and saved us in Christ Jesus."

Azariah himself gave special emphasis to celebrating communion as expressing the essence of Christian faith, but also as denoting its special promise for India. Dining with members of other castes was one of the great, lingering taboos of traditional Indian society. Azariah was far from the only missionary who observed that Christianity often progressed in India caste-by-caste in coordination with denomination-by-denomination. That is, when one denomination made progress in one caste, converts in other castes would seek out other denominations, so that caste divisions could be preserved in the new Christian churches. Azariah tried in many ways to break the iron grip of caste. In writing about the Lord's Supper, he featured fellowship among believers as one of the important results flowing from the meaning of this sacrament: "It saves you from any temptation to go far away from the Cross and Resurrection—objective acts which constitute the starting points of our Christian life. Whatever my feeling may be..., whatever my failures may be, my being is immersed in the contemplation of something that happened apart from myself and yet which is the pivot around which my life must move. And this creates in us a dependence upon another and a humility that are the prerequisites of any growth in the spiritual life."

As one of India's most respected Christian leaders, Azariah, not surprisingly, was caught up in the great debates over national independence that gained momentum from the 1920s. In these debates, Azariah's moderate position put him at odds with all extremes. Against those who wanted to defend British colonial rule to the end, he spoke out for Indian control over India's future. Against those who saw British colonial rule as only oppressive, he defended many aspects of what the *Raj* had brought to the subcontinent. In the 1930s, as Mahatma Gandhi's campaign for independence intensified, Azariah had some contact, both direct and indirect, with India's most revered leader. Insensitive actions by American missionaries, who complained rashly about Gandhi's intentions, and the implications of Gandhi's own plans to aid the lower-castes and untouchables, which often seemed to exclude any Christian participation, combined to tarnish Azariah's reputation in the eyes of many Indian nationalists. In fact, Susan Billington Harper has titled her comprehensive study of Azariah *In the Shadow of the Mahatma* to indicate how much she thinks that Azariah's activities during his own lifetime and his reputation afterwards have been eclipsed by the much greater attention given to Gandhi.

In other domains Azariah's efforts to bridge the best of the British missionary past with the best of the emerging Indian future were more obviously successful. Throughout his years as bishop he oversaw the construction of the Anglican Cathedral in Dornakal, which offers a subtle incorporation of Indian motifs into an overall Christian scheme. Thus, the nave of the Dornakal Cathedral Church of the Epiphany is upheld by twelve pillars standing for the twelve apostles; the interior is dominated by a large cross. But under the cross are found not only the emblems of the twelve apostles but also local emblems like the lotus flower, which is a symbol for India. In its outer prospect, unmistakable Christian motifs are joined by domes reminiscent of Muslim mosques and pillars similar to those found in South Indian Hindu temples. The cathedral was constructed with local labor with its fine work carved by hand. It stands, as Susan Billington Harper has put it, as "the bishop's most dramatic statement of Christianity's potential as 'fulfillment'—of good but incomplete Indian faiths and of beautiful but imperfect Indian cultures."

Azariah also guided his flocks carefully along the treacherous border between faithfulness to Christ and loyalty to India. For instance, he strongly urged church members to abstain from alcohol, partly from general principles, but even more because habitual drunkenness was long considered a lower-caste characteristic while abstinence had been reserved for the Brahmans. He was also a constant advocate for education, medical care, and economic development among the lower castes and Dalits whom the caste system had doomed to positions of social inferiority. With his wife Anbu, he promoted education for women and organized Mother's Unions in the villages. In all of this work, he was guided by his commitment to evangelism, orthodox theology, and the strengthening of the church. This commitment pushed reform of Indian society even as it proclaimed the Kingdom.

THE END OF A LIFE WELL LIVED

As Azariah finished his seventh decade he looked forward to retirement and to more leisure for writing, but it was not to be. In late December 1944 he traveled by bullock cart and foot to a tiny village, Parkal, that was surrounded by rice paddy fields. There he confirmed forty men and women in a mud and thatch village chapel. According to a Western observer who was with him, "They were ragged and not yet very advanced in ways of cleanliness and order, but with persistence the Bishop finally had them seated in orderly rows on the matcovered mud floor, and the lists of candidates by villages before him. Then came the period of 'examination,' an informal hour when the Bishop in his white cassock sat with them, friendly and fatherly, testing their knowledge of lyrics which told of the life and work of Christ, their understanding of baptism and the promises made, of the Lord's Prayer, the Creed, and asking questions about the witness of their own lives as Christians among their Hindu neighbors. Except for the ... teachers none among them were literate, and everything of necessity depended on very simple verbal instructions together with the living witness of the pastor and teachers in their midst. As he sat listening to their lyrics, teaching, asking questions, noting their answers, his face alight with interest and often amusement, he was observing not only the village groups but individuals."

On Christmas day Azariah preached his last sermon. It included an explanation of the Christian's joy: "The reasons for the joy? Christ came, and with Him *forgiveness of sins.* Christ came, and *He helps us to be brave* in times of trouble, poverty, sickness." Shortly thereafter the bishop went down with a fever, probably malaria contracted from contagion in the swampy paddies. He passed away on New Year's Day, 1945.

Services of mourning were held throughout the south of India and as far away as the Houses of Parliament in London. At the latter venue, the Archbishop of York spoke of Azariah's "two lasting memorials—a cathedral built in Indian style, and a greater memorial still in the lives of the thousands whom he converted to Christ." His friend Stephen Neill later wrote that "Vedanayagam

Samuel Azariah at the time of his death was far and away the most outstanding of Indian Christians, and one of the most eminent Church leaders in the world.... [N]ow he has gone, and those to whom his loss seems literally irreparable are an innumerable company."

SOURCES

This chapter is taken almost entirely from Susan Billington Harper, *In the Shadow of the Mahatma: Bishop V.S. Azariah and the Travails of Christianity in British India* (Grand Rapids: Eerdmans, 2000). This exhaustively researched volume is a treasure house of information and informed opinion on one of the twentieth century's greatest, and most admirable, Christian leaders. For Dr. Harper's insights boiled down to a bare minimum, see her article on Azariah in the *Oxford Dictionary of National Biography* (Oxford: Oxford University Press, 2004-2009). For outstanding background information, see Robert Eric Frykenberg, *Christianity in India: From Beginnings to the Present,* (New York: Oxford University Press, 2008); and on the part of Azariah at the Edinburgh Missionary Conference, Brian Stanley, *The World Missionary Conference, Edinburgh 1910* (Grand Rapids: Eerdmans, 2009).

10

SUNDAR SINGH 1889–1929?

MYSTERIOUS MYSTIC

The life of Sundar Singh illustrates why it can be so useful for American and European believers to learn about Christians from other places in the world. By Western standards, it was anything but a conventional life, which means that Western standards may not provide the best guides for coming to grips with what Singh was and did. During the 1920s he became well-known in Europe and America because of two lengthy trips he made from his native India, and also because of intense public debate concerning his character and his deeds. He has remained a well-known figure in some Christian circles, especially where spiritual or mystical piety is prized. In Western eyes he was an unusually striking figure, but for contradictory reasons. Some regarded him as a saint, others as an imposter. Given the difficulty in finding concrete verification about his early life as an Indian Christian holy man, it is wise to withhold judgment and instead concentrate on setting out the basic outlines of this noteworthy life.

Sadhu Sundar Singh

EARLY LIFE AND CALL

Sundar Singh was born on September 3, 1889, at Rampur in the Indian Punjab, the vast ancestral empire that encompasses much of what is now northwest India and eastern Pakistan. His wealthy Sikh family provided a first-class education that included study with a Brahman pundit and Sikh holy men. Sikhism, a reformed off-shoot of Hinduism, also incorporates elements of Islam, especially dedication to the one true God. From his mother, Singh received faithful habits of personal devotion; she inculcated a love of the Hindu sacred writings, like the *Bhagavad-Gita;* and she taught him to make prayer the absolute first action of every day. After his mother died when he was only fourteen years old, Singh despaired. He reacted with particular distaste when his father insisted that he attend a nearby school recently founded by Presbyterian missionaries. There he learned English and began to receive instruction in the Christian Scriptures. The young Sikh, who was already committed to rigorous spiritual searching, was torn with doubts about the path he should pursue.

Singh's inner turmoil came to a climax in December 1904 when he lashed out at his missionary teachers as imperial colonizers and then, in the company of teenaged peers, tore a Christian New Testament to pieces and threw the pages into a fire. Pride in this burst of anti-colonial "heroism" did not, however, calm his heart, where struggle instead seemed only to intensify. Three days after this event, his despair reached a climax. He arose well before dawn and asked God to show himself before first light; if he received no answer, he was resolved to commit suicide by laying his head on a railroad track. He later reported what happened with these words:

> I prayed and prayed, waiting for the time to take my last walk. At about 4:30 I saw something strange. There was a glow in the room. At first I thought there was a fire in the house, but looking through the door and windows, I could see no cause for the light. Then the thought came to me: perhaps this was an answer from God. So

> I returned to my accustomed place and prayed, looking into the strange light. Then I saw a figure in the light, strange but somehow familiar at once. It was neither Siva nor Krishna nor any of the other Hindu incarnations I had expected. Then I heard a voice speaking to me in Urdu: "Sundar, how long will you mock me? I have come to save you because you have prayed to find the way of truth. Why then don't you accept it?" It was then I saw the marks of blood on his hands and feet and knew that it was Jesus, the one proclaimed by the Christians. In amazement I fell at his feet. I was filled with deep sorrow and remorse for my insults and my irreverence, but also with a wonderful peace. This was the joy I had been seeking. This was heaven.... Then the vision was gone, though my peace and joy remained.

Immediately Sundar committed himself wholeheartedly to following Christ, despite intense opposition from his family. After long and arduous efforts to make the young man recant his newfound faith, the family ostracized him, partly for becoming a Christian and partly because he violated the standards of their caste. In the region where the Singh family lived the only Christians were members of the lowest caste with whom it was a great disgrace for a wellborn Sikh to associate. When Singh cut off his hair as a symbol of breaking with his past, the family responded by cutting him off.

THE SADHU

Singh not only held firm but also almost immediately began to act as a sadhu, or a religious mendicant. The word itself means "one who is on the right path." Sadhus were objects of respect as they traveled from village to village, moved freely among all castes and taught whoever would listen about the search for inward peace.

Christian sadhus were rare but not unknown. In Singh's case, unusual happenings soon attended his journeys. One of the first came when he was expelled from his home and, in search of somewhere to lay his head, sought out a leprosarium some distance away. On the road he ate food that a relative had provided as a seeming last gesture of kindness. But the food was poisoned and Singh arrived at the leprosarium in desperate physical condition. No sooner had he arrived than his symptoms, including bleeding from nose and mouth, immediately ceased and he felt himself healed by the direct touch of God. On his sixteenth birthday, September 3, 1905, Singh was baptized by an Anglican missionary. Thirty-three days later he appeared shoeless, dressed in the saffron robe of a sadhu, and began the journeys by foot that would occupy the next decade of his life. Soon he was known in Indian Christian circles as "the Apostle of the Bleeding Feet."

As a sadhu, Sundar Singh did not altogether shun formal contact with other Christian groups. For a brief period beginning in late 1906 he joined two American missionaries in creating an interracial, semimonastic religious order modeled on the example of the Franciscans. They called it "The Brotherhood of the Imitation of Jesus." Then from December 1909 to July 1910, he studied at the Anglican St. John's Divinity College in Lahore, which is now in the Pakistani part of the Punjab, directly west of Amritsar, India. These experiments were short-lived. Singh was in essence an Indian Christian for whom Western denominational traditions meant little. In his mind, and as indicated by the course of his life's work, the great necessity was to follow God, contemplate the ways of God, and work as a servant of God. This attitude meant that, while he sustained positive relations with believers in many different Christian traditions, the shape of his Christian faith was influenced more by historic Indian models of spirituality than by anything from the West. He once said that "Indians need the Water of Life, but not the European cup."

JOURNEYS AND WRITINGS

Controversy about Singh in the 1920s concerned reports about the travels he undertook soon after his baptism. In those early years his journeys took him to many isolated regions in northern India and, by his own account, over the high mountain passes into Tibet. Even as his conversion echoed the miraculous appearance of Jesus to the apostle Paul, so too did his reports imitate what the apostle had experienced in his missionary journeys. Singh told later biographers about many instances of miraculous deliverance, healing, ecstatic experiences, visions, visits of angels, and narrow escapes from death. He once fasted for forty days, nearly to the point of death, but with permanent spiritual enrichment. He also told about meeting in Tibet on three occasions a 300-year old Christian hermit, the Maharishi of Kailash, who had been baptized by a nephew of the pioneering Jesuit missionary, Saint Francis Xavier.

In 1916 the first book about Singh was published. It was written in Urdu by Alfred Zahir, an Indian Christian. When this volume began to circulate, Singh received invitations to speak in more Indian locales. Soon he was traveling to the south of the Indian sub-continent and broadening his circle of contacts.

One important new friend was Mrs. Rebecca Parker, a worker with the London Missionary Society who, alongside her husband, oversaw a number of ministries in southern India. She began a correspondence with the Sadhu that lasted until his death. In 1918 she also published the book that made Singh known in the Western world, *Sadhu Sundar Singh: Called of God.* There would be several later editions of this volume as well as other writings by Rebecca Parker devoted to Singh's life.

The spread of these books resulted in speaking tours in Malaya, China, Japan, and Burma. Then in January 1920, Singh set off on a worldwide journey that took him to Britain, the United States, and Australia. Singh's father, who had himself become a Christian believer in the years since the family ostracized the young Sundar, paid for the trip. This trip spread word about the Sadhu even further, with the result that in 1922 he embarked on a longer journey that took him for extended visits to several European countries.

The appeal of Sadhu Sundar Singh lay in the simplicity of his stories and parables, combined with the profundity that listeners found in what he said. The speeches and then the slim books he later published were often composed of dialogues. A "seeker" would pose questions and "sadhu" would respond. A first question was "I am searching for inner peace, but the many religions and philosophies I have studied fill me only with doubts and questions. I am no longer even sure if God exists." But then the questions went on to cover many aspects of human existence in relation to God—for example, "some say that to encounter God we must fulfill some special devotional exercise of contemplation. What does contemplation really mean?" and "So is suffering necessary for the spiritual life?"

Singh's answers to these queries pointed to trust in God; many spoke of the work done to and for humanity by "the Master," which was the Sadhu's name for Christ. So in response to the question about the existence of God, Singh responded that only fools denied the existence of God; just as foolish as atheism was the notion that God was completely mysterious and unknowable. To the question about contemplation he responded obliquely by saying that in prayer humans received "wonderful peace and calm ... from the presence of God in our souls." About suffering he stated that human experience of spiritual suffering was like the bitter shell of a walnut or the cocoon of a silkworm—both were restricting and difficult but led on to strong spiritual growth: "We do not attain real victory by escaping pain, but rather by discovering the grace to change pain into ease, death into life, and evil into good."

The Sadhu regularly used parable-like stories or extended analogies to convey his message. One story concerned a poor grass cutter who discovered a beautiful stone in the woods. Thinking that it was an object of great value, the grass cutter took it to a jeweler and asked him to verify the great treasure that had been found. The jeweler immediately recognized that it was only a shiny piece of cut glass, but as a compassionate person he did not respond directly. Rather, he asked the poor man to come work in his shop so that he might, with the added experience, answer his own query about what he had found. This the poor man did. Several weeks later, and now much wiser, he took out the piece of glass again and immediately recognized it as an item of no value. But so taken was the poor man with how kindly he had been treated that he went to the jeweler and told him that he wished to devote his whole life in service to the jeweler. Singh's conclusion drew the spiritual lesson: "In the same way, God leads back to truth those who have wandered into error. When they recognize the truth for themselves, they gladly and joyfully give themselves in obedient service."

Another question presented a seeker's desire to know whether God's existence could be proved. Singh's response was to say that "God has no need or desire for anyone to prove his existence. Our arguments are feeble, our minds limited.... God desires rather that we should enjoy his life-giving presence and so bear witness to something far more sublime and convincing than anything the rational mind can produce." He then fleshed out this answer with an analogy:

> Our spirits live and grow in our human bodies much like the chick develops inside the egg. If it were possible for the chick to be told that a great world waits beyond its shell, that this world is filled with fruits and flowers, rivers and great mountains, and that its own mother is also there waiting for it to be set free and to experience this splendor, the chick could still neither comprehend nor believe it. Even if one explained that its feathers and wings and eyes were developing so that it could fly and see, still it would not be able to believe it, nor would any proof be possible, until it broke through its shell.

And then, as was customary, he drove home the analogy by saying that spiritual life requires people to "break out of our material limitations and attain spiritual life" by accepting "the life-giving warmth of God's spirit, just as the chick receives its mother's warmth." Not to welcome that warmth was the way of danger since "without that warmth, we will not take on the nature of the Spirit, and we may die without ever hatching out of this material body."

After he had traveled in the West, Singh reflected unfavorably on the spiritual situation he found there. In India he reported that observers thought he was suffering from the cold northern climates he encountered on his journeys; the reality, he went on, was different; he had returned to India feeling oppressed by "the spiritual atmosphere" rather than the mere climate. What bothered him was the contrast with India where—despite poverty, idolatry, and other great problems—"one feels everywhere ... that there is a desire for higher things." By contrast, in the Western world there was far too much stress on "armed force, great power, and material things." Singh expressed his respect for the Western Christian heritage, but used another analogy as a warning: "At one time the ostrich could fly, but because the ostrich stopped using its wings, it became unable to fly. So are the people of Europe and America—they do not appreciate the faith of their forebearers and are fast losing it."

His judgment was particularly harsh on the United States: "Looking at the motto 'In God We Trust' on the American dollar one might think the Americans are very religious people, but the motto should read, 'In the dollar we trust.' Americans are seeking the almighty dollar, not the Almighty God."

CONTROVERSY

With his turban and dark beard, his saffron robe and shoeless feet, Singh was noticed wherever he traveled in Europe and America. Many in the West found his message powerfully attractive, but for different reasons. Evangelical audiences appreciated the miraculous parallels to the life of the apostle Paul and Singh's obvious dedication to Jesus, "the Master." Liberal Christians appreciated his openness to other Indian religions and his advocacy of a "fulfillment theory" that saw the higher forms of Sikhism and Hinduism as preparation for the message of Christ. Ecumenically minded Christians appreciated his indifference to denominational distinctives and his willingness to minister with Christian groups of any type.

One of these ecumenical leaders was the Swedish archbishop, Nathan Söderblom, who became a great promoter of the Sadhu. Connections with Söderblom, however, led to controversy. During Singh's visit to Sweden in 1922, there was much enthusiasm for his message, but also considerable criticism from academic Christians and secular skeptics who claimed that Singh's message was simplistic, his manner unsophisticated, and the stories about his early life probably untrue. Söderblom and other admirers of Singh rushed their defenses into print, and a literary battle ensued that soon spread to Germany and lasted for much of the rest of the 1920s. German critics in particular took aim, not so much at the content of what Singh said when he traveled in Europe, but at the stories of unusual events that had established his reputation in the first place. Using methods that had earlier been deployed to question supernatural aspects of Christian tradition and the Scripture, these critics demanded proof for the miracle stories about Singh and proclaimed that, without convincing demonstration, it was mere incredulity to believe them.

Adding fuel to this new fire was the one source of denominational strife that followed Singh from India. There a few Catholic publicists had questioned the saintly reputation that Singh had gained by arguing that no non-Catholic could possibly achieve the higher realms of sanctity. After Singh had traveled in Europe, a few German Catholics picked up this line of attack and expanded it into a full-scale denunciation of his ministry.

European criticism of Singh eventually reached a bizarre culmination. In Zürich, Switzerland, Oskar Pfister was a colleague and collaborator of Sigmund Freud who acquired what Freud called an obsession about the Sadhu. The obsession lasted for several years and culminated in a book in German entitled *The Legends of Sundar Singh,* in which Pfister depicted Singh as a psychopathic liar unable to distinguish truth from fiction.

As if to provide his detractors with more ammunition, Singh returned to India with a fascination for Emmanuel Swedenborg, whose biography he had encountered in travels in Scandinavia. Swedenborg was an eighteenth-century Swedish mystic and Christian philosopher who had received a series of visions he interpreted as a call to reform Christian doctrine and practice. Swedenborg's voluminous writings had long attracted a small circle of admirers in Western lands, which now grew to include Sundar Singh. After his return to India, Singh meditated much on Swedenborg, even to the point of reporting to Western correspondents like Archbishop Söderblom that he had spoken to the Swedish prophet in visions of his own.

LAST DAYS

By the time Singh returned to India in 1922 after the last of his foreign travels, his health was broken, and he became a recluse at a compound in the foothills of the Himalayas. While Europeans continued to debate the meaning of his life, Singh contented himself by corresponding with a wide circle of friends and by writing several small devotional volumes. To his friends he spoke often of his desire to journey once again across the mountains into Tibet. On several occasions he made plans to put that desire into effect, but was frustrated by ill health.

Finally in 1929 he made one final attempt. On April 18 Singh penned a last letter to Archbishop Söderblom in which he said "I am leaving for Tibet." In this letter he cited a biblical reference, Acts 20:24, that preserved the Pauline echoes in his life to the end. The verse was from the apostle's farewell words to the elders of Ephesus: "But none of these things move me, neither count I my life dear unto myself, so that I might finish my course with joy, and the ministry, which I have received of the Lord Jesus, to testify the gospel of the grace of God." Singh left for his journey on that day or shortly thereafter and was never heard from again. His body was not recovered. Four years later the official proclamation of his presumed death was noted with a lengthy obituary in the *London Times.*

In the West, Singh drew the attention of some as an exotic. But others in Europe and North America were attracted to him as a figure whose Christianity was untroubled by the disasters of modern warfare and as someone whose mystical faith easily overrode the challenges of secular science and unbelieving biblical criticism. The European and American controversies that swirled about Singh had a curious quality, which Eric Sharpe, the most careful student of Singh, has highlighted: "Those who had known him were unanimously his supporters; his enemies for the most part had never encountered him face to face."

At home in India, many looked upon Singh as living out an expressly Indian version of Christian faith. This is a significant matter since in the days of British rule over India, many Indians viewed Christianity as a simple accessory of British colonial power. A Christian sadhu was living testimony that the Christian faith might be more than just an adjunct to Western power.

SOURCES

An overview of Singh's life with a collection from his writings, from which the excerpts above are taken, is provided by Charles E. Moore, ed., *Sadhu Sundar Singh: Essential Writings* (Maryknoll, N.Y.: Orbis, 2005). All of Singh's published works were gathered into *The Christian Witness of Sadhu Sundar Singh: A Collection of His Writings* (Madras: Christian Literature Society, 1989). Several sympathetic but critically exact works on Singh have been offered by Eric J. Sharpe, including "Sadhu Sundar Singh and His Critics: An Episode in the Meeting of East and West," *Religion* 6 (Spring 1976):48-66 (the above quote from p.62); "The Legacy of Sadhu Sundar Singh," *International Bulletin of Missionary Research* 14 (October 1990):161-67; and *The Riddle of Sadhu Sundar Singh* (New Delhi: International Publications, 2003). Excellent background is found in Robert Eric Frykenberg, *Christianity in India: From Beginnings to the Present* (New York: Oxford University Press, 2008), with the quotation from Singh about "the European cup" on p.415.

KOREA

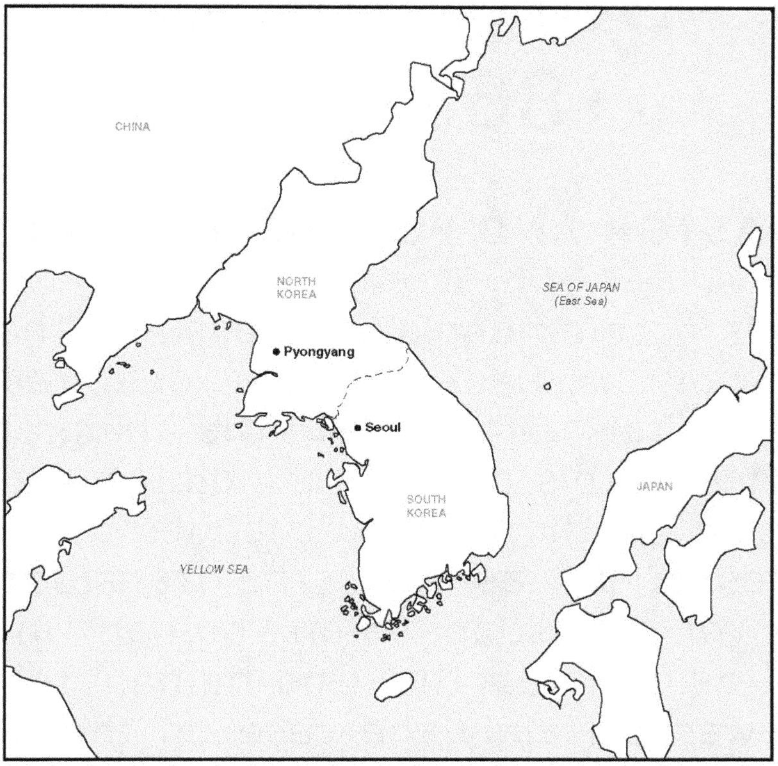
CHINA
NORTH KOREA
Pyongyang
Seoul
SOUTH KOREA
SEA OF JAPAN (East Sea)
JAPAN
YELLOW SEA

11

SUN CHU KIL
1869-1935

PASTOR AND FOUNDING FATHER

It is a commonplace to assume that the coming of Christianity involves deep religious change. Yet almost all the biographical sketches in this book also indicate that new Christian faith brings changes to other spheres of life as well. The transformative effect of Christianity on human interactions—as well as the God-human relationship—was certainly the case on the Korean peninsula when the faith took root there in the last years of the nineteenth century. The story of Sun Chu Kil is a good example of Christianity's wide impact, for he was not only a leader in one of the great revivals of the recent past but also a key figure in the dawning of modern Korean nationalism. His story—as passionate preacher, pacifist, and nationalist—highlights some of the unusual dynamics that have made Koreans such active participants in the recent world history of Christianity.

Sun Chu Kil (front row, second from right) with first ordained Korean Presbyterian clergymen

EARLY LIFE

Sun Chu Kil was born in March 1869, near the city of Pyongyang in what is now North Korea. Some of the difficulty for outsiders in understanding the story of modern Korean Christianity is suggested by the fact that different English-language accounts report his name as Kil Sŏnju, Kil Sŏn-chu, Kil Soon Joo, Sun-Joo Kil, Son Ju Keel, SeinJu Kil, Kiel Sun-Chu, and Gil Seon-Ju. In addition, sources do not always agree on the exact sequence of events in his life or on the exact role he played in the tumultuous events through which he lived. The main outlines, however, are clear enough.

Kil was born short years after a major outbreak of persecution against the small community of Korean Roman Catholics who had become Christians through the efforts of Catholic missionaries in China. Increased apprehension about the penetration of outsiders into Korea, along with the refusal of these Catholics to worship the spirit of ancestors, made them suspect in the eyes of Korea's Confucian rulers, the Joseon dynasty. The result was brutal suppression, with at least eight thousand mostly lay Korean Catholics martyred in the middle decades of the nineteenth century.

Kil's family was able to provide him with a good education; on his own he was drawn especially to Eastern mystical practices (a Korean variety of Taoism), which he cultivated from an early age. These practices included regular prayer, special journeys into the mountains to pray for up to one hundred days at a time, and also prayer very early in the morning. Kil's period of formal education was cut short by the need to assist in the family's store. His health was also damaged, with permanent impairment of his sight, when a gang of thugs administered a brutal beating to his family. Shortly thereafter, the family moved into the city of Pyongyang, which from that time was where Kil's spiritual development took place.

CHRISTIANITY SPREADS, THE NATION SUFFERS

By the time the family moved to Pyongyang, great political changes were sweeping over Korea; these changes also ushered in a new era for the peninsula's religious history. The Korean imperial dynasty had long been dominated by China, but as Japan pursued a course of rapid modernization (with selective Westernization), its influence grew in Korea as well (Kyoto, Japan, lies only 450 miles southeast of Seoul, the modern South Korean capital, which is itself only 150 miles south of Pyongyang). As a result, in 1876 Korea signed a treaty of friendship with Japan. Three years later China tried to reassert its authority against this Japanese move. When Korean soldiers mutinied as a protest against foreign intrusions, both Japan and China sent troops to defend their interests. By that time, however, another power—the United States—had begun to make its presence felt. In 1880 American diplomatic contacts were established with Korea; these initial contacts led two years later to a Korea-U.S. treaty that allowed Americans to trade and set up warehouses and residences in port cities. While this treaty was silent on religious questions, and also on the ultimate fate of Korea (situated as it was between two great Asian powers), some Koreans read the treaty as American approval for full-blown Korean independence. The treaty also marked an opening for American missionaries.

This treaty was signed in 1882. Kil's family moved to Pyongyang in 1885, the same year the first American missionaries arrived: Dr. Horace Allen, a physician; Henry Appenzeller, a Methodist minister; and Horace Underwood, a Presbyterian minister. The latter's brother, proprietor of the Underwood typewriter firm, put profits from this business to work in supporting the missionary work in Korea. Soon other missionaries arrived from the U.S. as well as from Canada, Australia and Scotland. By rendering critical medical assistance to the Korean royal family, by establishing hospitals and by setting up effective schools, the missionaries won almost immediate acceptance (and so showed how times had changed from the era when Koreans were put to death for becoming Catholics). For their part, the missionaries early on agreed to back a translation of the Bible into Hangul, the native Korean language that had been rarely used for printing out of deference to the Chinese-based language favored by elites. Almost immediately the Hangul Bible ignited tremendous interest in the population. The missionaries were also strongly influenced by the principles of John Nevius, a longtime American missionary to China who advocated self-propagation, self-government and self-support for new Christian churches. (As we have seen in several chapters, Nevius promoted in the Far East what Henry Venn advocated for England's Church Missionary Society in Africa and India.) Most importantly, the American and Scottish missionaries in Korea were not aligned with the colonial powers of China and Japan; they were thus in a position to encourage a faith that did not depend on the political and cultural subjection of the Korean people to neighboring countries.

Sun Chu Kil's path to Christianity was marked by a strong push and a strong pull. The push was a particular episode of disillusionment with the Taoist practices in which he had become adept. During a period of intense mountain prayer, a young woman approached him asking for spiritual guidance. The result, however, was not spiritual enlightenment but some kind of sexual indiscretion. Later Kil came to doubt the effectiveness of Taoism because it had not protected him in this encounter.

The pull came from positive contact with Korean converts and American missionaries. In 1897 a Korean friend, Song Sup Kim, and the American Presbyterian missionary Samuel Moffett urged Kil to read John Bunyan's *Pilgrim's Progress.* The book affected him deeply, as did articles from the *Christian News,* which Horace Underwood published out of Seoul. In a later testimony, Kil reported that during a time of prayer for repentance of his sins he had heard the sound of a flute and a loud voice repeatedly calling his name. His prayers became more intense; after spending the entire night in weeping and prayer, he was soundly converted.

Immediately he began to share the good news with his family, which at first resisted but then joined him by embracing the new religion. He also began attending the Ch'angdaehyun Church (Central Presbyterian) that Samuel Moffett had founded in Pyongyang. There his zeal and gifts were soon recognized, and in 1898 he was appointed a lay leader in this church.

Kil's rapid progress in Christian leadership corresponded with the deterioration of Korea's national position. As Japan expanded its influence through quarrels with China and Russia, it also began to flex its muscle on the peninsula. Kil's early involvement with Korean political history began in 1898, when he helped found the Pyongyang branch of the Independence Club, a national movement aimed at asserting the right of Koreans to rule themselves. The next year, on the day memorializing

Korea's founding as a nation, he offered a moving public address before thousands that upheld the necessity of Korea for the Koreans. Soon thereafter, however, the Independence Clubs were shut down as a threat to domestic and diplomatic peace.

As active as Kil became in politics, he was even busier in his life as a believer. In rapid-fire order, he took on a wide array of new responsibilities. These included founding a neighborhood school in Pyongyang to teach Christian principles to young people, an effort that would eventually grow into several respected educational institutions. He also helped create the first Women's Association in a Korean church and spoke up publicly for the rights of women. In this same regard, he led opposition to the traditional practice of seating men and women in separate sections of the sanctuary. He campaigned zealously against smoking and excessive drinking as modern habits that threatened the well-being of ordinary people. And he was a pioneer in evangelization efforts among industrial workers. In 1901 he was elected an elder of the Central Church; two years later he was named an assistant pastor and commissioned as an itinerant to oversee church planting and church nurture in an outlying district. And in 1903 he became a member of the first class in the Pyongyang

Presbyterian Seminary, yet another institution founded by Samuel Moffett in his effort to prepare Koreans for leadership in their own churches. What the flurry of Kil's own activities suggests is that Christianity was spreading rapidly as active Koreans joined discerning missionaries in propelling the faith forward.

While this expansion was taking place, Korea's political situation was declining rapidly. Military success by Japan, especially in the Russo-Japanese War, which ended in 1905, led to a much stronger military presence in Korea. That presence was formalized the same year with the creation of a Japanese protectorate over Korea. When King Kojong called on Koreans to resist this step by the Japanese, the call came to Kil as well as other leaders in Pyongyang. But Kil remained true to the nonviolent convictions he had already embraced and refused to take up arms. Nonetheless this turn in international affairs greatly troubled Kil and his colleagues.

The upshot generally was severe self-doubt among Koreans who had hoped they could take their place in the ranks of the world's modern nations. In 1906 the president of Emory University visited the country and offered this report: "Have you ever seen a broken hearted nation? ... broken hearted men and women out of whose pitiful lives every ray of hope seemed to have faded; ... a whole nation which seemed to be utterly dispirited. The Koreans seem to be without earthly hope, at least they seem to be utterly discouraged.... Japan's century-long aspirations are gratified and Korea's last hope of independence has failed."

REVIVAL

In these difficult circumstances the Pyongyang revival of 1907 took place—one of the most important landmarks in the modern history of Christianity. The critical events occurred in January 1907, but there had been preparations. Reports of the Welsh Revival of 1904-1905 were circulated in Korea. The Pyongyang Central Church was not the only place where earnest prayer had been offered for a similar outpouring of the Spirit. In 1906 Kil and a fellow elder had been involved in starting early-morning prayer meetings, which remain to this day a feature of Korean church life. They represent one of the ways in which ancestral forms of traditional Korean religion were infused with new Christian content. From early in the century, various groups of missionaries and Koreans had been praying for a special work of the Holy Spirit. In addition, for a "revival" to take place in the strict sense of the term (meaning "bringing back life"), it was necessary to have a substantial body of believers already in place who were longing for renewal. Korean leaders and missionaries had, in fact, been successful enough in their evangelistic efforts for such a body to emerge.

Presbyterian organization played a part as well, since the Pyongyang revival took place toward the end of a ten-day, regularly scheduled class for converts from throughout the area's churches. These classes offered biblical and theological learning while also providing the core constituency for large public meetings. About six hundred men had gathered for the 1907 class (instruction of women took place in outlying schools), with well over a thousand assembling for public meetings in the evenings.

When one of the missionaries paused in the course of the regular instruction to confess his own stubbornness and pride, the floodgates opened. Different accounts describe different sequences of what took place, but public confession of sin was certainly prominent. Kil himself made a memorable confession that he had profited inappropriately from a will that he had been asked to administer. Koreans confessed harboring secret resentment of missionaries. Confessions were attended by unusual personal struggle. In October 1907, the *London Times* carried a report by the Reverend Lord Gascoyne-Cecil in which he described what an eyewitness had told him:

> A rush of power from without seemed to take hold of the meeting. The Europeans described its manifestations as terrifying. Nearly everybody present was seized with the most poignant sense of mental anguish; before each one his own sins seemed to be rising in condemnation of his life. Some were springing to their feet pleading for an opportunity to relieve their consciences by making their abasement known, others were silent but rent with agony, clenching their fists and striking their heads against the ground in the struggle to resist the Power that would force them to confess their misdeeds. From 8 in the evening till 2 in the morning did this scene go on.

Prayer ascended from many voices at once, which began the continuing Korean practice of simultaneous group prayer.

After the initial night of confession and prayer, several succeeding nights followed in a similar pattern. It is reported that the local police heard about individuals confessing their crimes and so dispatched a member of the force to come and take notes for possible prosecution; in carrying out this assignment, the policeman was himself converted. Other conversions also took place. But the main impact was to deepen the faith of those who were already in the churches and who were inspired afresh for dedicated lives of consecrated service. It was also of great significance that, while missionaries participated in the revival, it was mainly a Korean event. The long-term result was to empower Koreans in carrying out tasks of evangelism and service.

Important steps for Korean oversight of Korean churches followed hard on the heels of the Pyongyang revival. In September 1907 the inaugural gathering of the Presbytery of the Korean Presbyterian Church assembled in Pyongyang. Samuel Moffett was elected the first moderator because at that time there were no ordained Korean ministers. But the last action of this inaugural Presbytery meeting was to ordain the first seven graduates of the new Presbyterian seminary, a class that included Sun Chu Kil. Very shortly thereafter Kil was appointed the lead pastor of the Central Presbyterian Church; in subsequent years Koreans took their place as moderators of the Presbyterian annual meetings. Other groups were not far behind, as indicated by the establishment in 1908 of the Korean Annual Conference of the Methodist Episcopal Church.

The combination of internal spiritual vitality and external organizational maturity left a different kind of impression on the visiting John R. Mott than the American visitor had recorded in 1906. Mott, the international head of the

YMCA whom we have met in his earlier dealings with V.S. Azariah, wrote these prescient words about what he witnessed in 1907: "During my recent tour in the Far East I formed the deep conviction that if the present work on the part of the cooperating missions in Korea is adequately sustained and enlarged in the immediate future, Korea will be the first nation in the non-Christian world to become a Christian nation. I know of no mission field where larger or more substantial results have been secured, in proportion to the expenditure, than in Korea."

SPIRIRITUAL ADVANCE, NATIONAL CRISIS

Once again, there is an eerie conjunction of spiritual advance and national crisis in the months immediately after the great revival. The same year as the Pyongyang revival, the Japanese forced King Kojong to abdicate in favor of his son, because the king was insisting on too much independence. The next year, 1908, when the Japanese resident general paraded the new king through Pyongyang and the north of Korea, Kil led Christians believers in refusing to display the Japanese flag alongside the Korean flag, as they had been ordered. In 1910 still worse was to come when Japan replaced Korea's protectorate status with full annexation into its imperial kingdom. Immediately Japan adopted measures to restrict use of the Korean language, counter expressions of Korean culture and transfer control of the Korean economy to Japanese. The very next year the Japanese pretended to discover a plot against their governor general, which gave them an excuse to incarcerate a number of Korean activists, including one of Sun Chu Kil's sons. This son was tortured during his imprisonment and died a few years after his release because of that ill treatment.

In these circumstances the new Christian churches were the strongest national organizations left under Koreans. The dawn prayer meetings and the practice of gathering believers for many services during the week excited Japanese suspicions, but for several years the churches were relatively free to keep going.

Internal church history was also moving fast. By 1912 the Presbyterians had expanded into seven regional presbyteries and so felt ready to establish a full general assembly. Kil was elected vice-moderator of the first general assembly and was asked to offer a public prayer for the World Alliance of Reformed Churches and the several national Presbyterian Churches (from Canada, the United States, Australia and Britain) that had sent their fraternal greetings.

Throughout these years, and until his death, Kil preached biblical messages in his own church, traveled regularly on evangelistic tours and expended great effort in mentoring younger men for the ministry. He also published a number of books that ranged from his Korean rendition of themes in *Pilgrim's Progress* and a Christian assessment of the Eastern philosophies he had studied before his conversion to many books of sermon outlines and biblical exposition. A helpful recent compilation of the sermon outlines by the Korean Institute for Advanced Theological Studies shows how he developed these themes: for example, "The Three Great Blessings of the Person in Christ" ("No Condemnation," "Escaping from the Pathway of Death" and "Righteousness Fulfilled") or "The Five Great Essentials of the Believer" (language, conduct, love, faith, holiness). All told, Kil preached over seventeen thousand sermons, shared responsibility for founding sixty different churches, and mentored eight hundred pastors and elders in their lives of Christian service.

THE MARCH FIRST INDEPENDENCE MOVEMENT

The tangled lines of church and political life continued to define Kil's life during the greatest moment in the history of Korean nationalism. In 1917, the American president Woodrow Wilson had come out strongly for the principle of national self-determination as part of his rationale for committing the United States to World War I. Korean patriots were naturally encouraged by this pronouncement. They were further encouraged by early signs from the Paris Peace Conference of 1919 that Wilson's principles might be put into actual practice. Nationalists from Korea sent petitions to this conference asking that self-determination for Korea be put on the agenda. In response, nothing happened. Instead, Japan continued to tighten its hold on the peninsula.

In early 1919, the abdicated King Kojong died unexpectedly. Because he had refused a Japanese request that he write to Paris assuring the delegates that Korea was satisfied with Japanese occupation, the rumor spread that he had been poisoned. This rumor convinced many Korean nationalists that only extreme measures could rescue them from the Japanese.

Japan, however, tried to proceed as if nothing was amiss. It decreed that the funeral for the ex-king would take place on March 3 in Seoul. For the first time since they fully occupied Korea in 1910, Japanese administrators also announced that Koreans would be free to travel to Seoul for this event without restriction. But already in January and early February plans were afoot to take advantage of the relaxed travel regulations to make a statement to the world. In these plans, church leaders, including Reverend Kil, took the lead. In response to requests coming from Seoul, Kil contacted fellow ministers and elders in the Presbyterian Church and further mobilized students and teachers in the broad network of missionary schools. (These schools had been restricted by the Japanese occupation but had nonetheless continued.) Soon negotiations broadened to include the YMCA, Koreans living in Tokyo and representatives of Chondokyo as well. Chondokyo was a loosely organized movement that combined elements of Taoism, shamanism and Korean Buddhism into a distinctively Korean expression of Eastern religion. Usually representatives of the churches and of Chondokyo were contentious enemies. Some church leaders objected to any cooperation—because they were so committed to evangelizing Chondokyo adherents and because they feared the Chondokyo leaders were prepared to use violence against the Japanese. But for this occasion in 1919, they set these objections aside, and church members joined Chondokyo members in order to work together for Korea.

The plan was to use the opportunity of King Kojong's funeral to publish a Declaration of

Korean Independence and so to shame the Japanese into granting national self-determination. Due to the presence of Christian leaders like Kil at the forefront of the movement, the action was to be nonviolent, with armed resistance and terrorist attacks against the Japanese strictly prohibited.

In his preparations for early March, Kil organized three groups in Pyongyang, which supplied many of the leaders. First were church officers, then the Women's Association of Pyongyang and finally the students in missionary schools. Their task was to build networks of communication, manufacture thousands of Korean flags and prepare to disseminate the Declaration of Independence once it was published. As was characteristic of much of his life's work, Kil urged his church colleagues to preach the gospel near and far even as they took on the task of promoting national independence. Kil himself sent on an associate to Seoul with authorization to affix his signature to the document while he preached at a Bible conference in the north of Korea that was scheduled to end on March 1. Because he knew how perilous his decision to join the independence movement had been, Kil gathered his family and committed it to the care of his wife before he left on his preaching mission. It is reported that his sermons at the Bible conference were particularly fervent.

Kil's plan was to arrive by train in Seoul on the first of March and then to take his place with other leaders of the movement. But events ran ahead of the original plan, which was to have thirty-three national leaders sign the declaration at a public park in the center of the city where a vast crowd gathered on March 1. At the last minute, the signers changed their mind, because they feared their provocative act might lead either to uncontrolled outbursts by the crowd or violent reactions by the police. They therefore put their names to the document in private at a restaurant, ate a meal together and then—most remarkably—telephoned the police to tell them what they had done. They were immediately arrested. The thirty-three signers included sixteen Christians, fifteen adherents of Chondokyo and two Buddhists. Kil's name, affixed by his surrogate, came second.

Meanwhile, back at the public park the crowd waited anxiously. They had unfurled the national flag, which had not been seen legally since 1910. Finally, a church school leader from an outlying town came to the platform and read the declaration. It began, "We herewith proclaim the independence of Korea and the liberty of the Korean people. We tell it to the world in witness of equality of all nations, and we pass it on to our posterity as their inherent right." At this reading, instructions were also relayed from the thirty-three signers that no violent acts be done against the Japanese, since these were "the acts of barbarians" and since such violence hurt the cause of independence. The document's main author was a writer and historian, Choe Nam-seon, who was not a Christian but who later said that the terms "independence, liberty, freedom, equality, and justice" were charged with Christian overtones.

Kil himself arrived too late to take part in activities at either the restaurant or the public park. When he was informed about what had happened to the other signers, he took himself to the police station where they were being held and gave himself up.

Throughout Korea, hundreds of thousands gathered on that March 1 to hear the declaration read and to demonstrate their support for independence. Where Christian churches had sprung up, the adherents often held the meetings in their buildings. There were very few incidents of Korean violence.

The reaction of the Japanese colonizers, however, was brutal. Not only was the mass rally in Seoul dispersed violently; but the authorities also lashed out at those they held responsible for the effort. Churches were special targets, with at least nineteen in the Pyongyang district badly damaged while Bibles, hymnbooks and other literature were destroyed. Total Christian adherence at the time amounted to 1 percent of the Korean population (roughly 200,000); it has been estimated that almost a fifth of that Christian population was brutalized as part of the Japanese response. One hundred and thirty-four Presbyterian pastors and elders were arrested. On one occasion, soldiers herded a village population into a Methodist church and set it aflame while shooting anyone who tried to escape. For the nation as a whole, as many as 50,000 Koreans were killed or wounded, while hundreds of thousands were imprisoned.

LAST YEARS

Sun Chu Kil was held in prison for two years. During those years he was transferred to seven different jails; at each one he preached boldly to other prisoners and his guards. He also used the time afforded by imprisonment to intensify his study of Scripture. Reportedly he read through the book of Revelation thousands of times during those years, with the result that whenever he preached from it thereafter he did so completely by memory.

The eschatological message of Revelation had been central to Kil's preaching before March 1919, but it became even stronger after he was released from prison. Themes of cataclysmic conflict, of God's protection for his children in violent times and of ultimate triumph for those who remained faithful unto death resonated with special force in Kil's day.

The Japanese occupation of Korea lasted until the end of the Second World War. Especially as tension gave way to warfare in Manchuria early in the 1930s, and as the Japanese attack on Pearl Harbor in 1941 drew near, restrictions multiplied for the Koreans, including the Korean churches. Poverty and disease added to the suffering of the Korean people.

Yet these very conditions help explain the dramatic turn to Christianity that took place after the Japanese were removed. During the nearly four decades of Japanese occupation, the churches had proven themselves as bastions of Korean life and as agents resisting the colonial power. Unlike the situation in much of Africa, India or Latin America—where Christianity was part of imperial domination—the new faith in Korea was clearly on the side of the people. When combined with the fervor of Korean believers themselves, the history of colonial oppression helps explain why John R. Mott's prediction of 1907 was at least partially fulfilled in the late 1940s and the decades that followed.

For Sun Chu Kil, the rest of his life was devoted to Christian work with as much zeal as before he was imprisoned. He remained the chief minister of Pyongyang's Central Presbyterian Church until 1926, when an internal conflict pushed him into the position of pastor emeritus. From that point he itinerated as a revival preacher, took several short term assignments and continued to publish sermon outlines and other edifying works. He was preaching at a Bible conference in South Pyongan province when on November 25, 1935, he collapsed. He died the next day without regaining consciousness. Five thousand people attended his funeral in Pyongyang, where the Reverend Jeong In-Gwa, chairman of the General Assembly of the Korean Presbyterian Church, delivered the sermon.

Some years earlier, the veteran Korean missionary Samuel Moffett spoke in general terms about the significance of individuals like Sun Chu Kil, his Presbyterian colleague and former student, when Moffett addressed the 1910 Edinburgh World Missionary Conference on the subject "The Place of the Native Church in the Work of Evangelization." As he looked back on the still-new church history of Korea, Moffett talked some about the efforts of missionaries but more about the zeal with which Koreans themselves were committed to their new faith: "Today in Korea probably more than in any other mission field ... will you find a Church which through its own labours and by means of its own pastors and evangelists, supported by the Korean Church, and by its own voluntary workers is pressing rapidly on to the evangelization of the whole country." Then Moffett summarized the rapid advance of Christian adherence in Korea from under one thousand in the early 1890s to a constituency of a quarter million in 1910. The key for Korea, in Moffett's view, was very much what it has been for almost all of the recently Christianized regions of the world, where new Christian communions have been "gathered very, very largely by the voluntary efforts of the Koreans themselves." In the process that Moffett described, Sun Chu Kil and like-minded believers were leading the way.

SOURCES

There are quite a few accounts of Kil's activity in the 1907 revival, although they do not agree on every detail of what happened. Fewer accounts treat his role in the March 1, 1919, movement, but the latter has been documented more securely than the former. In preparing this chapter the most helpful account of connections between religious and national life was the carefully documented study by In-su Kim, *Protestants and the Formation of Modern Korean Nationalism, 1885-1920: A Study of the Contributions of Horace G. Underwood and Sun Chu Kil* (New York: Peter Lang, 1996). Quotations from contemporaries are from this book, with the exception of the *Times* article mentioned below. In-su Kim also provided a short biography of Kil in *Dictionary of Asian Christianity,* ed. Scott Sunquist (Grand Rapids: Eerdmans, 2001), p.44. *Gil Seon-Ju: Essential Writings* (Seoul: The KIATS Press, 2008) offers a welcome collection of short writings and sermon outlines. L. George Paik's *The History of Protestant Missions in Korea, 1832-1910* (Seoul: Yonsei University Press, 1971 [first ed., 1927]) remains a classic account prepared by one of Korea's most distinguished modern educators and historians. The report from 1906 was by the Reverend Lord William Gascoyne-Cecil, "Mission Work in Korea," *London Times,* October 28, 1907, pp.2-3. The quotations from Samuel Moffett's 1910 address are from "The Place of the Native Church in the Work of Evangelization: A Paper Read at the World Missionary Conference," which was published in the *Union Seminary Magazine,* February-March 1911, pp.227-28 (entire article, pp.226-35).

Other helpful sources include William Blair and Bruce Hunt, *The Korean Pentecost and the Sufferings that Followed* (Edinburgh: Banner of Truth, 1977); Bonjour Bay, "The Pyongyang Great Revival in Korea and Spirit Baptism," *Evangelical Review of Theology* 31 (January 2007):4-16; Mark Shaw, "Above the 38th Parallel: The Korean Revival of 1907," in *Global Awakening: How the Twentieth-Century Revivals Triggered Christian Revolution* (Downers Grove, Ill.: IVP Academic, 2010), chap.2; and an address by Minho Song, "You Are the Rock of My Salvation: The Story of Rev. Kil Sun Joo and the Great Revival of 1907," July 27, 2009, Regent College (Vancouver). For what happened in Korea between the time of Kil's death and the end of the Japanese occupation, see James Huntley Grayson, "The Shinto Shrine Conflict and Protestant Martyrs in Korea, 1938-1945," *Missiology: An International Review* 29, no.3 (2001):287-305. For general treatments of Christianity in Korea, the writings of Samuel H. Moffett (the son of the Samuel Moffett mentioned above) are invaluable; for example, *A History of Christianity in Asia: Vol.II, 1500-1900* (Maryknoll, N.Y.: Orbis, 2005), pp.523-53. Special thanks also to Professor S. Steve Kang for help in preparing this chapter and also to Sam and Eileen Moffett for sharing personal sources about Korea's early Christian history.

CHINA

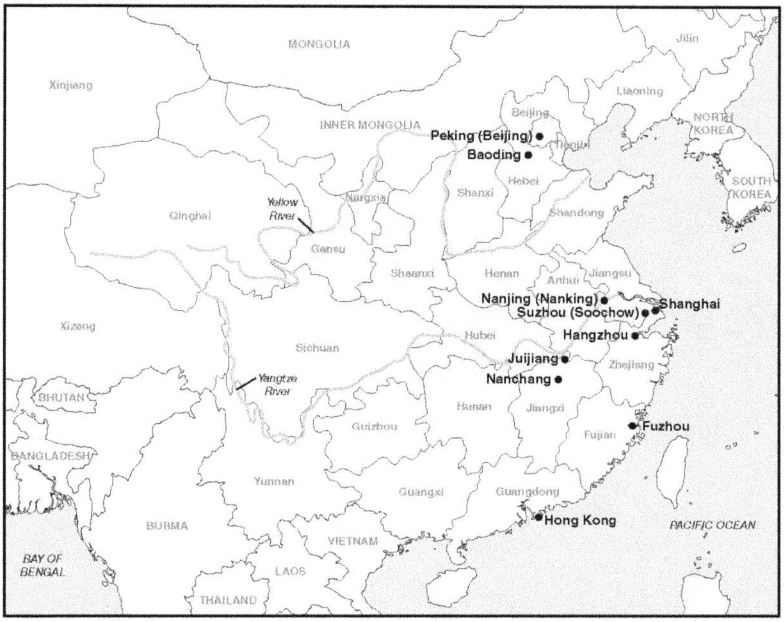
MONGOLIA
Jilin
Xinjiang
Liaoning
Beijing
NORTH KOREA
INNER MONGOLIA
Peking (Beijing)
Tianjin
Baoding
Hebei
SOUTH KOREA
Shanxi
Ningxia
Yellow River
Qinghai
Shandong
Gansu
Jiangsu
Shaanxi
Henan
Anhui
Nanjing (Nanking)
Shanghai
Suzhou (Soochow)
Xizang
Hubei
Hangzhou
Sichuan
Juijiang
Zhejiang
Nanchang
BHUTAN
Yangtze River
Hunan
Jiangxi
Fuzhou
Guizhou
Fujian
BANGLADESH
Yunnan
Guangxi
Guangdong
Hong Kong
BURMA
PACIFIC OCEAN
VIETNAM
BAY OF BENGAL
LAOS
THAILAND

12

DORA YU/YU CIDU 1873-1931

Dora Yu/Yu Cidu

CATALYST FOR AN ENDURING CHINESE FAITH

Since the early 1980s, the rest of the world has become aware of the surprising vitality of Christianity in the People's Republic of China. Despite determined attacks by the Communist regime of Mao Zedong (d. 1976), Christianity has not only survived but is expanding in many Chinese regions and many strata of Chinese society. The key to this development, which from a Western perspective has seemed so surprising, was the resilience of Chinese believers themselves. Through the Mao years of isolation and persecution, Chinese churches remained alive because they had been securely rooted in Chinese life before Mao.

At one time, Western missionaries seemed to be essential for Christianity in China, but that perception was amiss. The truly essential thing was the faith of intrepid Chinese believers like Dora Yu, who had passed away while the missionary presence was still at its height. Western missionaries were not irrelevant to what happened later, but the tree of faith that has become visible in recent decades grew substantially from seeds planted by Chinese Christians like Dora Yu.

THE WESTERN PERCEPTION

In 1932 the missionary Pearl S. Buck stood before two thousand Presbyterian women at the Astor Hotel in New York City and posed a question, "Is there a case for foreign missions?" With a scathing conclusion drawn from her own experience, she answered with a qualified, "Yes, barely." She then predicted, "We can have no assurance that if we withdrew from China today there would be any more permanent record left of our religious presence ... than is left there of the old Nestorian Church, a windblown, obliterated tablet upon a desert island." Buck was equating Christianity in China with the Christian missionaries in China.

In 1937 the exodus of Western missionaries from China began. As the first acts of World War II, Japan invaded China and prudent missionaries strategized retreat. By 1941 and Pearl Harbor, missionaries to China went back home if they were able and to Japanese prison camps if not. After the end of the war in 1945 some missionaries returned, but four years later Mao Zedong gathered the political survivors of thirty years' violent civil conflict and established himself as the head of the unified Communist People's Republic of China. The very next year, 1950, the new Communist regime slammed shut the doors on Western mission work.

Mission-founded schools, colleges, medical schools, hospitals and churches ceased to exist. Somewhere inside China remained as many as five million Catholic, Protestant, Orthodox and indigenous Christians, but they were loosely connected to each other if at all. In the 3,705,407-square-mile expanse of China's terrain less than 1 percent of the population professed Christian faith. In Christian churches throughout the rest of the world, returned missionaries and the vast numbers who supported missionary efforts in the Far East concluded that China was lost to Christianity. One hundred and fifty years of intense Protestant mission work, and much longer work by Catholics, had seemingly come to naught.

Yet during the succeeding thirty years of religious silence something unexpected was going on inside China. After the death of Mao in 1976, news trickled out of a gradual softening toward all religions. A few house churches in the countryside and in some cities began to meet openly. In 1979 registered "Three-Self Churches," which enjoyed government recognition, regained worship privileges—modified from the missionary years but still visibly Christian. By 1981, between fifteen and twenty thousand Protestants worshiped weekly in Shanghai—with little governmental objection. About the same time three thousand Roman Catholics made an unmolested public pilgrimage to the Church of Saint Maria near Shanghai. Stories of exponential growth among underground Christians fueled intense interest and speculation in the West.

In 1986, *Operation World* attempted a statistical evaluation. An accurate census was hard to come by, since only a few years earlier profession of Christianity could have meant a ten-year sentence to hard labor. But while the population of China had doubled since 1950, the number of Christians appeared to have multiplied nearly ten times. Five percent of Chinese people now called themselves Christians. Far from the casual cultural faith of "rice Christians" so deplored by Pearl Buck in the

1930s, Chinese Christians of the 1980s looked more like a fervent breed of spiritual survivors. *Operation World* enthused, "Praise [God] for ... the growth of the Church through the radiant witness of Christians, miracles of the Holy Spirit and mighty revivals. Never in history have so many been converted over such a short time."

Since 1986 the story has continued. No one knows the number of believers in China today, but church growth seems to have continued to outstrip population increase, in some places dramatically so. How did it happen? Who were the quiet, persistent, enduring Christians who had nurtured this growth? Where had they come from? How did they cultivate the skills needed for a church that not only endured but that multiplied during the dark years when Christianity was banned and well-known pastors were incarcerated in the camps?

It will help at this point to step back a couple of generations in Chinese history. Hundreds of Chinese leaders contributed to shaping what Chinese Christianity would become, but a single incident speaks to the germination of what became a great spiritual force.

DORA YU AND WATCHM AN NEE

The year is 1920. In Fuzhou, a southeast coastal city just across the strait from northern Taiwan, a rapt congregation gathers at the large ornate Tien'an Chapel to hear a revival preacher. Among the several hundred listeners sits Nee Shu-Tsu, a seventeen-year-old boy. By Chinese standards, he is a rebel: an excellent student but casual about school rules. His home life is not too good either, since his mother spends most of her days gambling the family funds at a mahjong table. The evangelist standing in the pulpit is a small, middle-aged Chinese woman, but she has experience and skill in holding the attention of a crowd. The boy listens to her words and returns sobered to his room to take up an intensely personal conversation with God.

That boy would later be known as Watchman Nee who, with the goal of "one church for every city or town," planted at least four hundred Christian churches over a thirty-year period of active ministry. Many of these churches were started in China's rural areas. Nee would write some forty books on Christian spiritual formation; the most widely read, *The Normal Christian Life,* is a collection of his speeches and essays. Nee himself would spend the last twenty years of his life in a Communist prison, where he died in 1972. But the churches he founded, and similar movements led by other indigenous leaders, possessed the resilience required for survival through very difficult times.

Who was the evangelist who sent the young Nee to his room for life-changing prayer? Her anglicized name was Dora Yu. Watchman Nee was only one of her better-known converts. Throughout China other young men and women were listening to Dora Yu and similar revival preachers, many of them missionary-taught Chinese. These young converts of the Chinese revivalists of the 1920s were crucial for the survival of the church in the dark years to come.

EARLY LIFE AND MINISTRY

Dora Yu was born in 1873 in the American Presbyterian Mission compound near Hangzhou, a southeastern coastal city of Zhejiang Province, about 120 miles south of Shanghai. Her father, a former physician, was studying there to become a "preacher." (Only Westerners could hold the higher and more remunerative rank of "pastor.") Dora's father had survived the Taiping Rebellion that began in 1851, a civil war with the dubious honor of being the bloodiest such conflict in human history. In thirteen years, twenty million people in central and southern China lost their lives. Dora's father survived in part because his surgical skills were needed.

Dora's grandfather had been Confucian, the most common religion or life-philosophy in China of that day, but her mother became a Christian as an adult and so did her father soon after the end of the Taiping Rebellion. About these early years Dora later wrote, "As far as I can remember I scarcely ever forgot to pray since I knew how to pray by myself; Christ was a very real Person to me, and I loved him." In her spiritual journal (frustratingly devoid of places, names and most dates), Dora describes herself as one who loved fields and flowers and hillsides, who almost never understood a joke because she took everything literally and who was absolutely intent on finishing a task in the correct order from first to last, so that "If I am speaking to one person, I do not seem to notice others around." As a sign of things to come, Dora remembers herself as a two-year-old lost on a solo nature ramble through grass and flowers to the great distress of her searching father. "This experience was ever to us a very real picture of Christ seeking his lost ones.... I know the great joy in the family when I was found."

Following in the footsteps of her father's first career, Dora at age fifteen went away to medical school in 1888. She never saw her parents again, as both became ill and died before she could return. She finished her medical training in 1896 after an unusually long course of eight years, probably due to poor supplies and on-again, off-again teachers at the Methodist-missionary-sponsored school. Her class numbered five graduates: three men and two women. Like many young Chinese women, Dora was engaged to be married; but unlike many other women of the era, Dora was allowed to participate in the choice of a husband. By age nineteen, however, she had decided that "marriage was a very serious act" that she did not want to pursue because, "first, I did not really care to live a married life; second, the fear of having my love to God divided; third, I did not wish to share my will with another." She was greatly relieved after much prayer when her fiancé's family agreed to end the engagement; she wrote, "I was fairly happy in those days when I became more accustomed to my lonely life."

The next phase, however, was far from happy; she called the years 1897-1903, which were spent in Korea as an associate of the Texas missionary Josephine Campbell, "wanderings in the wilderness." In hindsight Dora viewed the Korea trip as a mistake from the beginning because, "I accepted without asking my Heavenly Father's consent." It's hard to know from her journal (which focuses almost entirely on her inner spiritual world) what went wrong in Korea. It was probably a combination of overwork, minimal preparation, an unexpected failed romance, culture shock and the beginnings of the ill health that would plague the rest of her life. Dora, however, saw it as a time of spiritual refinement. "[God] took me right into His own hands and taught me many precious lessons, which at the time I did not understand, nor did I appreciate the hand of love which drew the plan of my path."

During the Korea years Dora experienced some of the mystical sides of Christianity. At one point she and a friend knelt in prayer for three hours begging to be filled with the Holy Spirit, yet no unusual sign of the Spirit appeared. So she tried again, this time alone in her room, determined not to leave until the Spirit manifested himself. (This attempt, too, seems not to have produced the result she was looking for.) Yet at a later time, in a vision, "I saw [Christ], my whole being seemed to become transparent, and I knew that I had been made white as snow. And I looked right up into that all-glorious and compassionate face, and said, 'Lord, I love You.' And he answered in a most tender and loving voice, 'Yes, I know you do, and I love you too.'" Although doctors had given up attempts to remedy her ills, Dora facilitated physical healing for others. Later, when her sister was near death with fever after giving birth to her sixth child, Dora earnestly prayed for healing and awoke the next morning to find the sister almost fully recovered.

In Korea, Dora worked hard as a physician, teacher, and Bible instructor and earned the praise of her Western colleagues. Miss Campbell reported, "Miss Yu ... being an Oriental, is getting the language much faster than I and is therefore a great help to me. She and our Korean teacher both write the classical language, which is read by all students of both countries, China and Korea.... She considers herself a missionary and is trusting to God and myself for support, asking nothing else."

One of Dora's many responsibilities was to train Korean women in their activities as "Bible women," a calling that missionaries recognized as critical to spreading the Christian faith. In the Confucian system "filial piety" outlined an orderly rank of responsibility based on superiority and subordination. Thus, older people were of higher value than younger ones; firstborn more valued than later-born; and men more valued than women. Because of deeply rooted cultural values, when Koreans and Chinese became Christians they often continued to work within the system of filial piety by separating genders for worship and spiritual teaching. So Bible women would travel to homes visiting other women who expressed interest in Christianity, as well as women already in the church. During these visits (usually reached on foot) the Bible women would teach the Scriptures to individual women and groups, pray with and for these women, and instruct them in holy living. In the single year of 1903, Dora Yu visited with 925 women and 211 children. She also worked on the campus of Paiwha School. Each morning she led the staff prayer meeting. She was the main speaker at the school's thrice-weekly chapel services, and she hosted 1,200 women visitors. In light of her many services to the American mission efforts in Seoul, the Americans began in 1901 to refer to her as a "missionary" instead of as a mere Bible woman.

But Dora's years in Korea were also very difficult. Much of the time she could not eat, so she drank only milk—which she milked from her own cow. She turned to self-medication and for two years took bromide, a common sedative of the era but one with side effects that likely contributed to her physical ills. At one point she had only twenty-six cents to her name. She was tempted to suicide but resisted, saying,

"No, I am going to wait for God's time." Dora Yu returned to China in 1903 at age thirty, a more sober, wiser, more spiritually attuned woman.

A CHINESE EVANGELIST

After considering various teaching and medical options, Dora decided to live quietly in Soochow "by faith" (without predictable income) with her sister whose family now included seven children. Dora grieved at their lack of deep commitment to Christ, so she instituted daily family Bible reading for the benefit of the children—which her sister soon sabotaged when it was her turn to lead by quoting the minimalist text, "Jesus wept," and rushing to breakfast. "And that," wrote Dora, "was the end of Scripture at breakfast." Mercifully for her sister, Dora soon found her own nearby accommodations. Mercifully for Dora, she was later able to see her sister, her sister's husband and their two oldest children experience "revival" and deepening of their faith so that they too joined in fervent evangelistic ministry.

By 1908 Dora Yu was speaking throughout eastern China and in circles far beyond the Methodists. Soon she was cooperating with leaders of the YMCA, with several missionary organizations and with a number of semiautonomous Chinese evangelists. Her revival preaching drew dozens, then hundreds and eventually more. In 1915 she opened her own Bible school and prayer house in Jiangwan, a southern suburb of Shanghai. Most of her early students were women, many of whom went on to become active preachers throughout China.

Despite evident success, Dora appears to have been relatively untouched by pride. Her journal records continuous humble dialogue with God, whom she felt privileged to serve. "God has all along been leading in that narrow path until it seems to me that even my Lord and I cannot walk *side by side*— I have to walk in Him and He in me. 'Abide in Me and I in you' is the wonderful truth!" Again, "It was not the gift of speech that was so important, but perfect obedience, being willing to be made a laughing-stock, if necessary, and just to bear witness to the Truth as He revealed it to me." Once, after she had taken part in what seemed to her an overly enthusiastic birthday celebration for two missionaries, she wrote these chiding words, "It is our privilege to give all the praises to the Creator, to whom all the glory and honour are due, and we should never allow it to remain with us ... [and] load our own souls down so as to prevent our maintaining our position in the heavenlies."

THE BIGGER PICTURE

By the 1910s, Dora Yu had become an influential Chinese evangelist. Her ministry was having a considerable effect in shaping the direction of Christianity in her native land. Yet it is also clear that, even as Dora influenced China, she was being influenced by Chinese developments in the early twentieth century. The relationship among Christian faith, Western imperial power and Chinese political development was especially important.

From almost every angle, the golden age of Chinese culture had passed by the time Dora Yu came on the scene. In the years 1839-1842, Britain had led Western powers in pushing themselves more directly into Chinese affairs. The goal was increased trade and freer access to Chinese goods and Chinese markets. The means to that end was Britain's protection of the opium trade between its Asian colonies and China. The resulting Opium War was successful from Britain's angle, since it secured protection for the trade in opium and also opened Chinese ports. For larger relations between China and the outside world, the Opium War was a disaster. The imposition of foreign imperial power constituted a blight that has colored Chinese attitudes toward the West to this day.

One of the byproducts of the Opium War was easier access to China for Western missionaries. This access had the positive effect of bringing some Chinese, like Dora Yu's family, into Christian faith. The negative effect was to link Christianity with Western imperial power. The result, as summarized by missiologist Ralph Covell, led to many difficulties: "From [the Opium War] until 1949, the gospel in China was proclaimed in the context of power."

China's loss of control over its own affairs continued after the Arrow War (Second Opium War), in which the Treaty of Tianjin (1858) opened ten more ports to unrestricted trade and allowed noncitizens (including missionaries) to travel throughout China. Missionaries took advantage by building churches and schools in many places. This effort opened doors for many Chinese, like Dora's father, but also created social tensions, as explained with some exaggeration by historian of China, R. Keith Schoppa: "The missionaries were convinced of their own superiority; educated Chinese saw all non-Chinese and their ideas as barbarian. The missionaries saw their teachings as Truth and the Chinese as benightedly superstitious; the Chinese saw themselves as grounded in realistic pragmatism and Christian teachings of a virgin birth or a father allowing his son to be crucified as scandalous and worse than superstitious."

In the period 1851 to 1864, a charismatic but unstable young man named Hong Xiuquan, who believed himself the younger brother of Jesus Christ, inspired the Taiping Rebellion. Xiuquan felt he had divine orders to "slay the demons," whom he took to be all Manchus, an ethnic people who had constituted China's ruling class since the seventeenth century. Dora Yu's father survived this war, but the Lower Yangtze macroregion alone suffered so many deaths that it did not recover prewar population levels for more than fifty years.

One result of Chinese internal turmoil was the discrediting of Confucianism. In 1905 the Dowager Empress Cixi (1835-1908), the last of the Manchu-related Qing dynasty, abolished the traditional Confucian civil service examination system in favor of a new scheme of general public education. For many, this seemingly minor shift in polity signaled the death of Confucianism. For more than a thousand years, China had cultured a brain trust of leaders through a three-tiered system of examinations whereby those who were sufficiently bright, wealthy and persistent could begin tutored study in early childhood to learn China's three thousand years of classical history, literature and Confucian philosophy. Then in young adulthood they would take a three-tiered layer of state examinations that only 1 to 3 percent of the students passed. From these few successful scholars China would choose her governmental officers and civil administrators. The educational shift begun in 1905 traded private classical education of the few for public practical education of many more. By 1930, 30 percent of all men were thought to be literate, which represented a broad advance. One of the consequences of this change in educational policy was to make mission schools a valued option, particularly in regions where public education was not yet fully operational.

DORA YUAS A CHINESE CHRISTIAN LEADER

Dora Yu's active ministry coincided with these momentous shifts in Chinese culture. Through her Christian faith, she had allied herself, to at least some degree, with foreign imperial powers. As a recipient of educational opportunities formerly reserved for male elites, she represented a practical repudiation of the Confucian past. Yet her personal dedication, her educational commitment, her ability in Chinese, her organizational gifts and her longing for spiritual authority—all of these identified her as a distinctly Chinese leader. She had become, in other words, a mediator between Christianity and Confucianism, and also between the religion of imperialists and the spiritual need of her own people.

By 1927, Dora Yu was well known to international circles of conservative Protestants. As a result she was invited to England by Reverend W.H. Aldis, the British home director of the China Inland Mission (CIM). As president of Keswick, he asked her to address the missionary conference that followed the annual Keswick convention. Keswick was the name given to the yearly convention of holiness-minded evangelicals whose regular meetings in the north of England had taken place since 1875. Summer by summer first hundreds and then thousands gathered for a week of worship, exhortation and teaching. Christian spirituality emphasized at Keswick focused on a "higher life" that called for a total relinquishing of self to God, so that ideally even the most minute decisions might become subject to an inner voice from God. Keswick spirituality also emphasized personal holiness as God's work of "sanctification," worldwide evangelism and unity among believers across denominational lines. In addition Keswick teachers taught that the second coming of Christ could occur at any time.

Dora Yu's gospel message was similar in many ways to the Keswick vision of Christian faith. She too pursued and preached deep personal inner holiness and constant surrender to God. In describing a revival from 1907, she wrote: "The Spirit of deep conviction fell upon us all; confessions and restitutions were made according to the Scriptures. The pastor of the church took two days to make confession to his church members, as he felt the sin of starving God's 'flock' by not feeding them with the Word of Life, and at the same time making them to serve him. The people first wept over their sins, and afterwards wept for joy." Dora would have known the terms (or at least the concepts) familiar to many conservative Protestants in Britain and the United States: "pray through," "get saved," "born again" (and sometimes born again and again), "full surrender," "second blessing," "tribulation." She may have been taught some of this theology by the missionary teachers of her youth; she doubtless studied Keswick themes in her active program of spiritual reading.

Like many other Chinese believers of her time, Dora Yu rejected modernistic forms of the faith such as Pearl Buck had begun to adopt before she left China in the mid 1930s. Dora was thus a natural ally for the Keswick conservatives to identify and to invite to their annual meeting. At Keswick in 1927, Dora Yu emphasized the bond she felt with the British believers whose convictions were so similar to her own. When she was introduced as a voice from China, she responded by emphasizing the oneness of all people who belong to Christ: "I am not the representative of China but of the Lord Jesus Christ, I belong to a Heavenly City." Her address then went on to plead passionately for Western churches to stop sending modernist missionaries to China; she feared that this kind of missionary would destroy the pure faith of Chinese believers. She particularly targeted teachings that opposed Christ's incarnation and divinity, his atoning work through death and resurrection, and his second coming. One account of her address reported that "Miss Dora Yu ... held the great crowd spellbound as she poured out her soul in impassioned words."

Silas Wu's important biography describes Dora Yu as (1) the foremost Chinese evangelist during the early part of the twentieth century; (2) the first crosscultural Chinese missionary of modern times; (3) the first Christian woman to found a prayer-based Bible school dedicated to the training of Chinese women workers for full-time ministry; (4) the only Chinese to be honored as a main speaker at the International Missionary Meeting of the 1927 Keswick Convention; and (5) a key first-generation Chinese revivalist who won others who would continue a distinctly Chinese evangelism in the 1930s and 1940s. Dora Yu was not alone in her efforts, but she was representative of the effective indigenous leaders who set a course for China's future.

Her status as a woman evangelist was, however, distinctive. Dora Yu was able to proclaim the gospel in China during a one-generation window of opportunity for women leaders. Confucian restrictions against women advancing to public leadership had softened by her time due to civil unrest and Western influence. At the same time, conservative reactions against modernist theology had not yet reached a consensus regarding gender roles. Dora Yu's spiritual granddaughters would rarely be allowed to publicly proclaim the gospel as she did. In Silas Wu's words, "A marked shift in gender leadership took place after the epic year 1927. Thereafter, the evangelical ministry of the first generation of female revivalists waned rapidly.... Leading young female evangelists suddenly stopped their public ministries and willingly receded into the background. A generation of male Chinese evangelicals carried on Dora Yu's spiritual ministry and raised Christian revivalism to a higher plane."

In 1931, four years after her appearance at Keswick, Dora Yu died in China of cancer at the age of fifty-eight. Her converts, including Watchman Nee and many other pastors and Bible women, would be active in the cities and countryside of China for many decades. Their ministry was crucial for the survival, and much more, of Christianity through difficult times. In an interesting conjunction of life courses, Dora Yu's speech at Keswick in 1927 nearly coincided with Mao Zedong's first successful organizing of farmers in his home province of Hunan. Decades later, the spiritual descendents of Dora Yu would be tested to the limit by the Communist regime that Mao and his comrades instituted. They would stand the test, at least in part, because she had done her work so faithfully.

SOURCES

The quotations revealing Dora Yu's inner spiritual world are from her autobiographical memoir, *God's Dealings with Dora Yu: A Chinese Messenger of the Cross* (London: Morgan & Scott, 1929). The quotations about Dora Yu from Silas Wu are from his book, *Dora Yu and Christian Revival in 20th Century China* (Boston: Pishon River Publications, 2002). This volume provides invaluable information, although Professor Wu has indicated that reliable detailed sources are scarce for some parts of Dora's life. R. Keith Schoppa, *The Columbia Guide to Modern Chinese History* (New York: Columbia University Press, 2000), is a useful general account (the quotation from this book is on p.19). Likewise for the specifically Christian story, Ralph R. Covell, *Confucius, the Buddha, and*

Christ: A History of the Gospel in Chinese (Maryknoll, N.Y.: Orbis, 1986), with quotation from p.83. Pearl S. Buck's *Is There a Case for Foreign Missions* (London: Methuen, 1933), is quoted from pp.49-50. Other books that were helpful for this chapter include Watchman Nee, *The Normal Christian Life* (London: Witness and Testimony Publishers, 1958); and John H. and Evelyn Nagai Berthrong, *Confucianism: A Short Introduction* (Oxford: Oneworld, 2000).

13

MARY STONE/SHI MEIYU 1873-1954

AGENT OF CHANGE

In 1881 a Chinese father walked purposefully down the streets of Jiujiang, in China's Jiangxi province, his small daughter cheerfully keeping pace at his side. Shi Meiyu was eight years old. Small for her age, she still drew attention. Most girls like her in this respectable section of town stayed at home nursing their recently broken foot bones while cheered by mother and grandmother about the handsome wealthy man who would one day marry them so that they would never need to walk much anyway. Other girls Meiyu's age, recovering from these injuries, practiced their new "lotus gait" of tiny tiptoed swaying steps so enticing to Chinese men and so troubling to Western visitors. But this father and his wife had other plans for their daughter. They were heading to the residence of Dr. Kate Bushnell, a missionary doctor serving under the Methodist Episcopal Church. When they arrived, Meiyu's father said, "Here is my little girl. I want you to make a doctor of her."

Mary Stone (Shi Meiyu) and Jennie Hughes

This request was no whim of the moment. Shi Meiyu's father was among the first Christian converts through the work of Methodist missionaries in central China. Her mother worked as principal of a school for girls and had further practiced her pedagogical skills at home. By the age of eight, under her mother's tutelage, Meiyu had already mastered a number of Chinese classics, the Gospel of Matthew and a Christian catechism. Meiyu's family departed from tradition in another area as well. A thousand-year custom dictated that mothers and grandmothers were responsible for binding the feet of young girls, but Meiyu's mother took this to mean it was also her privilege *not* to bind—which was the decision she and her husband made at Meiyu's birth. In order to show that Meiyu walked on natural feet not out of neglect or ignorance but by choice, Meiyu's mother kept her own feet bound. Only when Meiyu reached adulthood did her mother unbind her own feet.

Upon Dr. Kate Bushnell's recommendation, Meiyu's parents enrolled her in missionary Gertrude Howe's Rulison-Fish Memorial School. Howe had adopted a Chinese girl, Kang Cheng (Ida Kahn), as her own daughter. Kang Cheng and Shi Meiyu studied together as Gertrude Howe prepared to send both girls to medical school in her home state of Michigan. Along the way these two future doctors learned math, rhetoric, Latin, world history, physics and American history. By the time they reached Michigan their English was nearly impeccable.

CUSP OF CHANGE

Shi Meiyu was born on the cusp of great change in China, which her parents had wisely anticipated. Jiujiang, the city of her birth, was one of the "treaty ports" where China granted extra territorial rights to foreign powers after the Opium War of 1839-1842. Though more than 200 miles inland along the 3800-mile Yangtze River, it had been designated a port since 1861, a mere decade prior to Meiyu's birth. This status made possible uninterrupted Western trade that allowed opium to flow without restraint, the highest priority for

Western entrepreneurs. But it also brought in missionaries, teachers, doctors, Western ideas, and freedom for these newcomers to buy land and build schools, hospitals and churches. Shi Meiyu, whose parents were among the earliest Christian converts in Jiujiang, was born into this rapidly changing environment.

The decision by Meiyu's parents not to bind her feet reflected the tumult of the era. Foot binding had been practiced for about a thousand years, despite intermittent protests by various Chinese reformers. At the end of the nineteenth century, protests multiplied, much of it coming from the missionary community. Still, the practice remained mostly in place, because the bound and crippled lotus feet continued to signify an expectation of privilege, leisure and deference from males. Since unbound feet usually meant limited opportunity for marriage, Meiyu's parents knew they were taking a risk. But the tide was running their way. Less than forty years after Shi Meiyu's birth, the new Republic of China would ban foot binding altogether, making it punishable by death. Young Meiyu was among the first young girls in her area of China not to undergo the procedure. It was the first of her many firsts.

The practice of foot binding was far from the only matter undergoing unprecedented change. In the Jiujiang of Meiyu's childhood, not a single Chinese doctor (male or female) practiced Western medicine. Public schools did not exist. Wealthy families hired private tutors to prepare their sons for the civil service exams that could qualify them to serve as government officials. Only a few girls were educated, and most could not read. Yet within Meiyu's lifetime much of China adopted Western medicine and education. Some, like Meiyu's family, also became Christians.

In 1892 Shi Meiyu and her friend Kang Cheng completed their studies with Miss Howe, passed their entrance exams for medical school at the University of Michigan in Ann Arbor and traveled to the United States with most of their expenses paid by the Women's Foreign Missionary Society of the Methodist Episcopal Church. Women in medical school, even in the United States, were still rare. Only forty-five years earlier Elizabeth Blackwell had become the first American woman to earn a medical degree. Two other Chinese women preceded Meiyu and Cheng to the U.S. for medical study, but both Jin Yunmei (1885) and Xu Jinhong (1894) attended east coast schools open only to women. Meiyu and Cheng were the first Chinese women to attend a coeducational medical school in the United States. At the University of Michigan the only concession to female sensibilities was separate seating during anatomy and gynecology classes. Both young women did very well, even earning the best grades in some of their courses. By 1922, a mere twenty-five years later, more than two hundred Chinese women were studying medicine in the United States.

At the University of Michigan, the two Chinese women benefited from a recently upgraded curriculum. The school became famous for its early work in bacteriology, pharmacology, cardiovascular hemodynamics and (one of Meiyu's favorites) surgery—though she had to stand on a stool in order to work at the operating table. At this transitional state in modern medicine physicians knew that bacteria caused disease but had not yet developed antibiotics. Their best defense against illness was antiseptic cleanliness—which these two doctors later enforced with vigor in their Chinese hospitals.

AMERICAN-CHINESE CONNECTIONS

During the course of her studies at the University of Michigan, Shi Meiyu made two other important changes: she added an Americanized version of her name, Mary Stone, and she met Dr. Isaac Newton Danforth. The name change was a simple decision, made in concession to Michigan tongues that couldn't manage Chinese syllables. From that time on she alternated versions of her name depending on locale. After Dr. Isaac Newton Danforth, a urology surgeon at Northwestern Hospital in Chicago, supervised her clinical work in the summer of 1896, they became good friends. Before Mary Stone returned to China, Dr. Danforth trained her in the newest medical equipment including x-ray, introduced her to Chicago physicians and toured with her through major hospitals of the city. Evidently he sometimes had trouble keeping up with his agile guest because he complained, "The first thing I knew she would be right down by the operating table." Then he added, "She won the hearts of all with her charming ways, and got everything she wanted."

Dr. Stone and Dr. Kahn sailed back to China in the fall of 1896. Almost immediately they set up a medical dispensary in their home city of Jiujiang. Throughout the trip they had worried whether local people would accept them and their Western-style medicine. They needn't have feared. Thousands of firecrackers saluted the arrival of their ship, and in the first ten months they treated 2,300 patients and made hundreds of house calls. One peasant confided, "We are afraid of foreigners, but you understand our nature."

By 1898 Shi Meiyu was writing back to the United States: "An observer would think that we carried home but a slight idea of hygiene. Our hospital measures on the outside 28 by 21 Chinese feet ... and we have been compelled to crowd in twenty-one sleepers. We are looking forward all the time to signs or signals from the women of America to build our new hospital." This time the supporting signal did not come from the women of America but from Dr. Danforth, who offered to build a Chinese hospital in memory of his wife. Shi Meiyu put to work her visits to Chicago's finest hospitals, adapted these plans to the hot climate and walk-in visitors of China and with the help of her colleague Dr. Kang drew building plans later refined by a Chicago architect. What resulted in 1900 was, as described by a visitor some years later, "an airy, gray building, finished with white granite and limestone, plentifully supplied with comfortable verandas, and bearing over its pillared entrance the name 'Elizabeth Skelton Danforth Memorial Hospital.'" A photo of a two-storied, three-winged building laced with glass and verandas and sheltered by trees accompanied her apt description.

Sadly, Shi Meiyu and Kang Cheng were not able to immediately put the new hospital to use. Just as the building received its finishing touches, war broke out. The Boxer Rebellion of 1898-1900 particularly targeted Christian missionaries and their converts in central and northern China. In the summer of 1900, Shi and Kang had to evacuate and flee to Japan. Meiyu's father died in the uprising.

The two doctors along with Gertrude Howe returned in 1901 to find the hospital intact. They completed their moving-in process and began treating patients. In December of that year, the *China Daily Herald* described the official opening celebrated by officials from the Methodist Central China Mission. "Guests were at liberty to saunter across verandas and through the various wards ... convalescent's room, solarium, dark room, offices ... of this admirably planned hospital. The operating room with its skylight, its operating table of glass and enamel; the adjoining sterilizing room, containing apparatus for distilling, sterilizing ... the drug rooms are well stocked and furnished with ... a fine microscope ... and there is the nucleus of an excellent library." The same article spoke of "the two heroines of the occasion" who "kept modestly in the background." Doctors Shi Meiyu and Ida Kahn were twentyeight years old. During the first twelve months the Danforth Hospital was open, they treated nearly eight thousand patients.

MEDICINE AND EVANGELISM

Obviously the hospital needed support staff. A host of diseases and conditions awaited them each morning: measles, leprosy, typhoid, tuberculosis, open ulcers, harelip, and insanity, even at one point a fifty-two pound abdominal tumor. (Dr. Shi successfully removed it.) During their first year the two doctors had begun to train local women, perhaps two or three at a time, to assist in their work. Now Dr. Shi Meiyu set up a full-fledged nursing school. Once again she followed Western standards by requiring three years of training. In the curriculum she included not only medical and nursing skills but also Bible and Christian evangelism. Lacking textbooks in Chinese, she borrowed Western texts and translated them herself.

Since both doctors and nurses were in short supply, the nurses trained at Danforth had considerably more responsibility and authority than nurses in the United States. Both doctors saw nurses as independent healers in their own right. These nurses traveled out to the countryside, often accompanied by a Bible woman. They diagnosed disease and handed out medicines, conferring with the doctors only when needed. At one point Dr. Danforth offered to send an American-trained nurse to assist at the hospital, but Shi Meiyu declined, saying, "We want to convince the Chinese women that they are able to do things of which they have never dreamed."

Hospital stays were sometimes long, with fevers lasting weeks or months, not mere days. Shi Meiyu eventually built a small bungalow high in the hills outside the hospital so that in summer children with fevers could enjoy the cooler air of hills and trees. In 1908 a wing was added to the main hospital; in 1909 a home for nurses; in 1914 the Ida Bracey Cripples' Home for children with disabilities, named after a young invalid girl in New York.

In the cosmopolitan port city of Jiujiang the Danforth Hospital complex was by no means the only medical option. It was, however, the only option staffed by Chinese women trained in Western medicine. For some patients it was only one part of a smorgasbord of medical care, as they freely mixed what they received at Danforth with medical advice from traditional practitioners; the latter emphasized physical, emotional and spiritual balance through conversation, herbs and measuring the pulse from twelve sites of the body. Shi Meiyu rather indelicately referred to these traditional practitioners as quacks. For others, however, particularly women who would not consult a male doctor, and also for the poor who could not pay medical costs, Danforth became their only source of medical help.

In 1903 Dr. Kang received an invitation to open a medical facility in Nanchang, about one hundred miles south of Jiujiang, and after due consideration Kang Cheng and her adoptive mother Gertrude Howe moved there. Shi Meiyu continued the work at Danforth Hospital assisted by her sister Anna Shi, who had recently finished studies in evangelism in the United States. Like her two sisters, Meiyu and Phoebe, Anna had begun to study medicine, but early in her education she discovered that she herself was sick with tuberculosis. So she took a shorter program in evangelism taught by Methodist Episcopal Bishop Isaac W. Joyce and returned to China to assist Meiyu by managing a day school for children and a Bible Women's training college. By 1905, as tuberculosis was taking its relentless toll, it was plain that she could not work much longer.

The next year, 1906, was pivotal at Danforth. Meiyu's sister Anna died in March with grieving Meiyu in attendance until the end. She later wrote, "When my precious sister, Anna Stone, the sweet singer of 'Saved by Grace' and our evangelist in [Jiujiang] passed through the portals of Heaven ... never was Heaven so near and so real, nor earth so dull and bereft." But just one month earlier, American missionary Jennie Hughes had arrived at Danforth. Though originally assigned elsewhere, Jennie picked up the work of teaching evangelism and also filled a place in Meiyu's heart that had been left empty at her sister's death. Shi Meiyu and Jennie Hughes lived together for the next three decades, bringing some twenty needy children into their home, several of them distant relatives of Meiyu. Their first was an abandoned baby girl discovered by a mail carrier and brought in on Thanksgiving Day, 1906. Meiyu Shi eventually adopted four needy boys; the two "Aunties" raised them and several other needy children to adulthood.

The year 1906 was also a year of exhaustion and then sickness for Meiyu. After weeks of abdominal distress, which she suspected came from an inflamed appendix, the mission sent her to the United States for surgery and rest. By then she had been working at Danforth for nearly eleven years, had expanded the hospital from the size of single living room to a substantial campus of several buildings and was seeing (or overseeing) nearly a thousand patients a month. Her colleagues noticed visible signs of strain.

Meiyu and Jennie sailed for San Francisco in February of 1907 and from there traveled to Chicago to visit Mary's old friend and benefactor, Dr. Isaac Danforth. He performed an appendectomy, prescribed a month of recuperation and then sent the women off to Jennie's family in New Jersey for needed rest. Not surprisingly, Mary capitalized on the time by speaking about

China, recruiting new workers and fundraising at every opportunity.

Mary also used the time in America to update her medical skills once again by appealing to Dr. Danforth for in-hospital tutorials with specialists. By September 1907, Shi Meiyu was back in China at Danforth Hospital—seeing patients, teaching Bible at staff chapel meetings and constructing new buildings. Her status as a missionary physician sent out by the Methodist Episcopal Church enabled her to fundraise and recruit help just like any missionary from the States or Europe.

Shi Meiyu saw Danforth Hospital and its various accompanying buildings as functional ways of sharing the gospel of Christ. Her understanding of Christian faith included features of the social gospel but also stressed the reality of individual sin and the need to accept Christ as Savior. Margaret E. Burton writing in 1912 described a typical scene in a Danforth hospital ward:

> As the nurses were getting the patients settled for the night she noticed a low murmur which she did not at first understand until she saw that at every bed someone was in prayer. Here a mother was kneeling by the side of her little suffering son; there another mother of high rank was praying that the life of the baby by whose

> crib she knelt might be spared her. In one corner a woman had crept out of bed and was kneeling with her face to the floor; in other places those who were too sick to leave their beds were softly praying in them.

One of the factors that made this a typical scene was Shi Meiyu's determination that all nurses at Danforth also be Christian evangelists. In time this criterion would change at Danforth—with life-altering results for Meiyu—and for Christianity in China.

NEW DIRECTIONS

In 1918 Mary Stone and Jennie Hughes again returned to the United States, partly for medical treatment and also so that Mary could continue her postdoctoral education, this time at Johns Hopkins Medical School in Baltimore. Mary's sister Phoebe, also a medical doctor, took charge of Danforth during their two-year absence.

Meanwhile in California a seismic shift was taking place among the Methodists under whom Mary Stone had served since the days when that mission board funded her medical school education. Among Methodists a version of the fundamentalist-modernist division had arrived. In 1895 Methodist Episcopal Church pastors Phineas F. Bresee and Joseph Pomeroy broke from the Methodists and formed a new denomination in Los Angeles eventually known as the Church of the Nazarene. By 1908 fifteen other holiness groups, many from the Methodists, would join this new denomination. The Nazarenes emphasized urban ministry and evangelism, the absolute necessity of personal salvation, and holiness of life. This combination defined a faith quite similar to what Mary Stone practiced in China, but now that segment of historical Methodism had moved out of the parent denomination.

The division among American Methodists reflected some of the tensions that Stone and Hughes had experienced at Danforth as they juggled medical and spiritual care. In China they sought to blend the two efforts, as in the requirement that nurses function as evangelists. For her part Hughes also included science courses in the Knowles Training School for Bible Women, so that her students would receive the equivalent of a general high school education. Further tensions arose because both Mary Stone and Jennie Hughes were effective fundraisers, raising money directly rather than through the Methodist mission agency. Further, they were committed to local Chinese leadership and decision making rather than deferring to mission directives. It would not take much tension to break their ever-loosening connection with the American Methodists.

That tension broke in 1920 at the General Conference of the Methodist church in California, where Stone was a featured speaker. The Methodist board wanted Jennie Hughes to drop science from the curriculum of the Bible women. Jennie objected and resigned from the mission. Mary Stone followed suit. Both women returned to Jiujiang, gathered staff and belongings, and headed 430 miles northeast to the coastal city of Shanghai.

In her twenty years at Jiujiang, Shi Meiyu had trained some five hundred Chinese nurses. Nursing education continues there to this day, where at Jiujiang University's four campuses sixteen hundred full-time teachers instruct thirty thousand full-time Chinese students. The University traces its beginnings to 1901 and the Danforth School of Nursing.

BETHEL BANDS

As soon as they arrived in Shanghai, Shi and Hughes opened a new school. It was called Bethel: forty nurse-evangelists were the students, many brought from Danforth. They also established a sixteen-bed hospital as the first of an impressive collection of institutions: a high school for both boys and girls with dorms for each (1923); a three-story hospital (1925);

and a tabernacle meeting place seating one thousand people with dorm housing for four hundred (1927). By 1928 nursing and obstetric students numbered 137 with the continued assumption that all would do evangelism as well as public health and medical work. Meanwhile the two collaborators made a quick fundraising trip to the United States, where they also enrolled five of their students and adopted children in college. After returning to the Far East, they led an evangelistic team from Bethel for a year of mission work in Korea. This mission and the other ministries retained a strong dual foci, in Shi Meiyu's words: "As disease came through sin, ignorance, poverty and superstition, so the Gospel message of Health, Liberty, and the Abounding Life through Jesus Christ must be preached.... Then indeed our bodies are made Holy, fit temples for His continued indwelling." By the early 1930s about 200 nursing students were studying in Bethel's nursing evangelism program.

Throughout the 1930s "Bethel Bands" composed of both men and women were sent into the Chinese countryside to preach the gospel in sermon, song and testimony. Bethel evangelism resembled American revivalism, with emotional preaching as well as altar calls for salvation and full consecration. Jennie Hughes proclaimed, "Bethel believes in revival all year round." In the early 1930s a charismatic young preacher who had also studied science in the United States headed up one of the Bethel Bands. His name was John Sung, and his story is told in the next chapter.

The opening phases of World War II had a direct impact on the Bethel complex, which was hit by a Japanese bomb in 1937. Shi and Hughes worked their way south to safety in Hong Kong. At first, as she organized nursing students into Red Cross teams, Shi Meiyu hoped to rebuild. In December of 1937 she sent out a letter asking for one hundred thousand dollars to replace Bethel buildings. A few months later she reduced her request to fifty dollars a month to rent space for the school. But by then the Japanese occupation prevented even this modest effort. Eventually the two women sailed for Pasadena, California, where they spent the war years near Jennie's relatives.

A small Bethel organization remained in Hong Kong headed up by two of Jennie's adopted daughters. Mary and Jennie also created a small Bethel organization in California from which they planned to restart their work in China. But when the war ended, Dr. Mary Stone was seventy-three years old. She had already suffered the loss of treasured friends—her mentor Gertrude Howe in 1929 and in 1931 her colleague from student days, Dr. Kang Cheng.

Her lifelong coworker, friend and housemate Jennie Hughes died in 1951. Three years later Dr. Mary Stone followed: she was eighty-two years old.

LASTING LEGACY

A guiding clue for summarizing the lasting legacy of Dr. Shi Meiyu/Mary Stone comes from her preferred manner of dress. Doctor Shi spoke from both of her cultures by the clothes she wore, usually a Western style skirt with a Chinese tunic or top. Thus she brought Western medical education to China but then encouraged the Chinese to take charge of the work and decisions with as little Western influence as possible. Fundraising was among her greatest skills, and with these funds she produced prodigious results in buildings, institutions and people. How did she do it? Her own hard work exemplified the kind of commitment she expected from all who surrounded her. Her adage on economy combined Western principles of advancement with the Confucian sense of art and order: "Economy is the art which avoids all waste and extravagance and applies money to the best advantage."

Shi Meiyu insisted on combining medicine and evangelism; she saw them both as essential to human wholeness. For that principle she even gave up, at midlife, a campus of schools and a hospital and started all over. Her presence ensured that if you were among the thousands treated each year at Danforth or Bethel hospitals, you would have heard the gospel—probably at a time of need. Through this means, Christianity progressed in China during a time of strong missionary activity, but in preparation (as it turned out) for a time when the missionaries would be gone.

Shi Meiyu encouraged Chinese Christians to become self-reliant and independent. One might question the wisdom of her actions as she exercised local control over funds donated from abroad and as she rejected the loan of Western teacher-nurses to her school. One might argue with her ecclesiology as she created independent schools, evangelism teams, churches and the hospital at Bethel. But this independence and grass-roots, self-reliant leadership would enable Christianity to endure in China during a coming era when faith rooted in ecclesial structures would surely have collapsed.

SOURCES

This chapter drew extensively on Connie Anne Shemo, "An Army of Women: The Medical Ministries of Kang Cheng and Shi Meiyu, 1973-1937" (Ph.D. diss., State University of New York at Binghamton, 2002), which covers the sources of Mary Stone's life very well. Quotations are from this work and also from Margaret E. Burton, *Notable Women of Modern China* (New York: Fleming Revell, 1912). Mary Stone herself introduced a book by her longtime companion and coworker Jennie V. Hughes, *Chinese Heart-Throbs* (New York: Fleming Revell, 1920). Yading Li provides a biographical sketch of Mary Stone/Shi Meiyu in the online *Biographical Dictionary of Chinese Christianity* (http://www.bdcconline.net). Excellent treatment of Chinese believers from the first half of the twentieth century who had contacts with Americans and American education is found in the two volumes of *Salt and Light: Lives of Faith that Shaped Modern China,* ed. Carol Lee Hamrin and Stacey Bieler (Eugene, Ore.: Pickwick, 2009-2010). R. Keith Schoppa, *Modern Chinese History* (New York: Columbia University Press, 2000), and Daniel Bays, ed., *Christianity in China: From the Eighteenth Century to the Present* (Stanford: Stanford University Press, 1996), provided excellent background information.

Other useful material is available from Irene K. Sumner, "Nursing in Mission Stations: A Glimpse of Medical Work in China," *The American Journal of Nursing* 15 (January 1915):304-9; Edith L. Blumhofer and Randall Balmer, eds., *Modern Christian Revivals* (Urbana: University of Illinois Press, 1993); Lily Xiao Hong Lee and A.D. Stefanowska, eds. *Biographical Dictionary of Chinese Women: The Qing Period, 1644-1911* (Armonk, N.Y.: M.E. Sharpe, 1998); Howard Markel, "The University of Michigan Medical School, 1850-2000: An Example Worthy of Imitation," *Journal of the American Medical Association* 283 (February 16, 2000):915-20; and Weile Ye, *Seeking Modernity in China's Name: Chinese Students in the United States, 1900-1927* (Stanford: Stanford University Press, 2001). The website for Jiujiang University (www.jju.edu.cn/english/home.htm) contains information on this university today.

14

JOHN SUNG/SONG SHANGJIE 1901-1944

FIRESTORM EVANGE LIST

It is just before Christmas in 1926 at Calvary Baptist Church in New York. A small, haggard-looking student from nearby Union Theological Seminary sits in the audience. Union students don't often appear at this Baptist church, where fundamentalist John Roach Straton is the pastor, but this student has been to stranger places in his first term of studies at Union. Finding the seminary's liberal version of Christianity not to his liking, he has experimented with Buddhism, Taoism, mysticism and theosophy. He likes mysticism, but it offends his scientific mind, which has been trained in graduate-level chemistry. He feels a long way from his home in China and the rural Christian pastorate of his father. Maybe he will find solid theological footing from this respected Baptist preacher—or at least entertainment. The preliminaries over, the speaker appears, not the seasoned pastor he had expected but a young girl, age fifteen, dressed in white.

John Sung (Song Shangjie) (top row, first on left) with Bethel Band

Though young, she was no amateur. Uldine Utley preached the love of Jesus with simplicity, eloquence and quiet power. The seminarian journaled, "When she finished preaching, many people dashed forward weeping in repentance, including community leaders, government officials, as well as church pastors. I was so deeply impressed by her powerful sermon that I went back for more of her message four times." A wandering sheep was headed home.

BEGINNINGS

Song Shangjie was born in Hong Chek village, inland from China's southeast coast, on September 27, 1901, the sixth child in the family of an impoverished rural Methodist pastor. Like many in Chinese marriages of that era, Song's parents had been betrothed prior to either of their births. In this case the result was a devout Christian marrying a devout Buddhist. Shortly after the marriage Song's mother converted and received Christian baptism. Later when she was near death after her fifth pregnancy, she heard the voice of Jesus speaking to her and was instantly healed. Song spoke of this event as the time when his mother was "born again." Evidently his parents saw it that way too. Song was the next child born to them, and they nicknamed him Zhu En ("God's Grace") as a symbol of their now mutual faith.

By the age of twelve, Song was traveling with his father to worship sites that had sprung up in the wake of a vibrant revival three years earlier. If his father was ill or busy, Song would speak for him, first from memorized texts of his father's sermons and later from written expositions based on his own biblical study. Christians throughout the area began to call him "Little Pastor."

Though quick at reading, writing and memorization, Song was a difficult child, given to outbursts of anger. Still, a bright and active son had certain filial responsibilities. Song was expected to complete his education, earn enough money to send his brothers to school and marry a woman chosen for him by his parents. Song fulfilled those expectations, though reluctantly.

The lowered value of the American dollar after World War I opened the door for higher education in the United States. Through a missionary, Song received a full-tuition scholarship at Ohio Wesleyan University. Song's father agreed that he could go if he could find money for travel. Hearing of the opportunity and the dilemma, the Reverend's former students put together a six-hundred-dollar loan to fund the two-month trip. Song kept a careful record of each donation and vowed to repay the money as soon as possible. Once at Ohio Wesleyan he enjoyed the continued benefit of the shrunken dollar. The employment he quickly found allowed him to pay back his transportation loan in full, keeping a mere six dollars as pocket money with which to begin his college years.

STUDENT YEARS

Song concluded that the best way to economize was to shorten the educational timetable. At first, language was a barrier, but he mastered English in a few months. Then he cut the expected five years of college down to three, graduating with highest honors and a degree in chemistry, though he later admitted to cheating on his final exams. Meanwhile he had worked almost constantly at whatever jobs he could find that fit around his classes. In spite of an intense schedule, Song found time for spiritual tutelage under Dr. Rollin Walker, a professor of Bible at Ohio Wesleyan and also an itinerant preacher. Song soon called Rollin Walker "my American father."

Early in his academic career, Song experienced physical setbacks that would bother him the rest of his life. The problem was a high fever and "a huge abscess at the base of my spine." He agreed to surgery, then requested early discharge to cut costs. His doctor predicted that he would have problems with this "illness" as long as he lived—a prediction that came true, leading Song to call it "my thorn in the flesh." Meanwhile, at home, his parents selected a bride for him, a young peasant woman named Yu Jin Hua. After a brief exchange of photos and letters, Song reluctantly agreed to the future marriage—but only after finishing his education. Less than three years after entering the United States, his degree came with a gold medal and cash prize for physics and chemistry. The doorway was now open to graduate schools and scholarships.

Yet even as he triumphed academically, Song felt weakened spiritually, despite the fact that in his final year at Ohio Wesleyan he had formed an evangelistic band of students to minister in churches throughout central Ohio. His journal revealed the ill effects of pride: "I became arrogant because I thought I was more intelligent than others." Song also felt a measure of guilt for not following his original intent to become a student of theology.

Despite spiritual unease, he pushed on in chemistry. He had other offers but accepted admission into a master of science program at nearby Ohio State University. While participating fully in social life with other international students, Song finished his master's degree at Ohio State in less than a year. He assuaged his guilt about abandoning theological studies by hitchhiking to a summer Bible conference in Lake Geneva, Wisconsin, but then he ditched the meetings because they were "not exclusively devotional in nature." He returned to Ohio sick with fever and fatigue and received a diagnosis of tuberculosis. But "within three weeks, my tuberculosis left me."

Song's Christian life was bolstered in this period by the opportunity to hear Dr. E. Stanley Jones, a Methodist evangelist with long experience as a missionary in India, whom Song personally invited to campus. He may also have heard the revivalist Billy Sunday, who conducted several campaigns in central Ohio during Song's time there and whose energetic preaching style Song would later take much further.

In the spring of 1924 Song faced the future with conflicting motives. As he wrote to his parents, "Why does the Heavenly Father call me to bring revival to the country through Christianity and yet confer me with such a deep interest in Chemistry? It is still my intent to pursue my doctorate in Chemistry." With characteristic energy, Song learned German (a prerequisite for doctoral studies) and then with intense effort was able to graduate one year and nine months later from Ohio State University with a Ph.D. Somehow during that time he managed to exercise his "other calling" by preaching in a hundred churches, eventually receiving a "Preacher's License" from the Methodist church.

By March 1926, Song once again faced critical choices. For a while he taught at Ohio State while contemplating offers of teaching posts in the United States, Germany and China. But the pull of the ministry also remained strong. "One evening, as I sat to deliberate on my next course of action, the Lord's Word issued me a strong warning: 'What good will it be for a man if he gains the whole world, yet forfeits his soul?'" The next morning, he met with a representative of the Wesley Foundation who, observing that "you look far more like a preacher than a scientist," recommended that Song take up theological studies at Union Theological Seminary in New York, which he did, almost immediately.

FAITH CRISIS

Song's teachers at Union included the seminary's president Henry Sloan Coffin and Baptist Professor Harry Emerson Fosdick, who in addition to his teaching also pastored New York's new Riverside Church. Having spent the previous six years in intense study of science, Song now was given a full introduction to liberal Protestant scholarship at its peak. At least as he remembered the experience, he heard theologians speak of the Bible as a collection of myths, prayer as self-referential psychology, miracles as impossible, angels and demons as mythic, faith as a delusion, spiritual intensity as emotional disorder and Christ as only a high-principled human. Song soon rejected this kind of Christianity as "empty." In response he retreated to the religions of his homeland. The thoughtful philosophy of ancient Confucianism now made more sense. He read Taoist classics and chanted Buddhist scriptures.

At the end of his first term, perhaps as a diversion, he experimented once again with Christianity. This was when he encountered the child evangelist Uldine Utley. Mightily shaken by her gospel message, Song spent the remainder of his winter break reading Christian biographies and praying. When classes resumed, he rarely attended. His letters home sounded bland

and formulaic but what he wrote to his old teacher Dr. Rollin Walker at Ohio Wesleyan reflected intense spiritual struggle. Walker was worried by what he thought was an "overstrained brain" and so wrote to Henry Sloan Coffin about the possibility of medical intervention. Song later remembered about this period, "The heavy burden of my soul became heavier day by day until on February 10th I got to the point where I no longer had any desire to live."

Instead he experienced what he would later term his "born again" crisis. He described it with the mystical passion that would later characterize his Christian ministry.

> I wept and prayed in desperation.... The scenes of my own sinful life played out before my very eyes. [He dug to the bottom of a chest to find his Bible and began to read from Luke 23.] I felt as though my spirit had floated out of my body and was following Jesus, with the cross on His back, as He walked to Golgotha. I could also feel the weight of my manifold sins almost crushing me to death.... I dropped on my knees in humility, and pleaded with the Lord to cleanse me with His precious Blood.... Then the Lord said, "Son, your sins are forgiven!" I looked up at His face that was glowing with light and the marks on his hands, and he added, "You must

> change your name to John." The Lord explained that it was John the Baptist who had prepared the way for the Lord and made straight paths for Him.

John Sung (as he began to be known) experienced an immediate change. Instead of praying Buddhist chants quietly in his room he ran up and down the hallways shouting "Hallelujah" without noticing that it was now well after midnight. The next morning he announced his name change and asked to give a public testimony. He put aside his theology textbooks and started memorizing the Bible, which he rehearsed loudly along with Christian hymns, often through the night. He visited local pastors, demanding that they too repent of their sins, confess their unfaithfulness and sloth in preaching, and pray with him to receive God's forgiveness. One night he experienced a vision of himself in a coffin dressed in an academic gown and holding a diploma, and he heard a voice say, "John Sung is dead to the world." He awoke and prayed aloud to renounce all worldly things, including academics. Meanwhile, heeding the concern of Professor Walker at Ohio Wesleyan, Union's President Coffin arranged a medical intervention. John Sung spent the next six months in nearby Bloomingdale Psychiatric Hospital.

In the hospital, John Sung began a different kind of theological education. In his six months there, he read the Bible forty times—using a different technique of study with each journey from Genesis to Revelation. Eventually Dr. Walker, the professor he had called "my American father," traveled from Ohio to New York and with the help of the Chinese consulate arranged John's release. On October 11, 1927, John Sung boarded a ship in Seattle and headed home to China. While at sea, he held all of his academic diplomas and awards over the rail and dropped them into the sea. He saved only his Ph.D. diploma, which he would give to his parents.

TAKING CHINA BY STORM

Within a week of his arrival in China, John and his parents were at war. They expected him to assume a lucrative teaching position, put his younger brothers through school and get married. John wanted none of this. Instead, he longed to travel throughout China and preach the gospel to any who would listen, and he was more than willing to live on the donations his hearers chose to make. This familial civil war ended in a compromise.

During his years in the United States, John had managed to save seventeen hundred yuan, then about twelve hundred American dollars, which he gave to his family. He also took a part-time job teaching at a nearby school, which helped to educate his bothers. Then in November 1927 he met his betrothed wife Yu Jin Hua, lectured her about his higher commitments and married her two weeks later. Whenever his presence was not demanded at the school, he began to travel and preach. Not surprisingly, he lasted at this school less than a year.

By leaving his teaching job, John Sung was free to itinerate throughout his home province of Fujian, which begins about two hundred miles north of Hong Kong and stretches some four hundred miles along China's southeast coast and two hundred miles inland. Over the next three years he held evangelistic meetings at dozens of towns and cities throughout the province. Every few weeks Sung would return home for a few days with his wife in Han Jiang.

John's evangelistic style was energetic, even frenetic. As he zigzagged across the province he paired up with church leaders, students, and other traveling evangelists, both men and women. In his revival meetings some would sing, others would pray and most often John would preach. His activity matched Billy Sunday in his prime: running across the platform, leaping off it into the crowd, walking the aisles and gesticulating in a listener's face. The method was effective; at the end of his sermons many regularly came to the front to receive Christ.

Sung showed much less interest in home life. In February 1929 he recorded that when Hua was about to give birth to their first child, "Both she and her sister told me to stay at home. I told them that ... public duty had to come first ... and on no account should ministry work be held up." Only later did he return to visit his wife and new daughter, whom he named Genesis after the first book of the Bible. Succeeding children received names from the rest of the Pentateuch.

In October 1930 John details a visit home after the birth of his second child. "Our newborn baby was suffering from some congenital defects. Hua was down with ringworms and my daughter was having scabies. She was hoping that I could stay at home with her, but the day for the meeting at Nan Ri Island had arrived.... I encouraged Hua by telling her touching stories of past female saints: their labour for the family is the most beautiful cross." John arrived back home in late November where "Hua was cradling our sick son ... in deep sorrow. I tried to console her by saying that one had to experience suffering in life before one can empathize with someone else in a similar state." John remained home for a few days but left for

Shanghai a mere three days after the boy named Exodus died.

By 1930, John Sung had developed an evangelistic style that could sustain itself beyond a revival's "flash in the pan" excitement. As part of his preaching ministry he began to set up evangelistic bands and establish house churches, immediately dividing new converts into groups of three to five people (both men and women) and asking them to tell people about Jesus at least once a week. Many of these "bands" became traveling groups that scoured the countryside, villages and cities for potential converts. If churches could not absorb the new believers, Sung instructed them to meet in homes for worship, mutual confession, instruction and prayer. He calculated that in the single year of 1930 he set up a thousand of these assemblies. Meanwhile he urged potential leaders to attend several weeks of intensive Bible instruction, which he would lead himself from early morning until well into the night. The full impact of Sung's method would not be fully apparent until some years later when, under the Communist regimes, the churches in China were forced underground.

BETHEL BAND

In the early 1930s Sung's career entered a new phase. The team of Dr. Mary Stone (Shi

Meiyu) and American missionary Jennie Hughes (who are profiled in chapter 13) was heading up a complex of institutions and facilities in Shanghai that included a hospital, nursing school, Bible school, orphanage and worship space for more than a thousand. Each year they also organized dozens of "Bethel Bands" composed of three to five young adults who headed out to evangelize the city and countryside. John Sung came into this network when another pastor, Andrew Gih, recruited him. His three years of ministry with Pastor Gih would shift the shape of Christianity in China—and even begin to reshape his own soul.

In May 1931 three other Bethel men—Philip Lee, Frank Ling and Lincoln Nieh—joined Andrew and John to form the "Bethel Worldwide Evangelistic Band." From July 1931 to July 1932, this team traveled over 50,000 miles, held 1,200 meetings, preached to more than 400,000 people in thirteen provinces, registered more than 18,000 "decisions" resulting in 3,000 men and women newly committed to fulltime service in other small evangelistic bands. Cooperation between Gih and Sung sometimes faltered. When the two argued about who would preach when and where, they sometimes separated for a time or alternated as speakers.

In China during the early 1930s, revivals were serious events. The Bethel Band would preach up to three services a day, each lasting two hours or longer. If local buildings could not house the crowds, large makeshift sheds or tents were erected. In November 1931 Sung described the rhythm of a revival week:

> On the first day, I spoke on repentance—cutting the body. On the second day, it was salvation—draining away the pus. On the third day, I spoke of being born again—the removal of mortified flesh. And on the fourth day, it was on becoming holy—the clearing up of all things impure. On the fifth day, I spoke of being filled with the Holy Spirit—the use of medication. On the sixth day, I covered the topic of victory in the Lord, which is the stitching up of the open wound. On the seventh day, I talked about Christ's Second Coming—bandaging the wound.

Sung's preaching style was dramatic, even athletic. Sweat poured from his face as he acted out Bible stories with dramatic urgency. At one Presbyterian school for girls John preached about Naaman the Syrian, whom Elisha instructed to dip seven times into the Jordan River to be healed of his leprosy. John demonstrated by jumping off the platform seven times. Prayer was loud, long and simultaneous. Revival always opened with public confession of sin, beginning (John hoped) with local pastors—who might find his finger-pointing accusations prompting them to action. Despite regular complaints from neighbors about noise, all of this was amazingly effective as people crowded in line by the dozens and then hundreds to confess sins, make restitution and be reconciled to one another. Sung wrote of a Shanghai meeting in March 1931, "I pleaded with God not to allow me to feel proud because of the size of the congregation, as the place was overflowing with people. Praise the Lord! The Holy Spirit descended upon us like the wind, and the entire church echoed with sounds of weeping, prayer and confession."

In these revival meetings John Sung exorcised evil spirits, prayed repeatedly for those who needed healing from opium addiction, wrote worship songs to be used with his sermons, prayed for healing from various physical ills, ate little or nothing, taught the Bible chapter by chapter and slept whenever he could—more than once in a field.

In November 1931 the Bethel Worldwide Evangelistic Band entered the dangerous territories of Mongolia and Manchuria, where invading Japanese troops were wresting the sparsely populated territory from China. Only about one hundred and fifty people gathered at one meeting, but many had traveled several days to do so. John tried out a new sermon based on the eleventh chapter of John, the story of Lazarus's death, the grief of his sisters and the gradual putrefying of his body during four days in the grave. Then Sung invited his hearers to open their own coffins and pull out their own stinking sins—smoking, telling lies, lusting, plotting—and expose these sins to the Jesus who loved Lazarus enough to heal all of that decay and make him alive again. Revised and reused on many occasions during the next eight years, this sermon, titled "Open the Coffin," would become one of John Sung's most famous. It stressed a major tenant of Sung's Christianity, that true believers needed to confess their sins.

New Year's Day of 1932 found him back at the Bethel Complex in Shanghai, where by now Hua and their daughter Genesis had relocated. Three weeks later, on January 28, the "Battle for Shanghai" began, with Japanese bombs shaking the city. Most of Bethel's personnel evacuated, but when several students struggled through gunfire and bombs to arrive from distant provinces for the Bethel Short Term Bible School, John Sung opened a classroom and began teaching. In twenty-two days he marched his students chapter by chapter through twenty-three books of the Bible, occasionally ducking for cover from nearby explosions.

By March 2 he was headed south for four months of travel with his Bethel Band. While preaching in Hong Kong in early May, thirty-two people approached Sung after a service and asked to be baptized. "How can I do this when I myself have not been baptized?" he wrote. The problem was quickly solved when local pastor A.K. Reiton immersed John Sung, who then baptized his converts. Meanwhile back in Shanghai, Hua gave birth to a second daughter, whom they named Leviticus (Levi).

With constant travel and a grueling preaching schedule—as many as three two-hour sermons each day—John's health soon became an object of concern. Early on, Dr. Mary Stone of Bethel had suggested that he might have a weak heart and recommended a six-month rest. Sung declined. Soon afterward, a new convert observed that if John would "expend less energy" when he preached, he might live longer. This too he ignored.

Despite his physical weakness and deficiencies that even he recognized, Sung's work was having a dramatic effect on the shape of Christianity in China. He too was being changed. To his own surprise he began occasionally to speak in tongues and pray successfully for others to be healed. At the same time he valued ever more deeply love, "the greatest gift," which he recognized as often lacking in his own life. But later, after experiencing a personal baptism by the Holy Spirit, Sung came to think that all ministers who had not yet received this baptism should withdraw from ministry. And even as John Sung attempted to grow in Christlike love, his preaching became more censorious, with attacks on the cinema, parties and vacation cruises. He even advised Christians to observe Christmas (if they must) by celebrating the death of Herod! He could, however, be as hard on himself as on others, as when he acknowledged that he was the problem in incidents of ill will with his fellow workers. From John the apostle he gained hope for his own spiritual development, especially from the story that when the apostle was very old, he was said to have spoken only three words but said them over and over: "Love one another; love one another; love one another." John Sung even came to the point of urging pastors to devote themselves more lovingly to their families, advice he found difficult to follow himself.

In November 1933 Sung's ministry with Bethel came to an abrupt end. While on a southern tour, Andrew Gih received a telegram from Jennie Hughes, Mary Stone's partner as head of the Bethel ministries. Hughes ordered the Bethel Worldwide Evangelistic Band to return immediately to Shanghai to be dissolved.

She gave three reasons: John Sung did not preach the possibility of Christians becoming sinless; John drew too much attention to himself; and John was suspected of stealing money designated for evangelism. Sung agreed that he taught a different doctrine, but denied all wrongdoing. Nonetheless, Jennie Hughes ordered him to find alternative housing for his family. By mutual agreement Andrew Gih returned immediately to Shanghai, while John and the rest of the team finished their preaching in Changsha. Then John Sung returned to Bethel, suffered the indignity of having Hughes confiscate his archive of letters sent from believers throughout China and saw his family's possessions loaded up and carted away.

BEYOND CHINA

John Sung took about a month to prayerfully examine his own part in the demise of his Bethel Band. In mid-January 1934 he left Shanghai to organize and preach revivals throughout the five surrounding provinces—this time as an independent evangelist. For the next five years John Sung would again preach throughout most of eastern and central China, but he also branched out into Indonesia, Malaysia, the Philippines, Taiwan, Thailand, Java and Singapore. In so doing, he became the last mass evangelist to preach in these regions before they were closed by the Second World War.

Sung's revivals by now had taken on a set pattern. First came a call to public repentance where he insisted that people name their sins, write them on paper and personally present them. He followed this with a call to new birth. Next came teachings on the meaning of new life in Christ. Midway through a revival, he would begin calling converts to become evangelists themselves, forming bands of three to five people pledged to evangelize at least once a week. Next he would ask those who were willing to reject all other employment and offer themselves for "whole-time consecration." Only in the final days of a revival would Sung introduce the possibility of physical healing. He would kneel beside a petitioner, pray, dip his fingers in a bowl of oil and with a quick smack on the petitioner's head command healing in the name of Jesus Christ.

Sung often devoted the final evening of his meetings to testimonies, where people (often by the dozens) came to the front and in a few sentences told what had happened to them that week. These testimonies might run until nearly dawn of the day of Sung's departure. As crowds increased and as John

Sung's energy decreased, he was forced to develop a more efficient system. On the evening of the final meeting, people queued in long lines through the aisles, each person carrying a paper with his or her name followed by a single sentence. In that way the congregation could hear the testimonies of personal salvation or healing or blessing from hundreds of people in a single night. The next day John Sung would step onto a train or a ship and head for his next revival.

Meanwhile his family remained in Shanghai. A third daughter arrived on April 2, 1935. John dutifully named her Numbers along with a more traditional Chinese name. And in April 1937 their final child, a son, was born. John skipped the book of Deuteronomy and named him Joshua.

In June of 1939 while preaching in Siam (Thailand) John Sung was stung by bees and then got sick "because of food." From that point on his journals describe a steady physical decline. By early December Sung needed help getting dressed and had to be carried downstairs on the back of a friend. He preached propped up with a bed "on standby [near] the pulpit." By mid-December he was preaching on his knees and finally while lying on a couch, speaking not of sin but of "perfect love." In early January 1940 he began his last journey home, by way of Singapore and Hong Kong.

ENTERING THE TOMB

It took three years for John Sung to die. What had started as a bad case of hemorrhoids when he was still in college at Ohio Wesleyan was now compounded by tuberculosis of the bone with significant degeneration of his hip joints plus what was probably colon cancer. His journals and various surgeries describe a "fist sized" wound that eventually became "a foot deep." He wrote, "All this time I have been praying for others. Now others must pray for me."

The pattern—in shortening cycles—became surgery, slow recovery, reasonable health and even ministry, then relapse. In July 1941, Sung and Hua suffered news of the sickness and then death of four-year-old Joshua, their only surviving son, while in the care of his nanny in Shanghai, more than six hundred miles away. By the end of the summer the whole family moved from Shanghai to Peking, where Sung was receiving medical care.

During these three years, John journaled, composed songs of faith, and prayed with and for his three daughters. He told them stories, often allegories for communicating gospel truths. He saw each come to faith in Jesus. He also got to know his wife of fourteen years who patiently cared for him. As had been his lifelong practice, he continued to read eleven chapters of the Bible each day; when that became too difficult, others read to him. By the summer of 1944, his wounds were so deep and the pain so severe that doctors prescribed opium.

Hua sat with him through the night of August 18, knowing that the end was near. A light rain drizzled outside. She heard John muttering, his hands clasped in prayer. Then she prayed her own prayer, "O, Lord, don't take away your servant in the darkness of night.... I plead that you take him away in daylight." His daughter Levi recorded, "John's pulse started to recede at five o'clock in the early hours. At 7:07 he was taken away by the Lord, a peaceful smile on his face." Four days later Wang Mingdao, the subject of chapter 16, preached at the funeral of his brother evangelist.

LEGACY

The slow process of dying gave John Sung ample opportunity to reflect on both accomplishments and failures. Always an advocate of confession, he took his own medicine and confessed to God in writing: "I chased noisy children away during my sermons; I am lacking in love; I tend to exaggerate; when I had to deliver three sermons each day, I neglected my devotional studies; I stole the glory of God; I was arrogant and looked down on others." But even as he confessed his shortcomings, he also looked ahead confidently. In October 1940 he predicted in his journal that the missionaries and mission schools would one day be gone from China, but he was not worried: "God will raise His own lay disciples and those who are truly blessed will revive the church in China."

John Sung's style of evangelism was loud, abrasive and straightforward to the point of naiveté—yet remarkably effective. His practice of preaching where people lived, his demands for confession and personal reconciliation, his insistent Bible teaching, his stringent personal holiness, his preference for house churches separate from intricate layers of bureaucracy and his immediate commission of evangelistic bands that could replicate his efforts—all contributed to a sturdy brand of faith tailor-made to withstand the isolation and the persecution that soon befell Chinese Christians. Scholars estimate that, at the time of his death in 1944, 10 percent of all believers in China had experienced some direct contact with John Sung. Historian Daniel H. Bays has written, "Sung must be reckoned probably the single most powerful figure in Chinese revivalism in the mid-1930's." He encouraged a kind of

Christianity that would survive and spread in the dark years to come.

SOURCES

Almost all the quotations from John Sung and much other material in this chapter come from his own extensive journals that have been edited by his daughter Levi (Leviticus) Sung, *The Journal Once Lost: Extracts from the Diary of John Sung,* trans. Thng Pheng Soon (Singapore: Genesis Books, 2008). The history behind Sung's journal, forty diaries filled with tiny Chinese script, is itself revealing of much in the recent history of Chinese Christianity. In 1966, as a part of China's Cultural Revolution, Red Guards raided the home of Hua Sung, Sung's widow, and confiscated everything, including these diaries. Yet kindly local authorities recognized their value and kept them from being destroyed. In 1984 a school administrator ran into Leviticus and asked her if the family was interested in items that might have been confiscated. In a school storeroom filled with much other discarded material they found a dusty basket on top of which lay a photo of one of Levi's sisters. Beneath were the diaries, John Sung's poems, and essays that Hua Sung had written in memory of her husband. The journal is an invaluable resource, though of course subject to the limitation of all such records where other sources are not available for verifying the personal account.

Other useful material from and about John Sung is found in Timothy Tow, *John Sung My Teacher* (Singapore: Christian Life Publishers, 1985); Shangjie Song, *Forty John Sung Revival Sermons,* trans. Timothy Tow (Singapore: Alice Doo, 1978); Leslie T. Lyall, *John Sung* (London: China Inland Mission, 1954); and Ruth Tucker, "John Sung: Revival in the East," in *More Than Conquerors: Portraits of Believers from All Walks of Life,* ed. John Woodbridge (Chicago: Moody Press, 1992), pp.156-59. The quotation by Daniel Bays is from p.173 in his chapter on China in *Modern Christian Revivals,* ed. Edith L. Blumhofer and Randall Balmer (Urbana: University of Illinois Press, 1993). For helpful background information, see also Stacey Bieler, *"Patriots" or "Traitors"? A History of American-Educated Chinese Students* (Armonk, N.Y.: M.E. Sharpe, 2004); R. Keith Schoppa, *The Colombia Guide to Modern Chinese History* (New York: Columbia University Press, 2000); Scott W. Sunquist, ed., *A Dictionary of Asian Christianity* (Grand Rapids: Eerdmans, 2001); and especially Xi Lian, *Redeemed by Fire: The Rise of Popular Christianity in Modern China* (New Haven, Conn.: Yale University Press, 2010). On Uldine Utley, see Kristin Kobes Du Mez, "The Beauty of the Lilies: Femininity, Innocence, and the

Sweet Gospel of Uldine Utley," *Religion and American Culture* 15 (summer 2005):209-43.

15

YAO-TSUNG WU/WU YAOZONG 1893-1979

COMMUNIST AND CHRSTIAN

In 1930, Yao-Tsung Wu described the encounter that changed his life:

> It was about eleven years ago, in the home of one of my American friends, that I read for the first time in my life the Sermon on the Mount. After I had read it, my inner being seemed suddenly to be flooded with light, and my heart was filled with unusual happiness. What I had sought for diligently for more than ten years and had failed to find, was fully revealed to me in those three chapters. As to what it was that was revealed to me, I did not take the trouble to analyze at the time. What I felt was that every word in those three chapters spoke to me with a mighty force and was graven deep in my heart. At the same time I caught between the lines a glimpse of the speaker: that visage, its kindness mingled with courage and dignity, was the very incarnation of love. This matchless personality

seemed to bore its way into the core of my being; and tears suddenly burst from my eyes. Remorse for the past, consolation for the present, hope for the future, in that single instant seemed all to well up in my heart, and as though petrified by magic, I fell on my knees and cried out to that shining figure: "Lord, thou art my Saviour."

Yao-Tsung Wu (Wu Yaozong) with Mao Zedong

Wu was twenty-five years old when this happened. Shortly thereafter he made public profession of Christian faith at a YMCA rally led by the American Sherwood Eddy, the same leader who was also an important figure in the life of the Indian bishop V.S. Azariah. Y.T. Wu was so important for the later history of Christianity in China that we can only wonder how that history might have been different if this pensive young scholar had first encountered Christ in the gospel of John or in Paul's letter to the Romans. But he did not. It was the Jesus of the Sermon on the Mount who became Wu's lifelong guiding light, the central figure in a career defined by two purposes that he regarded as almost the same: love of Christ and love of country.

For Y.T. Wu, the imperatives of the Sermon on the Mount drove his determined pursuit of social justice. In the same essay from 1930 that contained the story of his conversion, Wu explained how he put to use Jesus' commands, "You cannot love both God and money," and, "Do to others what you would have them do to you." The issue was world food supply and its unequal distribution. For Wu, the love embodied in Jesus demanded a four-point strategy in respect to limited food resources:

1. The stronger ones will voluntarily let the weaker and more needy ones eat first.
2. If they are all in need of food, there will be an equal distribution of resources.
3. If no more food is available, some of them should be willing to starve in order that others may live.
4. Ways of increasing the food supply must be sought so that all may have enough to eat.

By contrast, without Christlike love, "all would begin to fight for the food, and not only the weak would suffer but even the strong would come off with broken heads and bleeding wounds, and in the end everyone's rice bowl would be smashed."

Guided by such an application of the Sermon on the Mount, Y.T. Wu would eventually repudiate much of the missionary Christianity of his youth and turn with hopefulness to the Chinese Communist Party. The result for the whole history of Christianity in China was momentous.

THE DEEPER PAST

Y.T. Wu's lifetime, 1893 to 1979, spanned an extraordinary era in China's history. He was born on November 4, 1893, in a non-Christian home in Guangdong province, in China's southeast coastal area. That same year, Mao Zedong was born into a peasant family in Hunan province in the Chinese interior. It is impossible to understand Wu's grasp of Christianity without also grasping the revolution that Mao brought to China. And it is impossible to grasp the character of that revolution without understanding what happened in the generations before Wu and Mao were born.

The Opium Wars, first 1839-1843 and again in the 1850s, had left China defeated and exploited by the Western powers. With Britain in the lead, these powers secured the right to sell opium in China. They also imposed a series of "unequal treaties" whereby China ceded sovereignty to Westerners over her port cities. With opium from the West came also Christian missionaries. For the most part they were people of deep faith and pure motives who themselves often criticized the opium trade severely. From the Western point of view, the missionaries were agents of civilization as well as of Christianity. They built schools, hospitals and churches while they trained local evangelists like John Sung. On the whole, Christian missionaries to China tried to do the right thing.

Yet in the minds of many Chinese, Western missionaries were forever tainted by their association with the rapacious opium trade, with opium addiction and with the loss of Chinese sovereignty. Y.T. Wu was one of those for whom the missionaries' association with Western imperial powers created lasting bitterness. In 1962, for example, he would describe the missionaries as imperialist agents who undermined the ability of the Chinese to determine their own futures and who participated in America's "overall plan for world domination."

But that conclusion gets us way ahead of this story. China's Boxer Rebellion, 1899-1900, occurred when Mao and Wu were still boys. The rebellion resulted in the brutal murder of thirty thousand Chinese Christians along with more than two hundred Christian missionaries in

China's northern provinces. This tumult may have gone unnoticed by the two boys growing up in the south of China. Yet the Boxer Rebellion signaled the hostility of impoverished peasants toward Western missions and their Chinese converts that Mao and Wu later came to share.

WU AND MAO

Through the first decades of the twentieth century, the life stories of Y.T. Wu and Mao Zedong moved in what looked like opposite directions. Wu attended the Customs College in Peking, then worked as a customs officer for seven years before being drawn into Christian ministry. Beginning in 1920, he came within the orbit of the YMCA, which brought him into contact with missionaries like Sherwood Eddy. Early on, Wu became convinced that the Chinese concept of reconciliation (in literal Chinese, "by love alone") embodied the ideal relational expression of Christianity. Meanwhile, influenced by English Quaker missionary Henry T. Hodgkin, Wu became a pacifist. In 1921 Wu was appointed executive secretary of the Christian Student Work Union (CSWU). In that position he advocated "peaceful noncooperation" in civil situations where love and force collided. As a way of promoting his convictions, Wu served the YMCA as chair of its Fellowship of Reconciliation and from 1931-1937 as editor of the Chinese journal *Reconciliation.*

Twice Wu's Western Christian connections gave him the opportunity to study in the United States. From 1924 to 1927 he attended the Union Theological Seminary in New York as well as nearby Columbia University and later Drew University in New Jersey. Part of his study focused on the pioneering psychologist William James, and James's concept of religion as an ineffable but unexplainable aspect of human existence. In the United States, Wu experienced the heyday of liberal Protestant theology. The same ideas that drove John Sung nearly mad at Union Seminary enchanted Yao-Tsung Wu. He relished the thinking of noted professors Reinhold Niebuhr, Henry Frederick Ward, John Dewey and Harry Emerson Fosdick. Their conceptions of justice, salvation and morality helped shape what later became Wu's Chinese version of America's "social gospel."

Beginning in 1939, after returning from a second period of study at Union in New York, Wu worked in the publications department of the YMCA in Shanghai, where he wrote dozens of articles and supervised the work of many others. He also traveled to India, where he met Gandhi. In 1942 Wu initiated *Tian Feng Monthly* along with *Christian Collection.* But when in the spring of 1949 Wu published a sharp attack on

Western missionaries titled "The Contemporary Tragedy of Christianity," he was forced to resign as head of the *Tian Feng* Society.

Meanwhile, the life of Mao Zedong was moving toward its rendezvous with Y.T. Wu. During his twenties and early thirties, while Wu was experiencing Christian conversion and education in the social gospel, Mao was organizing the peasant associations of Hunan in various forms of rebellion. He experimented with land reform and other strategies to empower the peasants. In 1921 Mao Zedong attended the first session of the National Congress of the Communist Party of China (CPC).

Oddly, Mao came to power through defeat. From 1930 to 1933, Nationalist Chinese forces led by Chiang Kaishek battled Mao's Communist troops in the area of their Jaingxi base in southeast China near Mao's home. But Chiang Kaishek suffered frequent interruptions to his military efforts because Japanese troops were invading from the north and Chiang had to leave off one battle in order to fight another. Finally, on a fifth attempt, Chiang succeeded in nearly crushing the Communist army. As a result, in October 1933, eighty-six thousand Communists from southeast China headed northwest on a circuitous march of nearly six thousand miles through bogs, mountain passes, hostile Tibetan troops, frostbite, starvation and even attacks by Nationalist bombs. More than a year later eight thousand people struggled on foot into Yan'an in Shaanxi province. They were the tough survivors of China's "Long March" and were now united under a single leader: Mao Zedong.

By the late 1930s, with Japan battering her northern borders, China could no longer afford a civil war between Communists (led by Mao) and Nationalists (led by Chiang). Resolution came when Chiang was kidnapped by his own forces and held for two weeks until he agreed to create a "united front" with Mao's Communists. In 1937 these forces joined against Japan, which had seized nearly one-third of China's north and east, including the capital city of Beijing. Several years before Europe, China was fighting the Second World War.

War is not an exercise in gentility, but Japan's infamous "Rape of Nanjing" from December 1937 through January 1938 drove the Chinese to crave an orderly society at any cost. The death and destruction—the rapes and assaults—the mutilation and barbarous slaughter of children—the tortures and extraordinary cruelty—all added up to massive fatalities, from 200,000 to 300,000 Chinese dead.

The struggle against Japan was arduous. Notwithstanding great ill will, Communists and Nationalists did manage to cooperate in that battle. The war in the East extended for eight full years, but at last Japan was defeated. After the war was over, the uneasy "united front" between the Nationalist followers of Chiang Kai-shek and the Communists of Mao Zedong soon came unglued; three more years of Chinese civil war ensued. In 1949 a generation of warfare came to an end when Chiang and his remaining followers fled to the island of Formosa (Taiwan) off China's southeast coast. The victorious Mao Zedong set up the People's Republic of China with himself as chairman. Communism ruled in mainland China.

The year 1949 was as momentous for China's Christian churches as for its political future. At this point Y.T. Wu's criticism of the missionaries allied him with China's new rulers. But for understanding why Wu would turn to Mao's new government, it is important to understand Wu's commitment to the social gospel.

THE SOCIAL GOSPEL OF Y.T. WU

The social gospel was not a Wu creation. Rather, it was a popular movement within the Christianity of North America from the late nineteenth century onward. In 1937, when Wu published eighteen articles under the general title "The Social Gospel," he brought to China what he had learned in America. The foundation was the justice system of Old Testament prophets as expanded by Jesus' Sermon on the Mount. The Japanese invasions of the late 1930s stimulated Wu's search for ways to fulfill Christ's command to love. He was fully convinced that this love had to result in both love of country and love of church. This conviction led Wu to translate what evangelicals considered spiritual truths into social realities. For Wu *salvation* meant a disinterestedness in self; the *cross* required that even if love leads to death, followers of Jesus must continue to love; *Christ on the cross* became the "revealer" of God as well as the Savior; and the *Great Commission* was a command to act in ways that improved human society by promoting dignity and human freedom.

In a 1937 essay, "Should Christianity Concern Itself in Social Reconstruction?" Wu argued that any division between a spiritual gospel and a social gospel was a false dichotomy because "the gospel of salvation is always social in nature, even when the specific characteristics of individual lives are taken fully into account." He then outlined four ways in which Christians should live out their salvation in the social context: first, encourage a deeper and more fearless study of the social teachings of Jesus; second, always stand on the side of the oppressed and the disinherited; third, have the courage and humility to learn from those who differ from us; fourth, fully surrender to Christ in obedience to his will. In summary he wrote, "Religion at its best does not stop with the personal, but it always begins with the personal."

WHY COMMUNIST?

By 1937 the Japanese had shocked Y.T. Wu out of any form of pacifism, but not out of Christianity. With political chaos all around, Wu continued to consider what it meant to live as a Christian, with special emphasis on social relations:

> From the very beginning, Christianity has been a social religion. If there is one idea that is central in Christ's teachings, it is the idea of fellowship. "I am the true vine; ye are the branches." And fellowship is essentially social in nature. Paul has put the same idea in an equally significant way in the simile of the body and its several members. The early Christian community for a time—though it may be under the influence of apocalyptic beliefs—even practiced communistic living. And down through the ages, the idea of a "Christendom" has served as the link that has joined together all believers in a great fellowship.

Under the pressure of events, Wu's social gospel evolved. First it meant pacifism, then noncooperation with the Japanese, then supporting military force against Japan, then participating in military actions and finally fully embracing armed violence exercised on behalf of social advocacy for the weak. Without giving up on Jesus' Sermon on the Mount, he increasingly came to believe that the best way to express love as described in the sermon was to forcibly eradicate social evil. The movement of his thought, with an anchor still in his early Christian vision, pointed Wu toward accommodation with the Communist system, which Wu came to feel was working out principles of the social gospel after its own fashion in the civil sphere. For him the apostle Paul's admonition for Christ-followers to act as individual parts of a single body was taking shape in the Communist ideal, "From each according to his abilities; to each according to his need."

The apparent practicality of Communism also seemed to fit with Confucian social thought, which the Chinese had embraced for more than a thousand years. Wu's social-gospel version of Christianity resembled the Confucian ideal with its grand tiers of filial responsibility that began with supreme loyalty to parents but still reserved a place for just treatment of one's enemies. By contrast with Confucianism, both

Christianity and Communism were relative newcomers to China. Likewise, both were brought by "missionary" effort, and both demanded a total life ideology. At least in some ways, Communism seemed to deliver on what Christianity promised. For a people divided by vast geography and culture, overrun by hostile neighbors, sadly behind Western standards of prosperity and wracked by a century of war, Communism offered much. It expressed Chinese nationalism and patriotism; it offered a strategy for modernization; and it provided a philosophy of human transformation. On the surface, what Communism offered did not, at least for some people like Y.T. Wu, conflict with Christianity.

In 1951 Wu explained how Christianity and Communism had come together for him. The article was titled "How the Communist Party Has Educated Me." At a time when professions of loyalty to the new regime had become as effusive as denunciations of the imperialist West were extreme, Wu's comments were relatively mild:

> First [Communism] has taught me the true meaning of the verse, "Love your enemies." Not long after I became a Christian I ... became a pacifist.... [Later,] I realized that it was the Communists who truly loved their enemies, for they on the one hand resolutely carried on war, and on the other

treated their Japanese prisoners with kindness.... Pacifism [is] an imperialist opiate to keep oppressed peoples quiet.

Second, ... imperialism really is the devil that Christians talk about. For the sake of a few it carries on aggression against the whole world.... Now I know that capitalism is an oppressive system....

Third, ... I [was] deeply influenced by those two agents of American imperialism, John R. Mott and Sherwood Eddy. Mott was ... spreading American imperialism throughout the world though Christianity. Eddy took the slogan of "reform" and preached the social gospel.... It drugged the people and sapped their revolutionary strength.

Fourth, the Communist party made me understand the true position of the proletariat. I had formerly thought that since all Christians are children of God they must be all members of one big family.... On the contrary, it is the duty of Christians to take with non-Christians [the duty] to oppose exploitation, oppression, and aggression, and to work for the true freedom and equality of all the people of the world.

Fifth, the Communist party has shown me the true relation between theory and practice, between faith and deeds.... If the "miracles" that Christianity believes in are true, then the fact that the Chinese Communist party in the short space of thirty years has enabled the Chinese people, exploited and oppressed for thousands of years, to stand upon their feet, and at the same time enabled the Chinese Christian church to throw off the shackles of imperialism, is a miracle of a sort hitherto unheard of.

Wu's five-point article spoke for viewpoints that had become common in the first years of Communist rule. Social reconstruction had begun, and Wu himself was being "reconstructed."

SOCIAL RECONSTRUCTION

The changes demanded by the new regime affected every aspect of religious life. Western observers knew most about the missionaries, but trauma for Chinese believers was much more severe.

Almost immediately after Mao's victory in 1949, "imperialist" missionaries were unwelcome; many soon began to leave. The hospitals, schools and orphanages they had built became government property with no financial compensation. By 1952 the missionary exodus was virtually complete. As reported by missionaries, there seemed no hope for the approximately one million Protestants and three million

Catholics who remained. Social reconstruction seemed likely to sweep them into the cultural dustbin of history.

Communist reconstruction of China's social structure was intended to be thorough. The pressure on Chinese believers took the form of denunciations, land reform and learning from the masses.

One of the most drastic means employed to enforce conformity to Communist norms was public denunciation. Especially painful were denunciation speeches, which became almost unbearable when they were delivered by individuals who had once been close to the victims. The speeches, which often served as public entertainment before large crowds, followed a prescribed pattern: first a violent attack on the person and his influence, then a list of the person's supposed crimes against China's government, and finally a commitment to live as a patriotic Communist and have no further association with this person. Outside observers knew most about denunciation of missionaries, but denunciations of Chinese believers were usually more brutally devastating.

Motives behind these denunciations varied. For some, survival was the issue. Refusing to take part could mean prison or even execution. But a Confucian sense of filial responsibility also played a role. Public duty, now defined as the

Chinese taking full control of China, seemed to demand a Christianity completely cleansed of all imperial influence. In the interest of national patriotism, these exercises in humiliation quickly and effectively ended direct Western influence among Chinese Christians. Public denunciations of Christians by Christians took place for a relatively short period, beginning in April 1951 and continuing for about fifteen months. During that time Y.T. Wu wrote with considerable pride in one report, "There have been 169 rather large scale denunciation meetings in 124 towns and cities around the country."

Land reform also began almost immediately upon Mao's assumption of national leadership. First, Communist agents gathered ownership information and made plans for redistributing all of the agricultural land of China. Local committees began by dispossessing current landlords, which could involve prison or execution for those considered cruel or unfair. In some areas mere ownership of land was itself grounds for execution. Then the organizing committees redistributed the land to the formerly landless peasants. The results, however, were short lived. Within about five years, China's small individual farms were recombined into ever-enlarging collectives composed of mess halls, child nurseries, housekeeping teams and vast laundries. Everyone worked and everyone shared.

Communists also sought to level the class structure. "Learning from the masses" became a required part of all higher education; in one common college schedule students spent eight months of the year in study, then three months in productive labor and finally one month for rest. Even those employed at high-profile jobs were expected to drop their pencils and paper and spend days or weeks working side by side with laborers, thus forging an identity with those of lesser skills and so "learning from the masses." For some who became targets for punishment, the "labor camp" was no mere exercise in reeducation; it became a life sentence.

The *Communist Manifesto,* published by Karl Marx and Friedrich Engels in 1848, provided a precedent for Christian leaders in China to author a similar document. In May 1950 Y.T. Wu—along with his YWCA colleague Cora Deng, Church of Christ secretary H.H. Ts'ui, Lutheran leader Ai Nein-san, Methodist Bishop Z.T. Kaung and theology professor T.C. Chao—consulted for several days with China's foreign minister Zhou Enlai on what an appropriate "Christian Manifesto" might look like. Wu wrote the final draft that was published in July 1950 and eventually signed by 400,000 Chinese

Christians, nearly half of all China's Protestants. While acknowledging the contribution of 140 years of Protestant missionary work in China, the three-page document included the prescribed denunciation of Christianity's imperialist connections and announced patriotic loyalty to the government of China. It then outlined a plan for Chinese Christian churches to function independently of any Western influence. The manifesto proclaimed a Chinese church whose affairs were managed by the Chinese themselves. It called Protestant Christian churches to self-respect, self-reliance, self-support, self-propagation and self-criticism.

SURVIVAL THROUGH THREE SELF

Y.T. Wu became a leading figure of the Three Self Patriotic Movement (TSPM, with the "three selfs" being self-support, self-government and self-propagation). This national organization was designed to organize all Protestant Christian churches throughout China. Wu was its official head beginning in 1954; until his death in 1979 he was also considered its key organizer and most important spokesperson. In 1957 a similar organization was created for China's Catholic churches, the Chinese Catholic Patriotic Association. As difficult as the Mao years would be for Protestants, they were even more draconian for Catholics, since Catholic loyalty to "a foreign power" (the pope) brought down the full weight of Communist suspicion, denunciation and persecution. The chapter in this book on Cardinal Ignatius Kung provides at least some hints of the difficulties faced by Chinese Catholics.

From Wu's perspective, acceptance of the TSPM as the official church approved by the Mao regime was a necessity if the faith was going to survive at all. Wu maintained this stance even when the regime was strangling the church. For example, by the fall of 1958, the TSPM had consolidated the once-numerous Protestant churches of Peking into only four congregations, geographically distributed. Moreover, it also signed on to a raft of restrictive regulations: all church committees and boards were dissolved; redundant pastors were required to take laboring jobs; all land, property and funds were turned over to the Three Self committee; church ritual was regularized in one standardized form; teaching about the return of Christ was prohibited; churches could not oppose marriages between believers and nonbelievers; the Little Flock congregations associated with Watchman Nee had to abolish their women's meetings, their weekly meetings for confessions and communion, and their rule against women speaking in church; the Salvation Army had to give up its military organization; Seventh-day Adventists had to abandon their daily morning prayer and their practice of tithing; faith healing was prohibited; and hymns along with Bible study materials had to be officially edited and approved before they could be used.

Wu did not invent the three-self concept. As we have seen, it had been proposed in the nineteenth century by Henry Venn (1796-1873), director of the Church Missionary Society, as a concept pushing churches from dependence on missionaries to a status "self-governing, self-supporting and self-extending." It was also articulated by Rufus Anderson (1796-1880) of the American Board of Commissioners for Foreign Missions; John Nevius (1829-1893), an influential missionary in Korea and China; and the Anglican missionary Roland Allen (1868-1947), who after witnessing the Boxer Rebellion of 1901 concluded that the only hope for Christianity in that part of the world was a Chinese church organized for the Chinese. Yet it was Y.T. Wu at this strategic moment in history who was given the responsibility of implementing the ideal, but under a regime with little sympathy for the Christian principles that inspired the ideal in the first place.

ASSESSMENT

The course that Y.T. Wu pursued can be easy to criticize, especially for those who did not face the life-or-death extremities of his situation. But approached cautiously, criticisms can be instructive. Wu's Christology in particular seemed thin—for example, his conclusion that Jesus "came to know God" or his attraction to Jesus' Sermon on the Mount, "not because he is 'God' but because he is a 'man,' a man just like ourselves." This concept of Christ was hardly adequate for any full-blown recognition of human sinfulness and thankful reception of divine mercy in Christ. Similarly, Wu's intense appreciation for God's immanence in the social gospel diminished his understanding of God's transcendence.

From the start, Wu tried to live out the love he saw in Jesus Christ with a twofold, wholehearted commitment to country and to church. It may have been an impossible combination. Observers must wonder about his choices when the interests of country and church collided. Where, in this formula, was love of God?

On the practical side, Wu's lack of concern for China's *other* Christians was a real problem. Catholics, whose Roman ecclesiology insisted on God-ordained papal authority, could never become "three self" in any true sense, and as a result they suffered horribly. In addition, the thousands of house churches that dotted China's towns and countryside throughout the Mao era likewise underwent intense persecution for failing to join the TSPM. Were these other Christians not also part of the "body" of Christ who also tried to live by the Sermon on the Mount? It is impossible not to wonder how the former pacifist Wu reconciled Christ's teachings on love as he condoned and even led the brutal denunciations of Christian brothers and then watched many languish in prison, or worse.

Yet criticism cannot be the only approach to assessing Y.T. Wu's life and times. In particular, the unusual circumstances of his career confront Christians worldwide with important questions. One concern is political accountability. In social structures where government and faith rarely oppose one another, Christians face less demanding political choices, but these choices still exist. Wu's lot was cast where they did conflict. Wu chose the treacherous road of trying to bring political and religious convictions together, despite potential contradictions. For Christians in the West, Wu's challenge is to realize that social and political realities demand sober Christian interaction, even when the demand is not obvious.

Wu also warned the West against equating Christianity with capitalism. His writings pointed out many areas where the uses of money and power needed explicit Christian assessment. His existential concern for the hungry, the poor and the powerless should be a challenge to other believers who think they have a better theology to put that theology to work in social and economic spheres.

Perhaps most important was Wu's effort to indigenize Christianity in China. For the last thirty years of his life, he tried to demonstrate how Chinese Christians could become patriotic citizens within a Communist government. In that effort he helped make Christianity a Chinese religion. Events since the easing of repression have shown how well that goal has been achieved, although the question remains open about Wu's exact role in making it happen.

LAST WORDS

Two Westerners have written with unusual care about the place of Y.T. Wu in the momentous recent history of Christianity in China. One has enjoyed extended direct experience of the changes since Mao's time; the other lived through the wrenching expulsion of the missionaries. Both offer measured judgments worthy of close attention.

Philip Wickeri is probably the Western scholar of the Chinese churches with the most extensive on-the-ground experience in China over the last three decades. He interprets Y.T. Wu and the TSPM as doing what had to be done in recognizing the new realities that had come to exist:

> Once there has been a political shift as momentous as that of the Chinese revolution, a church that merely struggles to hold onto its religious identity will have little to offer in the long run. Nor are Christians in a position to provide a theological critique of a revolution in which they have had little or no share.... For Chinese Protestants who discovered the meaning of Three-Self after 1949, this meant that they had to change the standpoint of the church ... to find some way of coming to terms with the Communist Party of China.

Francis Price Jones offered a perspective that comes closer to interpreting Chinese history as did figures like Wang Mingdao and Cardinal Ignatius Kung, who as other chapters in this book show resisted the Communist regime. Jones was a longtime missionary before 1949 who then suffered denunciations from Chinese friends and colleagues before he was expelled from the country. His evaluation was published in 1962, long before the

Chinese churches regained a measure of liberty. It involved a complex both/and:

> Mr. Wu threw himself into the task of preparing the church to accept the new regime. It seems clear that he was motivated by an honest conviction of the value of communism, a sincere love for the church, and a desire to save it from destruction. Approval cannot be given to all that he has done through the Three Self movement. He has allowed the church to become a "captive church," doing nothing but parrot the Communist line. But he undoubtedly felt that this was the only alternative to complete destruction. He was misled by too optimistic expectation of tolerance of religion from the Communist government and by a failure to appreciate the depth of the meaning in Tertullian's famous dictum that "The blood of the martyrs is the seed of the church."

The final word is Y.T. Wu's. In 1949, as Western missionaries exited China, most of them believed that their efforts had been in vain, that China was lost to Christianity, that unbelief would settle over China's vast landscape like a smothering red blanket. But Y.T. Wu saw a different future. In 1954, he wrote words that proved prophetic:

> Since liberation, we frequently hear Christians saying, "Has Christianity any future?" That is a strange question to be upon the lips of Christians. What has happened to our Christian faith? Do we believe that the eternal God who made heaven and earth exists today and will not exist tomorrow? Have we forgotten that the Christ whose life was full of mercy and truth is the same yesterday, today and forever? Do we believe that the Holy Spirit who has hitherto enlightened and guided our hearts, will now suddenly stop working? Not so. The eternal Triune God does not change with the times. It is not the faithfulness of God that we need be concerned about, but our own faithfulness. If we have deeds to match our faith, if we make an effective witness for Jesus Christ, then all our anxieties will have been found to have been needless.

The puzzle for interpretation concerns the role of Wu himself in bringing about the fulfillment of his prophecy. Did the TSPM, with its place at Mao's table and its wholehearted advocacy of Chinese Christianity defined only by the Chinese, preserve the necessary continuity for what would reemerge after Mao's repression eased? Or has the great surge of faith in recent

China happened despite Wu and the TSPM? Or was it some of both?

SOURCES

Y.T. Wu is his own best witness, especially through his essays in the *Chinese Recorder,* back files of which are available in at least some American libraries. Unfortunately, much that Wu did and wrote during the Mao years remains unavailable in the West. Wu's quotations from 1930 are from "Jesus as I Know Him," *Chinese Recorder* 61 (January 1930):75-95. His comments on the social gospel are from Wu, "Should Christianity Concern Itself in Social Reconstruction?" *Chinese Recorder* 68 (January 1937):21-24. Other quotations from Wu in this chapter are from Philip L. Wickeri's carefully documented *Seeking the Common Ground: Protestant Christianity, the Three-Self Movement and China's United Front* (Maryknoll, N.Y.: Orbis, 1988), p.134 (for denunciations of missionaries), pp.248-49 (Wu's prophetic words from 1954), and p.41 (Wickeri's own assessment from the end of the chapter). Examples of Wu's many other significant writings include "Whither the Chinese Church?" *Chinese Recorder* 67 (February 1936):71-75; "Christianity and China's Reconstruction," *Chinese Recorder* 67 (April 1936):208-15; "The Orient Reconsiders Christianity," *Christian Century,*

June 30, 1937, pp.835-38; and "U.S. Imperialism's 'New Strategy' in the 'Missionary Movement,'" *Peking Review* 5, no.22 (1962):10-13. An earlier work is Y.T. Wu with T.Z. Koo and E.R. Hughes, *The Jesus I Know: A Chinese Book Written for Chinese Youth* (Shanghai: privately printed, 1930).

Francis Price Jones's evaluation of Wu is quoted from his helpful book, *The Church in Communist China: A Protestant Appraisal* (New York: Friendship Press, 1962), pp.62-63. An even earlier assessment was provided in Jones, "The Christian Church in Communist China," *Far Eastern Survey* 24, no.12 (1955):184-88. Other useful work on Wu includes Ng Lee-ming, "A Study of Y.T. Wu," *Ching Feng* 14-15 (1971-1972):5-53; K.H. Ting, "What Can We Learn from Y.T. Wu Today?" *Chinese Theological Review* 4 (1989):34-43; and Chen Zemin, "Y.T. Wu: A Prophetic Theologian," *Chinese Theological Review* 10 (1995):148-57.

Excellent background material is found in Daniel H. Bays, ed., *Christianity in China: From the Eighteenth Century to the Present* (Stanford: Stanford University Press, 1996); Howard L. Boorman and Richard C. Howard, eds., *Biographical Dictionary of Republican China* (New York: Columbia University Press, 1970); R. Keith Schoppa, *The Columbia Guide to Modern Chinese History* (New York: Columbia University

Press, 2000): and Weili Ye, *Seeking Modernity in China's Name: Chinese Students in the United States, 1900-1927* (Stanford: Stanford University Press, 2001).

16

WANG MINGDAO
1900-1991

IMPRISONED BY CHOICE

On November 18, 1942, the pastor of Christian Tabernacle in Peking (now Beijing) received a hand-delivered personal letter. It was a summons to report immediately to the office of Japanese Military Police. Pastor Wang Mingdao was not surprised.

By this date Japanese invaders had already occupied the north of China for eight years. In the three previous years Japan had strengthened its authority over various civil affairs, including publications and churches. And Wang had resisted, not because he disliked the Japanese, though he had every reason to fear them. It was rather his independent streak, which had kept him aloof from church connections as well as suspicious of civil entanglement. Wang took very seriously the biblical command not to become yoked with unbelievers, a stance that brought him both advantages and disadvantages.

Wang Mingdao

In August 1939, when Japanese authorities had instructed Wang to insert four Japanese slogans of loyalty into his quarterly publication, *Spiritual Food,* he refused. Wang did, however, continue to publish and send to Japanese officials the requisite copies of his journal, but without the additions. Japanese authorities chose to ignore his gesture. Later, his staunch independence proved a benefit when in December 1941 Japan declared war on the United States and Britain. At that time all Chinese churches established by Western missionary societies were required to close and seal their doors, but Wang's Christian Tabernacle, with no history of missionary connections, was able to remain open, and hundreds of Chinese Christians continued to worship in its spare forty-by-seventy-foot space. Trouble arrived at his own door in April of 1942, when the remaining churches, now led by local Chinese, were required to join the North China Christian Federation in support of the government-mandated principles of "self-support, self-control and self-propagation." Wang again refused. His church was already practicing these principles, he replied, so to yoke with others of differing or lesser faith would defeat the three-self purposes this new organization supposedly supported.

Beneath the surface of Wang's stubborn independence lay two firm convictions: one spiritual and the other civil. On the spiritual front, Wang believed that he was responsible directly to God for the welfare of his church; he firmly believed that he and his church had to remain unpolluted by ecclesial ties, particularly with churches that did not distinguish between believers and unbelievers and that did not share his Bible-focused faith. On the political front, Wang suspected that civil affairs and ecclesial affairs did not mix well; he was convinced that in China the civil could easily dominate the religious and so impose a different form of "unequal yoke."

Wang Mingdao knew that he might go to jail for these beliefs. When in 1939 he had decided not to insert the required four Japanese slogans into *Spiritual Food,* his wife, Liu Jingwen, asked, "Are you prepared to be arrested, to be examined, and to be jailed?" He soberly considered before replying: "I am prepared." That crisis passed, but not the fortitude with which he faced such decisions. In October 1942 Wang instructed his church, "If I one day yield and lead our church to affiliate with the North China Christian Association, then you must all immediately throw me over. Do not again listen to my preaching."

So on November 18, 1942, Wang Mingdao prepared for prison. He packed his Bible, spectacle case, handkerchief, tooth brush, wool socks and donned three sets of clothing. "No matter what happens I shall not give in," he told his wife. Then, summons letter in hand, he walked to the police station.

Wang came back home the same day. The summons had been a false alarm. His name had gotten mixed with others who occupied formerly mission-owned property and who now had to turn it over to the Japanese. For another dozen years, Wang Mingdao continued as pastor at Christian Tabernacle, his preparation for prison a trial run for what came later.

Yet the Japanese summons had left the taste of fear in his mouth, along with increased faith in a sovereign God. So Wang could admit, "I am a human being. I have the thoughts of a human being, the feelings of a human being, the desires of a human being. I want to pass my time peacefully. I am afraid of physical pain and adversity." Yet when cautioned that the Japanese would as soon kill a Chinese man as an ant, he could retort, "What you say is true, but I am not an ant. I am the servant of the most high God. Unless God permits, no one can harm me." In August of 1955, the specter of prison would rise again, this time at the hands of the Communist government.

AT THE START

Wang Mingdao was born in Beijing in the midst of the Boxer Rebellion of 1900-1901, shortly after his father's death. His mother, Li Wenya, was married to Dr. Wang Dehao who worked at the Methodist Hospital in Beijing; the family lived on its campus. Four children had already been born, but three had died and only a six-year-old "elder sister" remained. The "Righteous Fists of Harmony," known in English as Boxers, were militants angered by the Western imperial presence. They were trained in martial arts and spiritual incantations. When they answered the Empress Dowager's call to "rid China of foreigners and Christians," the result was destruction and death for many with Western connections. Before she recalled her troops in the fall of 1901, 231 missionaries, 4000 Chinese Protestant Christians, and 30,000 Chinese Catholic Christians died. In May 1901,

Dr. Wang and his family—with Li Wenya in the final trimester of pregnancy—tried to escape by joining a somber march through the streets of Beijing, along with hundreds of other Christians and missionaries who took refuge at the enclosed property of the Foreign Legation. Once there, the family prepared for siege along with 2,500 other Chinese Christians and about a thousand soldiers and foreign civilians. Dr. Wang was among the wall watchers. What he saw outside and below convinced him that defeat at the hands of the Boxers was inevitable, that they would all die of violence or starvation. He took what he considered the only honorable way out and hanged himself. Five weeks later Li Wenya, still sequestered, gave birth to a son, whom she named Wang Tie, "Iron Wang." In August 1901, Allied forces arrived, the Empress Dowager evacuated to Xian and the siege on Beijing's Foreign Legation lifted.

Wang's family, however, had no place to live. Without a father employed at the mission hospital they could no longer stay in its compound. Li Wenya eventually received "forty taels of silver," imperial repayment for "damages suffered in the rebellion," which she used to buy a cluster of rooms around an open courtyard. There she took in some thirty lodgers while she and her two children settled into a single room. Throughout childhood Wang's courtyard playground consisted of the bawdy turmoil of Peking's lower classes. Later he wrote of lying, cursing, gambling, opium-smoking, stealing, promiscuous behavior, fighting, crude jokes, a husband who beat his wife bloody, the comings and goings of prostitutes and their customers. Sadly his mother fit fairly well into this culture. Li Wenya hated cooking, screamed insults at her children and extracted rent payments by whatever means possible. Yet in 1908 she did send her son to a nearby primary school run by the London Missionary Society.

The event was decisive. At school he studied arithmetic, history, ethics, Chinese literature and the writings of Confucius. He earned top examination scores and the attention of an able medical student who assisted the teacher. Even at this early age Wang was asking questions about the purpose of life and the nature of death, even as he grew to fear both. At age twelve he moved to a nearby boarding school, also mission run, which housed about thirty-five students. The obligatory Bible classes and chapel attendance meant little to him. Keeping his hair long meant more. When older students threatened to snip him bald, his courtyard manners returned as he stormed, "Whoever dares to do this, I will take the scissors and stab his eyes." He kept his hair and his dignity.

Later Wang spoke of the gritty poverty of those days with a measure of thanksgiving, "There are many sins you cannot commit without money."

Wang became a Christian at the age of fourteen, when an older student at the boarding school "led me to know God." The student had been influenced in his own spiritual growth by a book by H.L. Zia, a translator and editor for the YMCA. Wang's friend showed him "how to worship God ... to pray ... to read the Bible, how to examine myself daily and how to keep a diary. He gave me [Zia's] book ... entitled *A Help to Personal Development."* From infancy Wang had been surrounded by Christian influences. Not all the believers he knew lived exemplary lives, but when his new friend introduced Christ as Savior and Christ's teachings as a divine standard for living, fourteen-year-old Wang became a willing convert. "At Easter I was baptized in the chapel. I then considered myself a proper Christian."

Wang's daily self-inspection for sin soon extended outward as he urged teachers and students to act on the same behavior standards he had set for himself. If they resisted, he called them spiritual enemies; they in turn tagged him "Dr. Morality." It didn't help that the school was short of funds and therefore short of staff and so in need of fee-paying students regardless of their inclinations for or against Christianity.

CAREER OR CALLING

Shortly after his conversion Wang began to consider a life occupation. At first politics seemed to him the best way to defeat his fear of death. Acting on the proverb, "When a fox dies it leaves a skin; when a man dies he leaves a reputation," the fifteen-year-old Wang posted a picture of Abraham Lincoln above his bed and made plans for political studies at university. But he also sensed another call; perhaps God was leading him to become a preacher. But first he needed to overcome bad examples: "I had come across a lot of preachers who were worthless.... Some of them served the missionaries as cooks, cleaners, gatemen...; they learned a few passages of scripture, they sang a few hymns and went on to preach a few half-understood doctrines." His indecision weighed on him for three years; gradually he came to define the choice as between human pride and divine calling.

By the time Wang turned eighteen, circumstances made the decision for him. After being ill for nearly three months he had enough strength to sit for only two days of the five-day university exams. He then took one year of the two-year university preparation course, but in

1919 as part of the May 4 student demonstrations against Western imperialism, all schools went on strike. When schools reopened they also reorganized. To continue, Wang would have had to transfer to Jinan, some two hundred miles away. Because of filial responsibility to visit his mother who had been ill, Wang now saw university education as a divinely closed door. Reluctantly he accepted work as a teacher in a Presbyterian primary school in Baoding, one hundred miles south of Beijing. His salary of twelve dollars a month would almost pay for a monthly trip home to visit his mother.

Wang did not enjoy his teaching colleagues, whom he regarded as feeble in faith. Soon he withdrew from community meals because he was a vegetarian and because he did not care for their "lewd conversation." By contrast Wang certainly loved his students. Because he was sharp and could teach, he was assigned to work with the oldest group of students; soon he became their mentor, friend and spiritual guide. He also organized prayer meetings, Bible reading, times of confession and instruction in holy living that drew to some extent on his previous study of H.L. Zia. Wang loved seeing his students grow in faith and soon saw them as disciples and Christian brothers. As he watched their spiritual development, he began to appreciate the importance of spiritual rather than political influence. The result was serious consideration of a possible call from God. His colleagues at Baoding confirmed this move and began helping him plan and fund a ten-year program of theological education that included hopes for study abroad. In the summer of 1920 Wang chose his "adult name." He would become Wang "Ming-Dao." *Ming* means to "testify" or "certify," and *Dao* means "way" or "truth." Thus his name henceforth identified his calling as a preacher of the gospel of Christ.

But his second year at the Baoding school did not go well. At the opening of term Wang experienced various ailments, including difficulty with far vision, which would trouble him all of his life. By mid-fall he was also in the midst of another spiritual crisis. A newly arrived colleague with Pentecostal leanings preached a concept of sin that changed Wang's own thinking. Now he concluded that while he had resisted many evil actions, he had indulged in many evil motives, thoughts and purposes—pride being among the most insidious. A fresh round of self-examination and confession ensued until Wang eventually wrote, "No matter how good a man is, only let him be illumined by the Spirit of God and he becomes conscious of his own utter depravity.... I dedicated myself anew to [God].... From that day on my life was gradually but wonderfully changed."

This change was not happy for either Wang or the school. As part of his spiritual soul searching, Wang began to question his former baptism. Should he not be baptized again in the "biblical way," by immersion? In a Presbyterian school, where baptism symbolized God's act of covenanting with his people, to rebaptize was viewed more as a renunciation of God's grace than as a renewal of faith. While a little risqué conversation at the faculty lunch table did not bother Wang's colleagues, rebaptism struck at the core of their covenant theology. They told Wang that if he persisted, he would have to leave.

Wang, of course, persisted. On January 6, 1921, with another teacher named Ju and five students, Wang found a small spot of open water near an ice-covered bridge. Ju baptized Wang by immersion along with four of the students. Wang wrote, "I still remember how, as I came up out of the water, my long hair turned immediately into a stick of ice. As soon as I took off the thin garments they became hard and solid like thin boards." The fifth student, Shih Tien-min, did not participate in the baptism but did withdraw from school as an expression of unity with the others. Shih would become a career "fellow-servant" with Wang.

Now jobless, Wang Mingdao returned home. His mother and sister, who had expected lifelong financial support from his teaching career, railed at him relentlessly. His neighbors thought he had gone mad. Having lost hope of further theological education, Wang retreated to a nearby abandoned greenhouse to study the Bible and to pray. There he began again to face his childhood fears of both life and of death. "All of a sudden my heart was opened wide and I grasped the fact that Christ could give eternal life to all who believe in Him. In him is life.... He Himself rose from the dead.... I realized that death was not to be feared." A cousin, hearing that Wang was mentally ill, came to visit and offered his mountain home as a place of recovery. Wang read the Bible from beginning to end six times, remaining in this idyllic area near Crouching Tiger Mountain for two months.

At the end of May 1921, "Teacher Chun," a school friend who was worried about Wang's mental health invited him to Tsang-Hsien for a visit. Wang agreed, and when Chun found him quite sane, even "blessed by God," he invited Wang to preach. It was the beginning of hundreds, then thousands of sermons. In the next quarter century Wang preached in several hundred churches of thirty Christian denominations in twenty-eight provinces throughout China. He would also publish *Spiritual Food,* a quarterly journal of his sermons distributed for nearly thirty years to countless Chinese households. And he founded the Christian Church in Christ (CCiC) of Beijing, which would become a large and flourishing independent congregation. Later he would be known as the "Dean of House Churches of China."

THE HOME FRONT

His reputation throughout China, however, took time to develop. For several years between brief preaching tours Wang mostly remained at home with his mother and sister. He assuaged their resentment at this new calling by doing housework. "When I was sweeping I allowed not even the slightest dust to remain in the room. When I cooked the meals I made a point of making them perfectly palatable.... When I washed the clothes I made them perfectly clean.... In those days I had no hope of doing anything important.... Nor did I know what kind of work God would entrust to me in the future."

Then another life-changing event occurred. Wang Mingdao fell in love. At first he thought the diminutive Liu Jingwen was a mere child in her parents' household as they hosted him on several trips to the Nanking area. But when Jingwen filled in as substitute organist at one of his meetings in November of 1925, he looked again and realized that this "child" was an attractive and skilled young adult who was already working as a teacher. After a year of careful inquiries by their families that uncovered no objections, they became officially engaged in November 1926. Only then did the couple begin to correspond. In August 1928 Wang and Liu were married. Wang found instant acceptance in the household of his in-laws. In fact he had been attracted to the spiritual warmth and personal peace he encountered in their home long before he proposed to the daughter.

In his own family, however, the new couple suffered alternating bouts of stony silence and bitter accusation. Wang's mother and sister treated Jingwen as an inferior competing for Wang's affection, ordered her to do the most odious household tasks and then refused to eat with her. Even when Jingwen became seriously ill with tuberculosis, they insisted that she was merely trying to avoid work. Wang was able to avoid much of this turmoil by his frequent preaching tours, leaving the nineteen-year-old Jingwen at home to endure as best she could, which she seems to have carried off with grace and forgiveness. For his part, Wang wrote, "I stated on one occasion that I would rather sacrifice my wife than sacrifice my mother. But I realized afterwards that this was wrong ... In spite of this my mother still regarded me as an outsider." The couple lived in this embattled household for nine years. In 1929 their only child, a son whom they named Tianzhe, was born.

Like many church planters, Wang began with meetings in his own home, at first the renovated greenhouse in his mother's courtyard. Sometimes only a handful joined him for prayer and instruction. But within a few months growing numbers required larger quarters that could accommodate up to seventy people. In 1933 they rented a hall, which had room for two hundred with another hundred able to hear through winter cold and summer rain from a courtyard outside. In 1937 they built a "solid tent" that could hold eight hundred people wedged into its shelter. That year Wang Mingdao and Jingwen along with eight-year-old Tianzhe moved out of Li Wenya's household and into a home across the courtyard from their new Christian Tabernacle.

The unembellished white interior of Wang's Christian Tabernacle bespoke the purity and simplicity he demanded in theology. Only the pulpit and baptistery occupied front space, and even this was minimal in order to free up room for people. Wang taught and expected that lives would be changed by conversion. "We are very strict in receiving believers. Unless we are quite sure that a person has repented and believed in the Lord and is thereby saved we will on no account accept him for baptism." Demonstrating the visible evidence of a holy life might require as much as a three-year probation. Wang took no offerings and never preached about tithing. A collection box at the rear of the tabernacle provided sufficient funds for minimal expenses. There was no paid staff except for Wang, who was absent about six months of the year on preaching tours. In his absence, committed laypeople led the church. Foregoing even the title "Pastor," Wang used "Mr." to emphasize his independence from any ecclesial body except his own congregation.

Wang's personality disinclined him toward casual social connections. His theology warned him away from any dependence on unbelievers, based on the apostle Paul's instructions about being "unequally yoked together" in 2 Corinthians 6. Wang's views came from Jesus' teachings to "Give to Caesar what is Caesar's and to God what is God's," with the call of God trumping national loyalty in any potential conflict (Mt 22:21). When the Communists rose to power in China, with Chairman Mao's determination to draw all religious groups into the government-controlled Three Self churches, Wang Mingdao's convictions made a clash with the state inevitable. The collision was postponed only because Wang's complete independence from any Western organization ruled him out as an immediate threat and because he was already operating under three-self principles in the strictest sense of the term. Yet by the early 1950s, Wang knew that he was in danger and would have to make a choice.

In the spring of 1954 the Three Self Patriotic Movement (TSPM) ordered all churches in Beijing to send delegates to an "accusation meeting" against Wang. When this meeting took place, he sat through it all without uttering a word. The chairman called for either imprisonment or death, but only a quarter of those present agreed. The remainder sat silent or in tears.

Although Wang remained silent when publicly accused, he was otherwise engaged in a whirlwind of activity—writing a flurry of articles and books aimed at encouraging Bible-based Christian life and criticizing what he labeled as the watered-down religion offered by Y.T. Wu and other Three Self leaders. At home in the Tabernacle, he taught his followers that suffering must be expected and that persecution would bring its own purifying power. He also implored his congregation to stand firm for the truth of Christ in the hard days to come.

On August 7, 1955, the day arrived, Wang conducted a usual Sunday morning worship at the Tabernacle, jammed full of apprehensive members and not a few infiltrators. Two or three hundred stood outside to hear fragments of the service. In the afternoon he presided over the Lord's Supper for some two hundred congregants and then led an evening prayer service lasting until after ten p.m. Afterward Wang and Jingwen walked home through the dark courtyard. Thomas Harvey records what happened next:

> In their bedroom, Wang removed his shirt and sat down to read some letters.... Jingwen thought she heard a noise on the roof, so she went out to investigate. She entered the hall and found herself face to face with a police officer armed with a pistol. He stifled her before she could cry out, sat her down on a chair, and handcuffed her. Meanwhile, Wang continued to read his mail. "Don't move!" he suddenly heard behind him. Wang turned slowly to find two police officers in his room, one with a gun trained on him. Several other policemen quickly entered the room, and an arrest warrant was presented to Wang as the others began to search the room.

> By the time Wang was cuffed and led downstairs, Jingwen was nowhere to be seen. A thunderstorm was rolling in swiftly as Wang was led into the courtyard, where some thirty officers milled about. Upset, Wang asked where his wife was. The officers replied that she had been arrested and taken away. Wang began to cry out for help and yelled, "False arrest!" To stifle his cries, the police officers threw a cloak over him, knocking off his glasses in the process.

Wang Mingdao and his wife, along with eighteen leaders of various Beijing churches, were imprisoned in separate places. Jingwen could sometimes catch a glimpse of her husband through distant courtyards, but without his glasses he could not see her; he thought himself entirely alone.

SIDELINED

Wang Mingdao would live another thirty-six years, but from that moment his public ministry was finished. The purpose of imprisoning dissidents was to "reeducate" them, and Communist methods were thorough and effective. Wang collapsed within days. The opening round came the morning after his arrest, following a sleepless night endured on a small bed, lying between two other prisoners intent on tormenting him.

> *Interrogator:* Are you or are you not opposed to the Three-Self Movement?
>
> *Wang:* I am opposed, but that is a religious question and not a crime; opposing the Three-Self offends no law of the state.
>
> *Interrogator:* That is where you are wrong; opposing the Three-Self Movement is a crime.

Eventually Wang would admit to this "crime," along with dozens more, mostly twisted truths or outright lies.

Throughout the next months Wang wrote and rewrote his confession, with officials finding inadequacies in each draft and requiring further additions, until finally in late summer 1956, his written confession was deemed satisfactory. On September 30, 1956, Wang Mingdao entered the YMCA headquarters that sponsored the Three Self churches headed up by Y.T. Wu. In front of one hundred Three Self leaders Wang read his seven-page confession in a quiet voice without raising his eyes. Polite applause followed. Only then was Jingwen released from prison and together they returned home. Across the courtyard, the Tabernacle remained sealed shut by order of public security.

Prison diet and restraint had left them both weak and ill. Wang had eaten only "corn flour bread" for most of the year. Both had had little opportunity for sleep. Jingwen remained solid in faith and relatively optimistic, but she soon found that her husband needed her protection. Wang sank into depression; she feared he would follow his father's path of suicide. Once she had to restrain him from pouring boiling water over his own head. Another time she had to wash his mouth after he had stuffed it with blistering lime. Over and over they received material from Three Self churches: programs, agendas, prayer letters, notices about information meetings, Bible studies, sermon notes, prayer requests, invitations to preach. Over and over Jingwen replied, "We are not ready yet." Wang ignored them entirely. Twice a month they went to the police station for a required check. They made an attempt to move to Shanghai, where their son lived near Jingwen's mother. This was, of course, denied. Old friends and coworkers lost faith in them, and sometimes in Christ. The Wangs stopped meeting with police and made plans to change their names and quietly move out to the countryside.

On April 29, 1958, the government acted again. Wang had not fulfilled his responsibility to join the Three Self movement. The Wangs were again arrested and imprisoned. This time Jingwen got a fifteen-year sentence, and Wang got life. Wang's life sentence, which was finally announced in 1963, triggered an unexpected result. This final sentence stimulated him to recall biblical texts memorized at a much earlier age, including Micah 7:7-9:

> But as for me, I watch in hope for the LORD,
> I wait for God my Savior;
> my God will hear me....
> Because I have sinned against him,
> I will bear the LORD's wrath, until he pleads my case. (NIV)

As his life sentence began, Wang Mingdao's faith returned.

Over the years the Wangs were moved several times from one prison to another, sometimes in the same area and occasionally catching a glimpse of each other but never being allowed to speak. Sometimes they nearly starved; sometimes they ate well. Often they were put to work: Jingwen knitted sweaters; Wang painted eyes on toy cats. Eventually they were allowed reading and writing material. Jingwen learned to read the newspaper and Wang wrote a spiritual confession, but this time for himself. He also wrote grievance letters and "suggestions" to prison officials. In later years, after officials gave up reeducating Wang, his son sent him some five hundred books, which prompted interesting conversations with various prison staff who sometimes borrowed from his library. Tianzhe also sent his parents clothing and food.

Both Jingwen and Wang suffered episodic torment from other prisoners. In 1966, Wang was transferred to the Datong mining camp. After Wang made a number of intemperate comments about Chinese political leaders, the camp manager selected nine tough inmates to live with Wang. For five months day and night he suffered torture at the hands of this "Battalion of Nine." In February 1970 Jingwen became the object of her cellmates' wrath, one of whom was imprisoned for murder. Night after night she suffered hair-pulling, kicks and slaps. Jingwen wrote a letter quoting Mao Zedong's statements guaranteeing Chinese freedom and ended with, "There is freedom of belief in China. I don't want to be beaten by those who have beaten their own children to death." The beating stopped for a time.

In April 1974, Jingwen completed her fifteen-year prison sentence, and Tianzhe was eventually able to take her home to live near him, his wife and daughter in Shanghai. While in prison Jingwen had developed high blood pressure and lost the vision of one eye because of untreated glaucoma. She would soon lose vision in the other eye as well.

By 1979 the world political scene had changed. Mao Zedong was dead. Sino-American diplomatic relationships were reestablished, and China allowed more access into the country. Human rights organizations in both Europe and the United States began to make public inquiries about political prisoners in China. In May 1979 Dr. Sheng Xianzhi, the son of a Presbyterian pastor, traveled from the United States to visit his father's old friend. Learning that Wang was still housed at the Yingying Labor Camp, Dr. Sheng visited the camp but was not able to find Wang. He left a letter, a pair of gloves and a flashlight, hoping to provide tangible evidence that someone outside of China was interested in Wang. The letter attracted the attention of the international press both in Germany and the United States, and diplomatic wheels began to turn.

RELUCTANT RELEASE

In November 1979, Tianzhe received a telegram saying, "Come and take Wang Mingdao home as soon as possible." Tianzhe quickly arranged the trip. It seems, however, that no one informed the seventy-nine-year-old Wang, who had grown accustomed to his jail home full of books.

> "Why are you here?" he asked his son.
>
> "To take you home."
>
> "I won't leave. Go back and tell Mum that I'm fine here."

"You must go," said the prison director.

"Before I go, the government must admit three things. They must admit that they wrongly arrested me, that they wrongly sentenced me and that they have wrongly imprisoned me for over twenty years. If they don't put this in writing, I won't leave."

Tianzhe departed without his father, leaving behind dozens of boiled eggs he had prepared for their train trip home.

Prison diplomatic wheels continued to turn, eventually taking Wang's demands into consideration. On December 29 prison officials engaged Wang in one of his favorite topics of conversation, the comparative merits of sprinkling and immersion in Christian baptism. They then convinced him to take a little vacation in a visitor's quarters outside the prison walls. Wang grudgingly assented, provided they would help him haul his books and other belongings up the eighty-one steps to his new abode, which they did. They even provided other "guests" to help him with meals in his new temporary lodgings. Then the prison gates clanged shut with Wang on the outside. Wang took a couple of days to consider his new situation. On New Year's Eve he sent a postcard to his son. "Tianzhe: Decided to go to Shanghai. Come to get me soon. Dad"

Wang and Jingwen spent their remaining days together in Shanghai. By this time Wang was nearly deaf and Jingwen totally blind. Their son and other relatives and friends cared for them. Guests from the West came to visit, including Billy and Ruth Graham on April 23, 1988. Maintaining his lifelong battle, Wang received the Grahams only grudgingly, because they had, of necessity, obtained permission from the Three Self Church in order to pay him a visit. Ruth Graham was able to arrange for Dr. David McIntyre of Seattle to visit, with the result that in May of 1991, Jingwen recovered sight in one eye. But not much time remained for either Wang or Jingwen. On July 28, 1991, Wang Mingdao died of a blood clot in the brain. Nine months later Jingwen became ill and within three days was diagnosed with stomach cancer complicated by pneumonia. She joined her husband in death on April 18, 1992.

What happened to the thousands of people who had been influenced by Wang Mingdao's teaching, preaching and writing before he went into prison at the age of fifty-five? Some joined the Three Self Church. A few gave up their faith altogether. But most held firm by taking their convictions underground. Many of them formed quiet, small, mobile house churches, first by the hundreds, then thousands and tens of thousands. They were self-governing, self-supporting, self-propagating churches in the most unencumbered way possible.

While Wang served his life term in prison, the churches in China were manifesting resolve that burst forth in public once the Cultural Revolution was over and the restrictions of Mao eased. Wang's legacy remains controversial, in large part because of his uncompromising criticism of other Chinese believers who did not remain as independent as he did. Yet as a force for both inspiration and division, the life of Wang Mingdao testified to the resilience of Chinese believers and pointed the way to the remarkable Christian expansion of recent decades.

SOURCES

The quotations in this chapter from Wang himself come from a book of autobiographical writings edited and translated by Arthur Reynolds: Wang Ming Dao, *A Stone Made Smooth* (Southampton, U.K.: Mayflower Christian Books, 1981). Reynolds was also the translator and editor of sermons that first appeared in Wang's *Spiritual Food Quarterly,* published as Wang Ming-Dao, *Spiritual Food: Twenty Messages* (Southampton, U.K.: Mayflower Christian Books, 1983). For thoughtful integration of biographical information into the history of the era, as well as for special material on Wang's time in prison, this chapter made use of Thomas Alan Harvey, *Acquainted with Grief: Wang Mingdao's Stand for the Persecuted Church in China* (Grand Rapids: Brazos, 2002). Also unusually helpful for those prison years is a book by Stephen Wang, *The Long Road to Freedom: The Story of Wang Mingdao* (Kent, Tenn.: Sovereign World, 2002). Stephen Wang became a Christian under Wang Mingdao's ministry and was a part of his church in Beijing. He later joined Inter-Varsity Christian Fellowship's literature ministry in Shanghai. In August 1955 Stephen Wang was among those arrested with Wang and Jingwen. He too spent the next twenty-two years in prison and labor camps. Much of his writing about Wang in those years came from what he witnessed personally.

Other useful material is provided by Tony Lambert, "Wang Mingdao: A Christian in Conflict with the State," in *Answer of a Good Conscience* (London: Westminster Conference, 1997); Samuel Mau-Cheng Lee, "A comparative Study of Leadership Selection Processes among Four Chinese Leaders" (D. Miss. thesis, Fuller Theological Seminary, 1985); and Timothy Tow, *Wang Ming Tao and Charismatism* (Singapore: Christian Life Publishers, 1989). An outstanding general history is Xi Lian, *Redeemed by Fire: The Rise of Popular Christianity in Modern China*

(New Haven, Conn.: Yale University Press, 2010).

17

IGNATIUS CARDINAL KUNG/KUNG PIN-MEI 1901-2000

A CATHOLIC VALIANT FOR TRUTH

After the death of Mao Zedong in 1976, Deng Xiaoping emerged from the maneuvering for power that followed to become the leader of China's Communist Party. Deng moved cautiously to open up Chinese society, first by beginning the economic reforms that have led to China's current place of preeminence in the global market. Incremental relaxation followed for culture and communications—and also for religion, but at a slower pace. One of the signs of gradual retreat from the closed society of Mao's day was an increasing number of invitations to foreigners to visit China. In 1984 one who received such an invitation was Jaime Sin, the Roman Catholic cardinal archbishop of Manila in the Philippines who later became famous for leading the People Power revolution that ousted the Filipino dictator Ferdinand Marcos. During his visit to China, Cardinal Sin came in contact with another Catholic leader who, in his own way, was as much an inspiration to faithful Catholics in China as Sin was to his flock in the Philippines.

Ignatius Cardinal Kung (Kung Pin-Mei)

This leader was Ignatius Kung Pin-Mei (sometimes spelled Gong Pinmei), who in 1950 had become the bishop of Shanghai. Since 1955, however, Bishop Kung had been in prison. From that time until his meeting with Cardinal Sin, the bishop had had no contact with any fellow Catholic and no communication of any sort with the outside world. (He did not even know about the Second Vatican Council.) He had been sent to prison for refusing to break ties with the pope in Rome but also for denying the legality of an alternative Catholic Church that the Communist government had set up as an autonomous Chinese organization in competition with Catholics loyal to the pope.

But now with Deng Xiaoping in power the regime was trying to display its liberality, and so a banquet was arranged for the visiting Filipino cardinal where the Chinese bishop would also be in attendance. The event was carefully staged to ensure that Kung and Sin had no chance to talk in private; instead, they were seated at opposite ends of the banquet table with something like twenty Communist officials and leaders of the CCPA separating them. In this strained atmosphere, Cardinal Sin suggested that each person offer a song for the entertainment of the others. When it came to Bishop Kung, he stood up, looked at his fellow bishop and sang "Tu es Petrus et super hanc petram aedificabo ecclesiam meam," which is the Latin Vulgate for Jesus' words from Matthew 16:18, "You are Peter, and on this rock I will build my church." As soon as someone from the CCPA recognized what Bishop Kung was singing, he tried to get the song stopped, but it was too late. In his first contact in thirty years with a Catholic from outside China, Bishop Kung was showing that his fidelity to the pope, who in Catholic doctrine is the successor of Peter as head of the church, remained firm. After Cardinal Sin left China, he reported the incident to the Vatican with word that Bishop Kung was resolute in his faith.

In John Bunyan's classic allegory of the Christian life, *Pilgrim's Progress,* there is a character, Mr. Valiant-for-Truth, who stands for persistence, dedication and courage under fire. The name has been apt for many Christian believers over the course of the last century, including this indomitable Chinese bishop.

What neither Cardinal Sin nor Bishop Kung knew in 1985 was that two Catholic cardinals had attended their banquet. In 1979, Pope John Paul II had named Bishop Kung to the college of cardinals, but *in pectore* (literally, in the heart or breast). Such appointments are made when publicizing them would endanger either the person named or the church community the person serves. Cardinal Kung did not learn of his appointment until he personally visited Pope John Paul II in 1989, and it was not until two years later, in 1991, that the appointment was announced to the world.

EARLY LIFE

Ignatius Kung Pin-Mei was born in the outskirts of Shanghai on August 2, 1901, to a family whose Catholic heritage went back at least five generations. He came into the world only shortly after the Boxer Rebellion of 1900, during which scores of Western missionaries and thousands of Chinese believers had been killed. He would live through tumultuous times of church expansion, intense persecution and the reemergence of flourishing Christian churches.

The future cardinal's education was overseen by members of Catholic religious orders who trained him in the Chinese classics as well as in Catholic doctrine. When he was eighteen years old, Ignatius Kung entered the diocesan seminary in Shanghai, the great port city that was also headquarters for many of the Christian organizations operating in China during the early part of the twentieth century. He was ordained a priest in May 1930, after having served for many years as a Latin teacher and administrator at schools run by the Jesuits in Shanghai. During this period Kung earned a reputation as an effective administrator and a serious-minded churchman. He was consecrated bishop of Soochow (also Suzhou or Souchou) on October 7, 1949, six days after the Chinese civil war ended with the establishment of the People's Republic of China under the victorious Mao Zedong. A year later Kung became the first native Chinese bishop of Shanghai. At the same time he was appointed administrator also of Nanjing (Nanking) and asked to continue supervision of Suzhou. In Bishop Kung's hands, in other words, lay the administration of three of China's largest cities where Catholic communities had existed since the sixteenth century.

The history of modern Catholicism in China began when the pioneering Jesuit missionary Francis Xavier visited the island of Shangchuan briefly before his death in 1552, even as he was awaiting passage to the Chinese mainland. Under the leadership of unusually talented Jesuits who followed in Xavier's train, the Catholic faith was established in several major cities and also in many rural regions. Scholars and teachers like Matteo Ricci (1552-1610) worked assiduously to master Chinese language and literature, to translate Catholic doctrine into Chinese idioms and to make themselves useful for the emperor and his court. The result was often controversy and disappointment: the fortunes of the church fluctuated depending on the emperor's dictates, and Catholics in Europe regularly questioned the way Jesuits translated Catholic thought and practice into Chinese. Nonetheless, an ongoing Catholic Church did emerge, surviving even the period when the Jesuit order was dissolved from the 1770s to the 1810s. Ignatius Kung's training by the Jesuits as well as his family's Catholic heritage, in other words, made him a self-confident Chinese Christian and not the recent convert of an imperial or alien faith.

BISHOP KUNG

As part of his duties as bishop, Kung worked hard to encourage lay Catholics, in large part because he foresaw the possibility of trials afflicting the church from either the civil war between Nationalists and Communists or from an unfavorable government in power. One of the prime vehicles of that encouragement was his support for the Legion of Mary, a movement founded in Ireland in 1921 that by the late 1940s had spread throughout much of the world. The legionnaires pledged themselves to regular prayer, small-group meetings under the direction of local priests or the bishop, and outreach into the community. That outreach was evangelistic, with members of the legion active in passing out Catholic literature, but also philanthropic, with members visiting prisons, providing for the homeless and carrying out other deeds of mercy. In the first years of Communist rule, the lay members of the legion also began to take on several tasks that had usually fallen to priests and nuns, like visiting the sick and teaching catechism to young people and converts.

Communist officials distrusted the legion because of its autonomy (a potential competition to the state) and soon took steps to suppress its activities. They also pretended that the "legion" was an "army" of reactionary fascists. In Shanghai a decree from October 1951 banned the legion, ordered its members to register with the government and arrested three foreign priests who had worked for the movement—in the words of the authorities, "three imperialist elements who organized the reactionary organization 'Legion of Mary' and directed its counterrevolutionary activities."

Bishop Kung then showed the mettle that would sustain him through great stress when he declared 1952 as a Marian year in Shanghai. This special observance included an uninterrupted twenty-four-hour recitation of the rosary in front of a statue of Our Lady of Fatima, which throughout the year toured the parishes of the Shanghai diocese. The bishop himself personally led a special rosary at Christ the King Church in Shanghai, whose priests had been arrested at the same time as the crackdown on the Legion of Mary. He prayed, "Holy Mother, we do not ask you for a miracle. We do not beg you to stop the persecutions. But we beg you to support us who are very weak."

When the Communists came to power in 1949, Catholics made up about two-thirds of China's Christian population of three to four million. Among Christian groups, they were singled out for special attention from the new government because of the structure that tied Chinese Catholics to the pope and international Catholicism. All Christians in China were accused of being lackeys of imperialist forces; all soon experienced the expulsion of foreign workers. In 1951, as Protestant missionaries were leaving the country, so also was the emissary of the pope expelled. As part of the effort to organize Chinese institutions for the Chinese, Protestants led in proclaiming the three-self principles of self-governance, self-support and self-propagation. The Three Self Patriotic Movement (TSPM) was the government's vehicle to organize all Protestant denominations into one organization that could be guided by a central planning committee and cooperate in promoting the social goals of the Communist party. Y.T. Wu's decision to cast his lot with the TSPM is told in chapter fifteen. The Catholic counterpart to the Three Self Patriotic Movement was the Chinese Catholic Patriotic Association, or CCPA; Catholics spoke of the Three Autonomies, which the CCPA was to implement.

These were difficult days for all Christians in China, but especially for Roman Catholics. As evident from the career of Wang Mingdao (chapter 16) much disagreement existed among Protestants about how fully to cooperate with the Three Self Patriotic Movement. But by their very nature as Christian movements whose connections with foreign interests were informal and not doctrinal, Protestants enjoyed a certain flexibility toward the new regime that Catholics, with their church defined by its connection to Rome, did not. (In fact, students of the recent explosion of Christian groups in China ascribe survival under the intense persecution of Mao's Cultural Revolution, 1966-1976, to the capacity of at least some Chinese Christian groups to operate as grassroots, locally organized, lay-directed, and self-organizing movements.)

In the early years of the Communist era, the Chinese authorities used pressure, intimidation, harassment and occasional arrests to push Catholics into renouncing ties with Rome. Eventually the CCPA was established as the organizational vehicle for receiving those Catholics who were willing to denounce Rome and organize on their own. For Bishop Kung, whose entire conception of Christianity was defined by loyalty to the pope, this move was completely unacceptable.

IMPRISONMENT

Years of tense negotiations and increasingly tighter restrictions came to a climax on September 8, 1955, when the bishop and more than two hundred other Shanghai Catholics, priests and laypeople, were arrested. Many of the laypeople were members of the Legion of Mary who had continued what Catholics call a "lay apostolate" in defiance of official directives. The bishop was subjected to intense interrogation, which led officials to conclude that he was ready to cooperate. He was then paraded publicly into Shanghai's Dog Racing Stadium for a "struggle session" in which it was expected that he would publicly announce his break from the pope. Instead, when the diminutive bishop, barely five feet tall, was put in front of the microphone, he shouted "Long live Christ the King, long live the pope." He was immediately silenced, dragged back to prison and was not seen for the next five years.

In 1960, Kung went on trial for treason; "leading a counterrevolutionary clique under the cloak of religion" was the official charge. He was convicted and then sentenced to life in prison. Before the trial he was given yet another chance to break with Rome. He told his interrogators: "I am a Roman Catholic Bishop. If I denounce the holy father, not only would I not be a bishop, I would not even be a Catholic. You can cut off my head, but you can never take away my duties."

For the next twenty-five years Bishop Kung was kept in isolation intermixed with outdoor work details. The work details sometimes required him to drive water buffaloes in the rice fields. For this whole period his only religious contacts were with officials of the CCPA. He was deprived of all books (including the Bible), the Catholic missal, the crucifix, and correspondence with the outside world and even with his family. He was not allowed to say Mass. After his release from prison, the cardinal reported that he had spent much time in prayer, and particularly in saying the rosary. When asked how he said the rosary when the authorities did not allow him to have beads, he pointed to his ten fingers. Somehow through it all he kept a sense of proportion, even of humor. When he was asked in later years how he managed to remain so fit, he replied "no cholesterol."

Occasionally during his work assignments, Kung would have opportunities for brief conversations with other prisoners. One of them, an academic named Yi Lifa who was imprisoned for spying, later came to the United States and taught at the University of Iowa. He reported that he had encountered the bishop at a labor camp and that the bishop continued to pray, "morning and evening, while working with the water buffaloes." Yi Lifa also testified that Bishop Kung had persuaded him not to commit suicide when Yi became despondent over his own imprisoned plight.

Bishop Kung was not permitted paper or writing materials, but he did once succeed in composing a brief "Meditation On the Crucifixion of Jesus" written on a scrap of thin rice paper that was then smuggled outside of China. Here is a portion of that meditation:

> Jesus accepted suffering inflicted by every kind of person. The apostles betrayed Him, the Jews made accusations against

Him, the Gentiles cursed Him, and high priests, officials, soldiers, and other people all determined to kill Him. Because Jesus suffered in order to save all classes of people, so He accepted sufferings caused by all kinds of people, including all of us. Are we not increasing His suffering by our lack of faith, committing sin and not loving His Sacred Heart.

Where was our Blessed Mother at that time? She was weeping beside the Cross, watching Her son suffer. This was not just the human life between mother and son. She united her love of Jesus with her love for all mankind, offering it in sacrifice to God the Father for the salvation of the whole world. Our Lady is indeed the Mother of our salvation.

Each and every one of us should imitate Our Blessed Lady, contemplating Jesus on the Cross. We should offer our sufferings in reparation for our sins and those of others, asking for mercy and forgiveness and not fail to respond to the graces Jesus obtained for us through His Passion.

Pope John Paul II made Kung a cardinal *in pectore* after he had been in prison for nineteen years. About the time of the dramatic banquet with Cardinal Sin, Kung was released from prison for what the authorities called "health reasons." He was paroled on July 3, 1985; he was eighty-four years old; he had spent more than a third of his life in prison.

FREEDOM

In January 1988, Chinese news agencies published an announcement declaring that the bishop had received his full civil rights. The announcement was ambiguous, since it could be read to suggest that Kung had admitted his errors but also that the authorities, rather than Kung, had relented.

In May 1988, Kung received permission to travel to the United States to receive medical help for his hearing and for heart problems. A nephew who had emigrated to the U.S. arranged details. The next year Kung traveled to Rome and received news from the pope personally of his selection as a cardinal ten years before. That announcement was not, however, made public until a formal ceremony at the Vatican on June 28, 1991. In front of nine thousand visitors in the Vatican's Audience Hall, Kung was carried in his wheelchair to the foot of the papal dais. He then arose, set aside his cane and walked up the steps to kneel at the feet of the pope. John Paul II raised the aged cleric to his feet and put the cardinal's red hat on his head. The audience responded with a standing ovation lasting seven minutes.

Despite his years and failing health, Cardinal Kung traveled widely throughout the United States and beyond. He said Mass in many parishes and spoke on television and at Catholic conferences. He repeatedly called attention to the continued persecution of the Roman Catholic Church in China. In response to that publicity the Chinese government revoked his passport in March 1998, which meant that he was officially in exile. The cardinal's nephew in 1991 established the Cardinal Kung Foundation, which since that time has worked to publicize persecution of Catholics in China and to disseminate information about Chinese Catholics who, like the cardinal, have maintained their loyalty to the pope.

In May 1995, Kung participated in a triple jubilee Mass, held in his honor in Stamford, Connecticut. It was to commemorate the sixty-fifth anniversary of his ordination to the priesthood, with forty-five years of episcopal ordination and fifteen years since being elevated to the College of Cardinals. One of the main celebrants was Dominic Tang Yiming, archbishop of Canton, who like Kung had been incarcerated for many years (in his case, twenty-two years) and who had also been exiled. During his long years in prison, Dominic Tang repeatedly prayed a prayer composed by Ignatius of Loyola, founder of the Jesuit order: "Take, O Lord, and receive all my liberty, my memory, my understanding, and entire will, all that I have and possess. You have given them to me; I return them.... Give me only your love and your grace, for these are enough for me."

Another priest taking part in this Mass was George Wong, also a Jesuit, whom Bishop Kung had ordained in 1951. Reverend Wong had spent over fifteen years in prison because after he was arrested he refused to sign a statement naming the bishop an "imperialist stooge."

Philomena Hsieh was another expatriate who attended the Mass in 1995. She had been a university student and active in the Legion of Mary when she was arrested along with Bishop Kung on September 8, 1955. At the dinner for those attending this special commemoration forty years later, she told Cardinal Kung that through her youth "in dungeons and fields, performing hard labor," it was his example of fidelity that had given her and her fellows the courage to go on.

The Cardinal lived another five years after this landmark reunion Mass. Shortly before he died, he received a message from Cardinal Joseph Ratzinger, later Pope Benedict XVI: "In the decades of fidelity to the Church, you have followed the example of Christ the Good Shepherd and even in the face of great suffering, have not ceased to proclaim the truth of the

Gospel by your words and example. For your faithful witness to Christ, the Church is deeply grateful." The motto that Kung chose for his cardinal's coat of arms was "One Fold and One Shepherd." After Kung's death on March 12, 2000, his body was transferred to a chapel at the Santa Clara Mission Cemetery in California.

Ten years after the Cardinal's death a memorial mass was celebrated in his honor at the Basilica of St. John the Evangelist in Stamford, Connecticut. At that time Monsignor Stephen DiGiovanni of the basilica announced that he was soliciting written recollections from those who knew Cardinal Kung so that he might advance the cause for the Cardinal's canonization as a saint.

Cardinal Kung's body now lies in a vault above the ground at the cemetery in California. It is disposed in this way in order to await transportation for final burial at the foot of the altar of his cathedral in Shanghai. The day of that reinterment may not be far off. Since Cardinal Kung's death, negotiations between the Vatican and the Chinese government have moved cautiously toward reconciliation between the CCPA and Chinese Catholics loyal to the pope.

The pace of reconciliation slowed in the year 2000 when Pope John Paul II canonized 120 Catholics who had been killed for their faith in

China from the mid-seventeenth to the early twentieth century. Chinese authorities strenuously objected to this announcement, which was made on the anniversary of the founding of the Communist state in 1949. Yet despite lingering controversy over these "Chinese martyrs," increased contact among the interested parties has been taking place.

In 2007, Pope Benedict announced that some bishops ordained by the CCPA had requested full communion with Rome, and that he had granted them full episcopal authority. At the same time, the pope also pointed out that there remained many points of tension, including the presence of CCPA bishops who had not sought reconciliation with Rome. But even with much remaining to be worked out, the situation for Catholics in China is now closer to normalcy than at any time since the early 1950s. Since the easing of official restrictions, non-Catholic Christian groups—in a huge variety—have proliferated more rapidly than Catholics. In 2005 it was estimated that the number of Chinese Catholics in fellowship with Rome had risen to over eight million, with another four million affiliated with the CCPA. What it will mean if Catholics are allowed to sing "Tu es Petrus," publicly and in Chinese translation, no one can tell.

SOURCES

Much of the basic information on Kung Pin-Mei, including the account of the banquet with Cardinal Sin, comes from the website of the Cardinal Kung Foundation (www.cardinalkungfoundation.org). Material on the Legion of Mary is from James T. Myers, *Enemies Without Guns: The Catholic Church in the People's Republic of China* (New York: Paragon House, 1991), which includes much other material on its subject. A report on the commemorative Mass from 1995 is found in George M. Anderson, "Witnessing for the Faith in China's Prisons," *America* 173 (July 29, 1995):16-21. The testimony of Yi Lifa is found in John F. Burns, "China Releases a Catholic Bishop Who Was Jailed Nearly 30 Years," *New York Times,* July 4, 1985, p. A-1. We also thank Joseph Kung for his helpful assistance.

AFTERWORD

The stories told in this book are meant to stand on their own. This intention is reinforced by an observation from the history of Christianity itself. In many places and regions of church history, it has been all too easy for members of one Christian tradition to rush prematurely toward assessment, evaluation, appropriation or judgment when confronted for the first time by another Christian tradition. This drive for assessment is natural and can be useful. Others may and should engage in such criticism of the world's newer expressions of Christianity. But our effort has been guided by the conviction that it is important first simply to know before trying to judge.

Nonetheless, a few general matters fairly cry out for attention in response to the seventeen biographies we have narrated. To consider such matters briefly may also highlight themes that could be used for discussing the lives described in these chapters.

One obvious generalization is that Christianity in the twenty-first century has become even more **diverse** than in the past, where great diversity had already existed from the earliest Christian centuries. It is enough to think of a practical exercise in evangelism where the directors were William Wadé Harris, Simeon

Nsibambi, John Sung and Pandita Ramabai to recognize the multiplicity within world Christianity. The same could be said for a seminar on Christian participation in politics conducted by John Chilembwe, Albert Luthuli, Cardinal Kung and Sun Chu Kil. If this book had contained a few more sketches of Roman Catholic figures, it would have been clear that unusual diversity now exists within the world's largest church by itself. But even with the lives chosen for consideration here, multiple forms of diversity are obvious. The degree to which appreciation, critical scrutiny, cautious appropriation or regretful rejection should guide the growing number of connections among Christian traditions is one of the important issues raised by the potpourri of lives we have introduced.

Even more pertinent may be the way that learning about believers from outside the West shows the prevalence of **tenacity** in the midst of **deprivation** and **conflict.** Every one of the individuals we have profiled was "heroic" in some legitimate sense of the term. That is, of course, a main reason why sources about their lives written in English have reached the Western world. But it should be obvious that for every "hero" whose life enjoyed a written record, there were countless fellow believers whose lives remain unrecorded, or recorded only in local records inaccessible to the outside.

The sobering truth is that, whether we consider the Boxer Rebellion, the more general effects of Western imperialism, the spread of Communist regimes or the rise of African dictators, we are living in the Age of Martyrs. Never before has Tertullian's famous epigram from the early third century been truer than it is today: "The blood of the martyrs is the seed of the church." Even where duress stops short of martyrdom, a great number of the world's believing communities have suffered markedly for following Christ.

Such reflections might lead to serious thinking among those of us in the West who suffer rarely if at all for our Christian profession. But there are other kinds of reflection involving the West that point in a different direction. One of the repeated phenomena in the book's seventeen biographies is how often a spark lit by **missionary-native contact** initiated remarkable Christian expansion through native agency. Whether John Chilembwe's relationship to Joseph Booth, Pandita Ramabai's to the Community of Saint Mary the Virgin or Sun Chu Kil's to Samuel Moffett, the actions of missionaries were crucial to the indigenous growth of the faith. One of the byproducts of becoming more alert to the indigenous character of Christian expansion is likely to be fresh appreciation for the importance of mission work. To be sure, that importance will not be framed as in former times when the missionary could be depicted as the cause, guide and guardian of Christian life wherever it existed. Rather, recognition of the missionary as one important cog in a divine economy of many cogs—where the whole enterprise of expansion and maturation is bigger than any one perspective can comprehend—is likely to grow from a better understanding of world Christian history.

Also obvious from the lives that we have presented is the power of **cultural instincts.** Mary Stone, John Chilembwe, the Sadhu Sundar Singh and others learned about Western cultural assumptions when they lived or traveled in Europe and the United States. The elements of Christianity they stressed on their own turf reflected, by contrast, the cultural assumptions of their indigenous regions. William Wadé Harris was precise about physical objects and spiritually relaxed about polygamy, likewise Pandita Ramabai about organizing schools (precise) and denominational differences (relaxed). One of the great benefits to arise from trying to learn about Christ-followers from other places is to make us more self-conscious about our own cultural assumptions. The end product of this process need not be cultural relativism but rather greater clarity about the profusion of God's work in creating so many cultures and his power in illuminating the entire rainbow of human cultural diversity by the grace of Christ.

Finally, even passing awareness of lives from the new Christian homelands underscores what all believers know but all too easily forget. The **Scriptures** remain a powerful, life-transforming force. The **fellowship** of believers takes many forms, but is an essential element of Christian vitality. The **Holy Spirit** is everywhere active in drawing people to the Father through the Son and in guiding them into service for the kingdom. Reports of the Spirit's unmediated activity—through dreams, audible voices, direct visions of Christ—may be startling for many of us in the West, but that activity has become the norm for the majority Christian world. Time-tested Christian truths sometimes seem trite when they have been confessed for many centuries in the same place. There are, however, few activities that so easily rekindle confidence in such foundational realities than to see them at work in regions and among people where the eternal Christ is being confessed anew.

FOR FURTHER READING

Besides the particular sources of special value for the individual biographical studies, which are specified after each chapter, the following list offers outstanding surveys and interpretations of world Christian history in general. A more extensive sample from an ever-expanding bibliography of useful works is found in Mark A. Noll, *The New Shape of World Christianity: How American Experience Reflects Global Faith* (Downers Grove, Ill.: IVP Academic, 2009), pp.201-6. The *International Bulletin of Missionary Research* is the premier journal in English for general research in world Christianity. Four times a year its articles, reports and reviews offer unusually reliable help in bringing the new world picture into focus. It is sponsored by the Overseas Missionary Study Center (www.omsc.org).

Allen, John L., Jr. *The Future Church: How Ten Trends are Revolutionizing the Catholic Church.* New York: Doubleday, 2009.

Anderson, Allan. *An Introduction to Pentecostalism: Global Charismatic Christianity.* New York: Cambridge, 2004.

Bamat, Thomas, and Jean-Paul Wiest, eds. *Popular Catholicism in a World Church: Seven Case Studies in Inculturation.* Maryknoll, N.Y.: Orbis, 1999.

Barrett, David, George T. Kurian and Todd M. Johnson. *World Christian Encyclopedia.* 2 vols. 2nd ed. New York: Oxford University Press, 2001.

Cox, Jeffrey. *The British Missionary Enterprise Since 1700.* New York: Routledge, 2008.

Freston, Paul. *Evangelicals and Politics in Asia, Africa and Latin America.* New York: Cambridge University Press, 2001.

______. *Protestant Political Parties: A Global Survey.* Burlington, Vt.: Ashgate, 2004.

González, Justo L. *The Changing Shape of Church History.* St. Louis: Chalice, 2002.

Hanciles, Jehu. *Beyond Christendom: Globalization, African Migration and the Transformation of the West.* Maryknoll, N.Y.: Orbis, 2008.

Hastings, Adrian, ed. *A World History of Christianity.* Grand Rapids: Eerdmans, 1999.

Hutchinson, Mark, and Ogbu Kalu, eds. *A Global Faith: Essays on Evangelization and Globalization.* Sydney: Centre for the Study of Australian Christianity, 1998.

Irwin, Dale T., and Scott W. Sunquist. *History of the World Christian Movement.* Vol.1, *Earliest Christianity to 1453.* Maryknoll, N.Y.: Orbis, 2001. (Written intentionally to reflect the present-day diversity of world Christianity.)

Jenkins, Philip. *The Next Christendom: The Coming of Global Christianity.* New York: Oxford University Press, 1999.

______. *The New Faces of Christianity: Believing the Bible in the Global South.* New York: Oxford University Press, 2006.

Johnson, Todd M., and Kenneth R. Ross, eds. *Atlas of Global Christianity.* Edinburgh: Edinburgh University Press, 2009.

Koschorke, Klaus, Frieder Ludwig and Mariano Delgado, eds. *A History of Christianity in Asia, Africa, and Latin America, 1450-1990: A Documentary Sourcebook.* Grand Rapids: Eerdmans, 2007.

Mandryk, Jason. *Operation World 2010: The Definitive Prayer Guide for Every Nation.* 7th ed. Colorado Springs: Biblica Publishing, 2010.

Martin, David. *Pentecostalism: The World Their Parish.* Oxford: Blackwell, 2002.

Marty, Martin E. *The Christian World: A Global History.* New York: Modern Library, 2007.

McLeod, Hugh, ed. *The Cambridge History of Christianity.* Vol.9, *World Christianities, c.1914–c.2000.* New York: Cambridge University Press, 2006.

Mullen, Robert Bruce. *A Short World History of Christianity.* Louisville: Westminster John Knox, 2008.

Robert, Dana Lee. *Christian Mission: How Christianity Became a World Religion.* Malden, Mass.: Wiley-Blackwell, 2009.

Sanneh, Lamin. *Disciples of All Nations: Pillars of World Christianity.* New York: Oxford University Press, 2008.

______. *Translating the Message: The Missionary Impact on Culture.* Maryknoll, N.Y.: Orbis, 1989.

_____. *Whose Religion Is Christianity? The Gospel Beyond the West.* Grand Rapids: Eerdmans, 2003.

Shaw, Mark. *Global Awakening: How 20th-Century Revivals Triggered a Christian Revolution.* Downers Grove, Ill.: IVP Academic, 2010.

Shenk, Wilbert R., ed. *Enlarging the Story: Perspectives in Writing World Christian History.* Maryknoll, N.Y.: Orbis, 2002.

Stanley, Brian. *The World Missionary Conference, Edinburgh 1910.* Grand Rapids: Eerdmans, 2009.

Walls, Andrew F. *The Cross-Cultural Process in Christian History.* Maryknoll, N.Y.: Orbis, 2002.

_____. *The Missionary Movement in Christian History.* Maryknoll, N.Y.: Orbis, 1996.

Image Credit

Chapter 1

Bernard Mizeki: From Jean Farrant, *Mashonland Martyr; Bernard Mizeki and the Pioneer Church* (Cape Town: Oxford University Press, 1966), between pp. 68-69, figures 3 and 4. Used by permission of Oxford University Press. www.oup.com

Chapter 2

John Chilembwe: From George Shepperson, *Independent African; John Chilembwe and the Origins, Setting and Significance of the Nyasaland Native Rising of 1915* (Edinburgh: Edinburgh University Press, 1958), after p. 87. © George Shepperson. Used by permission.

Chapter 3

Albert Luthuli: Keystone/Getty Images. Used by permission.

Chapter 4

William: Wadé Harris Personal photo provided by David Shank. Used by permission.

Chapter 5

Byang Kato: Personal photo provided by James E. Plueddemann. Used by permission.

Chapter 6

Simeon Nsibambi: From Henry Martyn Centre for Mission Studies, Cambridge, U.K. Used by permission of the Joe Church family.

Chapter 7

Janani Luwum: Keystone/Getty Images. Used by permission.

Chapter 8

Pandita Ramabai: From Clementina Butler, *Pandita Ramabai Sarasvati; pioneer in the movement for the education of the child-widow of India* (New York: Fleming H. Revell, 1922), opposite title page.

Chapter 9

V. S. Azariah: From Sherwood Eddy, *India Awakening* (New York, Missionary Education Movement of the United States and Canada, 1911), between pp.204-5.

Chapter 10

Sundar Singh: Basel Mission Archives/Basel Mission Holdings, no. QS-30.017.0013. Used by permission.

Chapter 11

Sun Chu Kil: Personal photo provided by Samuel and Eileen Moffett. Used by permission.

Chapter 12

Dora Yu/Yu Cidu: From *Silas Wu, Dora Yu and Christian Revival in 20th Century China* (Boston: Pishon River Publications, 2002), cover photo. © Silas Wu. Used by permission.

Chapter 13

Mary Stone/Shi Meiyu: Taken from Jennie V. Hughes, *Chinese Heart-Throbs* (New York: Fleming H. Revell, 1920), opposite title page.

Chapter 14

John Sung: From Leslie T. Lyall, *John Sung* (London: China Inland Mission, 1954), p.93. Copyright OMF International. Used by permission. www.omf.org.uk

Chapter 15

Yao-Tsung Wu/Wu Yaozong: From *Three-self patriotic movement of the protestant churches in China* (Shanghai: Amity Printing Company, Ltd., 2000) p.6. Every reasonable effort has been made to secure permission from the publisher.

Chapter 16

Wang Mingdao: From Leslie T. Lyall, *John Sung* (London: China Inland Mission, 1954), p.212.

Copyright OMF International. Used by permission. www.omf.org.uk

Chapter 17

Ignatius Cardinal Kung/Kung Pin-Mei: From Joseph Kung, The Cardinal Kung Foundation, Stamford, CT. www.cardinalkungfoundation.org. Used by permission.

Front Cover Flap

A tattered Hindu pilgrim girl becomes one of India's most influential Christians of the twentieth century.

An African herder boy grows up to be archbishop of a large Anglican flock in Uganda and is martyred under Idi Amin.

A brilliant Chinese pastor's kid, spiritually adrift in his studies in the U.S., goes on to become one of the most powerful figures in Chinese revivalism in the 1930s.

With the recent growth of Christianity in Africa and Asia, a robust company of saints has left footprints in the soil of these new Christian heartlands.

In seventeen fascinating and inspiring narratives Mark Noll and Carolyn Nystrom introduce us to a variety of Christians in Africa and Asia who lived remarkable lives of faith and leadership in the midst of trying circumstances. Spanning a century, from the 1880s to the 1980s, their stories sparkle with the vitality of Christian faith lived out in a diversity of global contexts.

This kaleidoscopic witness to the power of the gospel will both inspire and educate.

Whether for a class in global Christianity or for a personal journey to other times and places of faith, *Clouds of Witnesses* is a book that tugs at our curiosity and resists being laid down. An engaging traveling companion to Mark Noll's award-winning book *The New Shape of World Christianity.*

Back Cover Flap

MARK A. NOLL is Francis McAnaney Professor of History at the University of Notre Dame. Some of his many books are *The Civil War as a Theological Crisis, The Rise of Evangelicalism, The Old Religion in a New World, Is the Reformation Over?* and *The New Shape of World Christianity.*

CRROLYN NYSTROM is a freelance writer based in the western Chicago suburbs. She has written more than seventy-five books and Bible study guides and served as general editor for the Christian Classics series.

Back Cover Material

THESE SEVENTEEN PROFILES OF CHRISTIANS FROM AFRICA AND ASIA GIVE TEXTURED DETAIL TO THE TAPESTRY OF GLOBAL CHRISTIANITY.

"*Clouds of Witnesses* powerfully portrays the lives, ministries and contributions of leading non-Western Christians in a diversity of contexts and Christian traditions. This unique collection provides a timely reminder that non-Western Christianities, now the dominant form of the faith, were forged in historical situations that are far removed from the purview of most Western Christians.... The voices that speak in this volume speak to the whole church."

JEHU J. HANCILES, Fuller Theological Seminary

"Few are unaware of Christianity's decline across old Christendom, its stasis in neo-Christendom and its astonishing post-colonial growth across much of the non-Western world. Nevertheless, the 'streetlight effect' evident in standard church histories means that we know scarcely anything about those men and women chiefly responsible for the most remarkable demographic surge in the history of the church. As a happy exception to that rule, this book reminds us that Christianity is a *world* religion, and provides Christians everywhere with cause to celebrate."

JONATHAN J. BONK, Overseas Ministries Study Center

"The book of Revelation reminds us that the company of the saints encompasses those from every nation, tribe, people and tongue, but too many volumes of modern Christian biography appear to restrict the saints to those of European descent. This rich collection of pen portraits corrects the imbalance and reminds us of the wonderful variety of the worldwide people of God.... This book will expand your horizons, instruct your mind and challenge the level of your spiritual commitment."

BRIAN STANLEY, University of Edinburgh

"Here are seventeen disciples from Asia and Africa with hearts for their people and heads that grasp the big picture. Hear their voices."

MIRIAM ADENEY, Seattle Pacific University

A

B

M

U

V

W

Books For ALL Kinds of Readers

At ReadHowYouWant we understand that one size does not fit all types of readers. Our innovative, patent pending technology allows us to design new formats to make reading easier and more enjoyable for you. This helps improve your speed of reading and your comprehension. Our EasyRead printed books have been optimized to improve word recognition, ease eye tracking by adjusting word and line spacing as well as minimizing hyphenation. Our EasyRead SuperLarge editions have been developed to make reading easier and more accessible for vision-impaired readers. We offer Braille and DAISY formats of our books and all popular E-Book formats.

We are continually introducing new formats based upon research and reader preferences. Visit our web-site to see all of our formats and learn how you can Personalize our books for yourself or as gifts. Sign up to Become A RHYW Registered Reader.

www.readhowyouwant.com

Printed in the USA
CPSIA information can be obtained
at www.ICGtesting.com
LVHW062038310823
756761LV00044B/845

9 781459 621640